Art for the Ladylike

AN AUTOBIOGRAPHY
THROUGH OTHER LIVES

WHITNEY OTTO

MAD CREEK BOOKS, AN IMPRINT OF
THE OHIO STATE UNIVERSITY PRESS
COLUMBUS

Published by Mad Creek Books, an imprint of The Ohio State University Press.

Library of Congress Cataloging-in-Publication Data
Names: Otto, Whitney, author.
Title: Art for the ladylike : an autobiography through other lives / Whitney Otto.
Other titles: 21st century essays.
Description: Columbus : Mad Creek Books, an imprint of The Ohio State University
    Press, [2021] | Series: 21st century essays | Summary: "Personal essays exploring
    how biography, art history, photography, feminism, careerism, and motherhood
    are woven throughout the author's life and the lives of Sally Mann, Imogen
    Cunningham, Judy Dater, Ruth Orkin, Tina Modotti, Lee Miller, Madame
    Yvonne, and Grete Stern"—Provided by publisher.
Identifiers: LCCN 2020041934 | ISBN 9780814257821 (trade paperback) | ISBN
    0814257828 (trade paperback) | ISBN 9780814281017 (ebook) | ISBN 081428101X
    (ebook)
Subjects: LCSH: Otto, Whitney. | Women authors, American. | Women
    photographers.
Classification: LCC PS3565.T795 Z46 2021 | DDC 814/.00803552—dc23
LC record available at https://lccn.loc.gov/2020041934

Cover design by Regina Starace
Text design by Juliet Williams
Type set in Adobe Garamond Pro

∞ The paper used in this publication meets the minimum requirements of the
American National Standard for Information Sciences—Permanence of Paper for
Printed Library Materials. ANSI Z39.48-1992.

For John and Morganfield

It is difficult for a woman to define her feelings in language
which is chiefly made by men to express theirs.
—Thomas Hardy, *Far from the Madding Crowd*

I was seduced by money, by love.
Now I just love art.
—Man Ray (later in life, from Hollywood)

I love to do portraits of smart women, beautiful women,
babies when I must. Men are very difficult to please.
—Man Ray, 1932

I hate writing. I love having written.
—Dorothy Parker

CONTENTS

An Introduction in Three Parts and a Final Thought   1

Goodnight Kiss: Sally Mann   7

Inventing the Male Nude: Imogen Cunningham   45

The Woman with the Mink Sleeves: Judy Dater   75

Don't Be Afraid to Travel Alone: Ruth Orkin   111

The Sentimental Problem of Tina Modotti: Tina Modotti   145

A War of My Own: Lee Miller   183

Be Original or Die!: Madame Yevonde   221

Psychoanalysis Will Help You: Grete Stern   269

Epilogue: Revisiting *The Advantages of Being a Woman Artist,* Thoughts on Writing, and One Question   303

Acknowledgments   309

About the Author   311

AN INTRODUCTION IN THREE PARTS AND A FINAL THOUGHT

I.

If an autobiography tells the story of a life then this "autobiography"—these women, these other artists, these bits and pieces from my past, my thoughts—this *is* what the story of my life looks like. Imagine one of those "hidden puzzle" pictures in the children's magazine *Highlights,* where someone has drawn, say a city scene, asking the reader to locate the "hidden" butterfly, the bucket, the book, the ax, the horse, and the hat that are really all there, in plain sight. You just have to readjust your idea about the city scene; to see past the bus stop and the cars, to notice the butterfly.

So, I've been chipping away at this book since 2002, writing a nearly complete first draft at that time. I would put it down, then pick it up, then write something else, then pick it up, then put it down, then write something else, then pick it up and so on. It's said that "life is short and art is long"; it turns out that writing about art is even longer. I wasn't always sure what I was writing, until I understood it as autobiography; that we are the things we love.

2 · WHITNEY OTTO

II.

Are women photographers fundamentally different from male photographers? Taking a picture can be an aggressive, predatory, and often public act; one "takes" or "shoots" a subject (women are often raised to be quieter, more circumspect). Photographing a person is a form of staring. It's been said that men watch women overtly, while women watch discreetly. Is there any social effect when a woman is explicit in her observing? Is there something disquieting about a woman who is clearly paying close attention?

III.

When Georgia O'Keeffe was trying to find herself as a painter, before Stieglitz, before New York, and the flowers and the desert and the fame, she wrote:

I can't live where I want to, I can't go where I want to go, I can't do what I want to, I can't even say what I want to. I decided I was a very stupid fool not to at least paint as I wanted to.

This was my mantra as a young woman just leaving college, feeling limited and lost, and knowing what I wanted to do (write) without knowing exactly how to do it. For now, this quote must suffice as the stated intention of this book of essays.

*

A few quotes pinned to the wall above my desk:

Incredible that the novel should be so hard—each morning dreading it. Do I fear finishing it? Is that it? Fear that it is not the masterpiece that I planned?

—Dawn Powell, writing in her diary about
The Wicked Pavilion

*

Van Gogh confided to his brother, Theo, that he still occasionally felt *a terrible need of—shall I say the word?—religion. Then I go out at night and paint the stars.*

(Note: How else to explain all this sitting alone in a room and talking to yourself, then writing it down?)

*

Martin Puryear, artist on art:

I didn't approach the prospect of being an artist with the notion that anything was guaranteed, or that I had a right to anything, least of all success. It's the kind of life you go into with a lot of hope, but you really take your chances. The reward has been the chance I've had to live a life that involves doing what I love more than anything else, and having that be at the center of my life rather than on the periphery.

*

He forces you to use the word "beautiful." What more do you want?
(Note: Robert Motherwell talking about Joseph Cornell.)

*

Joni Mitchell on happiness:

You can strive and strive and strive to be happy, but happiness will sneak up on you in the most peculiar ways. Some days the way the light strikes things. Or for some beautifully immature reason, like finding myself running to the kitchen to make myself some toast. Happiness comes to me even on a bad day. In very very strange ways.

(Note: How else to explain all this sitting alone in a room and talking to yourself, then writing it down?)

*

"I love this city" she wrote in a notebook in 1947, *"its clean cut look, its sky, its buildings, its scientific, cruel, romantic quality."*
—Louise Bourgeois

*

And now that you don't have to be perfect, you can be good.
—John Steinbeck, *East of Eden*

*

And Frank O'Hara:
Each time my heart is broken it makes me feel more adventurous (and how the same names keep recurring on that interminable list!), but one of these days there'll be nothing left with which to venture forth.

*

These quotes are mostly about love, but they also could be about writing and being a writer. Go back and read them again with that in mind, and they will tell you more about how I feel about what I do, and how much it means to me, and how hard it can be when things go a little sideways, and how great it can be when it all comes together.

A Final Thought

Thus, reader, I am myself the matter of my book; you would be unreasonable to spend your leisure on so frivolous and vain a subject.

—Michel de Montaigne, *Essays*

GOODNIGHT KISS

Sally Mann

Cloud movements, erratic storms, lightning all occur so fleetingly that only the photograph holds them long enough to be savored. Ruth Orkin, yes. Children, too. Everything about them resembles weather: Their bodies and emotions in a constant state of flux, their curiosity, their intellects, their interior lives.

Kids are careless early chapters that only adults see as stories they mistakenly believe they can write. Maybe you have to be a novelist (and I'm clearing my throat here) to understand that characters—let alone flesh and blood beings—have fates nearly impossible to determine. Just when you think you've worked out the particulars of their lives, they turn around and surprise you. And that's what happens on a good day.

And maybe that's the very thing that makes artist mothers good (and, sometimes not so good, their attention elsewhere) parents, the way in which they take their hands off the controls because they understand all too well that they can't really make anything happen; they can only set the stage, establish the circumstances, furnish the props before allowing the whole thing to unfold.

Or, if you're Sally Mann, you turn your minimally edited children's lives into art. They start, you stop, then you visually record what it looks like when you step back, and watch.

1.

I had in my purse a folded, used looking piece of heavy yellow construction paper that read, in black felt-tip pen: *More Sally Mann locked in the case!* Then, in smaller red-inked letters, *ask for help.* . . . This was in the early 1990s when I pulled this message where it hung from a shelf in the extensive photography section of Powell's Bookstore in Portland, Oregon, where Sally Mann's books should be. The issue is Mann's *Immediate Family.*

Let me offer a little context; the other monographs on display on the day I found the note were as follows: Joel-Peter Witkin's stitched up, autopsied models; Frances Glessner Lee's collection of eighteen graphic crime scene dioramas, known as *The Nutshell Diaries of Unexplained Death,* little dollhouse rooms of violence, a kind of cousin to Weegee's journalistic photographs of real-life crime scenes, all rivers and aqueducts and sprays of blood. There was Diane Arbus's modern-day slide-shows of dislocation and discomfort featuring such subjects as giants, circus performers, unsettling twins; Mapplethorpe's muscled men in sexually explicit poses, including the now-infamous self-portrait with a rectally inserted bullwhip. Dorothea Lange's rural Great Depression poverty; Pierre et Gilles' cabaret-touched sparkling sailor boys; James VanDerZee's 1920s Harlem crossdressers, and dead children, referencing Victorian memento mori. Claude Cahun and Marianne Moore, stepsisters (their parents marrying a few years *after* the girls met), as well as lifelong lovers and artistic collaborators, taking marvelous pictures illustrating the flexibility of imagination and gender. Yasumasa Morimura's appropriation photographs where he appears, respectively, as Frida Kahlo, Rrose Selavy (Duchamp's female alter-ego, who also made her own art), Diego Velasquez's little seventeenth-century Spanish princess of *Las Meninas,* among others. There are piles of corpses, rotting and spilling out of train cars in Lee Miller's concentration camp photos, along with the group suicide of a Nazi official, his entire family peacefully strewn about their fastidious library. Helmut Newton and his fabulous fetish girls, sometimes bound and collapsed in the trunk of a car. Hans Bellmer's pictures of homemade life-sized pubescent dolls in the 1930s. The dolls were sexualized, often missing limbs, and included a doll of his lover.

On those shelves of photographed, highly personalized worlds, were housewives, *memento mori,* transgender people, crossdressers, nudes of every stripe and taste and age; the young, the old, the haves and have nots. War zones, refugee camps, funeral homes. Filmed humanity, an enormous everybody, all bound into volumes and sold at the largest independent bookstore in America, all are present . . . except for the family photos that Sally Mann took of her three children.

Mann's *Immediate Family,* locked in a case, isn't even a first edition. So what's so precious about it? Is it signed? It is not. If there's no measurable value to this particular book as an object, then the assumption is that it is being sequestered for content, and given the controversy that surrounded *Immediate Family* when it was published in 1992, I'm not surprised.

2.

A little general background: Just two years prior to the publication of *Immediate Family,* Jock Sturges, a photographer whose photographs included portraiture of adolescents (and some children on the verge of adolescence), was having his own problems with the law. In 1990, the FBI led a raid on his California photography studio, claiming that his pictures constituted child pornography. It should be noted that Sturges also filmed families (adults *and* children). There was a similar and subsequent charge brought against Barnes & Noble bookstores in Alabama and Tennessee in 1998 because they were selling Sturges' books. Though the charges were later dropped, suspicions of child pornography still cling to the photographer's work.

It's the casual nudity that draws the accusations of child pornography. Without the framing of High Art, many people find naked models discomfiting (worse if they're really young), as if there's no difference between a Sturges photograph and peeping into the neighbor's bedroom window. At the same time, artists are natural observers, which might come awfully close at times to voyeurism.

It's romantic to accept, even to admire the tortured artist, nearly destroyed (or fully destroyed) by the need to make art. We love the imagined sacrifice, the descent into unsavory addictions, the forgiven acts of selfishness and cruelty. It's Picasso kicking his women around; it's Hemingway with a shotgun in his mouth.

It's less romantic to think of artists among us, watching, listening, borrowing from our unguarded moments, because those activities no longer just involve *them;* they involve *us.*

"I've always been fascinated by physical, sexual, and psychological change," Sturges said. It's so ordinary, so unexceptional, *growing up,* so what makes it art? Maybe the very everydayness of Sturges's pictures makes it easier to declare it pornographic. What about intention and context? How much do they count?

Sturges photographed many of his subjects for more than twenty years. Alfred Stieglitz said that his ideal project would be to film someone from the cradle to the grave. Michael Apted's ongoing *Up* series continues to search for the "boy in the man," recording his subjects every seven years, beginning when they were seven years old (the latest installment is *63 Up: 2020*).

Richard Linklater gave us the marvelous twelve-year experiment, *Boyhood*. It's selective to accept parents as the only adults allowed to continually record their offspring's milestones (birthdays, graduations, school play, soccer tournament, along with vacations and holidays), having, and *sharing*, these visual biographies. If they put up iPhone videos or pictures of their children in swimsuits, year after year, aren't they recording the passage of time through the body?

Aren't Joel-Peter Witkin and Diane Arbus's pictures indicating an interest with physical and psychological states that are as intimate as Sturges's?

We love stories. We live beginnings and middles and ends. We like narrative order.

3.

The sixty photographs included in *Immediate Family* were culled by Mann, with the assistance of her children, out of some two hundred prints. They were made over a period of ten years at a remote cabin in rural Virginia, usually in the summer because, said Mann, "Nothing happens during the other seasons." Summer, too, is associated with childhood, freedom, possibility, and play. Images include her children, naked and clothed (far more often clothed). They are playing games, or sleeping, or swimming or playing dress up, complete with candy cigarettes, spinning out a common childhood fantasy of adulthood (when I was a kid, we would sometimes roll up paper to create our own "cigarettes"). One girl swings, nude, from a giant hay hook. They are also shown with the usual childhood bumps and bruises, a cut here, a little blood there. There is urine and dirt. There are roller skates and pearl necklaces and animals. The children don't seem to mind the camera, which is incredible luck because one really senses that they are allowing the pictures to be taken, which pretty much discredits the idea of exploitation, one of the many criticisms leveled at Mann.

"When I want to use a photograph, I contact each person, explain the context in which I wish to exhibit or publish that picture, and get permission for that specific purpose. I've had a number of American adolescents who, when they hit high school, said, 'I really don't want to see these pictures published right now,' and they were immediately pulled. . . . It's not unusual for them to change their minds at a later time." This is Sturges talking about his professional relationship with his subjects and their preferences. He says that he's never asked a model to sign a release that would surrender his or her rights, allowing him to show the pictures at his discretion; he asks each and every time. (Mann has mentioned that there were one or two pictures her son didn't want shown because he felt they made him look like a "dork.")

Kids are not clueless; they aren't unaware or without any sort of opinions except the ones that adults force on them. Pure innocence is a fantasy, an idea that serves adults more than it does children (sometimes in unsavory ways). It's a notion rooted in nostalgia. They're exposed to the adult world all the time—in the home, in the media—so really, when we decide who they are, or what they don't know (and this stance often masquerades as protection, which is a different thing entirely, a more complex act), we make them reflections of our thought, as opposed to seeing them for themselves. The modern American child isn't as unsullied as we like to think; they just don't have the maturity and world experience to process what they know.

In the *Art:21* documentary for PBS, a now-grown Virginia Mann (Mann's youngest child) said, "Every time she [Sally Mann] looks at something, she's looking at it as an artist. It's so much of her energy. And so we lost, to some extent, a mother, but gained a friend and an artistic accomplice."

An accomplice.

*

Mann said, ". . . I struggle with enormous discrepancies: between the reality of motherhood and the image of it, between my love for my home and the need to travel, the occasional despair and the muse, so tenuously moored, all visit their needs upon me . . . ."

Ruth Orkin said, of her decades-long photographic series, *A World Through My Window,* "Now that I think about it, I don't see how anyone but a housewife could have got all this done." She's talking about taking pictures, from her apartment window, of Central Park and the New York skyline, every day, at various times of the day, through all the seasons, while staying home with her two children. She said that she never set out to be a scenic photographer but "eventually I started taking pictures, not only because it [the park, the skyline] was there, but because I was there." Orkin also took pictures of her children, her daily companions.

When Imogen Cunningham was home with her three children, day in, day out, she, too, produced numerous shots, often nude, of her boys. She said, "The reason I really turned to plants was because I couldn't get out of my own backyard when my children were small. That was when I started photographing what I had in my garden."

And Mann said, "The children were there so I took pictures of the children. Not that I'm interested in the children that much or photographing them. It's just that they were there."

They were there. I was there. We were there. The skyline was there. The plants were there. The park was there.

Film photographers habitually keep track of time; how much time elapses in exposing a shot; how much time in and out of the various chemicals of the darkroom; how much time until the light goes. A mother also lives by the clock. I always wore a watch when my son was small; I, too, watched the light because I needed to know where my child was at all times. Did he need to be picked up, dropped off, fed, bathed, awakened, wrestled into bed. He has thirty minutes to play video games. He has one hour to read a book. Forty-five minutes for homework. Yes, you can go to a friend's house, but be back in two hours.

You have to imagine creative women, women who were career photographers (as Mann, Orkin, and Cunningham were) before becoming mothers, then consider the times in which they lived (Orkin and Cunningham) to understand what it must have been like to have the desire, the "enormous discrepancies," and be tethered to the home. Neither Orkin's nor Cunningham's images of their children are sentimental, because being with children every day leaches sentimentality out of the experience.

As a culture, we expect women—*mothers*—to be selfless, tireless, protective and nurturing. We have to think of them in that manner; the alternative is too alarming. This is only one of the reasons we are even more troubled by terrible mothers than we are by terrible fathers (there are reasons to be troubled by them as well). The minute there is the slightest hint of a mother not being selfless, tireless, protective, and nurturing, there's a disturbance in the universe.

I'm not talking about the currently in-vogue idea of The Bad Mother, which often strikes me as a kind of brag. A bourgeoise brag, if you will, as if there's something rebellious in the notion of allowing your kids five unscheduled minutes. But scratch the surface and you'll find that these Bad Mothers make sure their kids have private schools (or very good public schools, more and more an oxymoron), travel, computers, and lessons, allowing them, the mothers, to run around and complain about the stress of it all. I get that the Bad Mother thing is ironic yet pushed up against the "good mothers" (who presumably do the same things as the bad mothers but without faux complaint) offers a debate that leaves no space for the truly confusing contradictions and tangled emotions of motherhood.

Then there's the artist mother. A classic "bad mother." Not the posturing, pretend-negligent braggart, but someone who wrestles with the push-and-pull love for the two opposing poles of creation and children. (Maybe the only way to alleviate guilt if you are an artist-mother is to include your kids in your art.)

Mann's pictures of her children aren't solely about the experience of childhood—the naked frolicking in the pond, the roller skates, the candy cigarettes, the bloody nose, the urine-soaked sheets—they're also about motherhood. They're about Mann's "enormous discrepancies," her inconvenient and conflicting desires to be here and to be elsewhere (sometimes, for the woman artist/mother, being "elsewhere" can mean being in your own head). They're about wanting to watch her children without interfering, trying to capture the evanescence of childhood, that most fleeting of all moments. (Maybe motherhood is fleeting, too.)

When Mann was photographing she said that her children ceased to be her children, and instead became her models; the woman artist doesn't stop seeing or feeling or experiencing the world as an artist because she has children. That impulse, that *tendency* doesn't go dormant.

Here's another way to think of professional women who happen to be artists now in the midst of domestic life: For centuries men photographed or painted the women in their households: wives, mistresses, children, housekeepers, mothers, and no one thinks that the resulting picture—even if it's nude, even if it's post- or pre-coital, even if it's a mistress and the artist has a wife—is anything other than part of their body of work. Does Vermeer cease to be a painter and become a father who wants a likeness of his daughter? No one talks about the possible humiliation and embarrassment of Mrs. Stieglitz and her daughter, Kitty, when her husband was making sexual nudes of Georgia O'Keeffe and showing them publicly. Vermeer, Stieglitz are always considered artists, and the art they make of the children and lovers is always Art. Regardless of the impact of their pictures on their subjects or the other people in their lives, or the circumstances (hanging around the house; apres sex), it is allowed (it is forgiven) because it's Vermeer. Because it's Stieglitz.

In the *Art:21* documentary about Mann, her son, Emmett, calls his mother "Sally Mann," using both names as if their relationship has a formal, professional aspect. Virginia Mann also sometimes speaks of her mother as if she isn't in the room when she is sitting right there. It's as if there is the professional distance of artist and subject: an unexpected objectivity.

4.

I've always struggled with closeness because I've so often longed to be unencumbered. This doesn't mean I've wanted to be alone; I've wanted relationships that offer a fair amount of breathing room with minimal demands. This sort of arrangement is possible between adults, but unrealistic with a child, especially when your child makes you want to stop time, because your heart can't catch up to the seemingly accelerated changes. How ideal to be a mother/photographer, capturing pieces of their lives. How perfect the way photography travels that line between too much and too distant.

5.

The cabin that serves as the setting for *Immediate Family* is Edenic, a little paradise where children live unsupervised lives of swimming, basking, and imaginative play. The adults are shadowy background figures, engaged in their own lives. The sun always shines, the cabin is rustic enough to withstand children and inviting enough to want to spend time, the lake beckons. The life depicted in Mann's photos appears ridiculously perfect. Mann said, "I wanted the family pictures to look effortless. To look like snapshots." There's something undeniably lovely about this idea, the effortless, unstudied approach that fits right in with the relaxed atmosphere.

Then why did so many writers and critics get so charged up about a parent's vacation photos?

Here's my decades-long theory: It has to do with Nature.

Nature is neither pure nor good nor corrupt nor evil. It's indifferent, behaving according to its own properties and laws without making moral judgments. The most destructive weather (tornados, hurricanes) or events (earthquakes, floods, volcanic eruptions) are not personal. This, of course, has often been a tough concept for human beings, as we tend to like cause-and-effect. So we invented immortals with moral failings, and call a thunderclap a tantrum, as if these fits of anger or jealousy or love are a comfort. Religion is another series of explanations. *Twister*, a Nineties big budget movie that was more an illustration of the art of selling out than it was about a weather condition, has one of its central characters, a scientist (!) relating to tornadoes in a rather personal manner. One "murdered" her family, and she's out for revenge (!!), which pretty much involves tying herself to a post and staring up in the eye of the tornado (!!!). Implausibility and lousy storytelling aside, the real failure of this film is that *Nature never does anything personally to anyone. Ever.*

This idea of tragedy always being someone's fault is fueled by our litigious society; in this way we are more primitive and more greedy than our ancestors who knew, on some level, that shit just happens.

We love nature when we believe it to be beautiful and kind. We love children because we believe them to be gentle and innocent.

I think Mann riles people because she places her children squarely within Nature, in a natural state, following their own desires and whims. There is no such thing as legislation in nature so, it follows, that there can be no sexually prohibitive laws: no underage sex, no rape, no incest. In this regard, everything is permitted. This is one of the reasons why one cannot be sentimental about the natural world; siblings mate, animal parents force their children from the nest or the den as they begin to compete for food and mates. Young males may be banished from the herd until they are strong enough to challenge a dominant male who will, inevitably, be defeated. These dark impulses may too have once been human impulses, but they aren't allowed in modern civilization; we find them too barbaric.

Placing a child (nude) in the context of Nature, then glimpsing the occasional adult in the far reaches of the frame (clothed), can highlight the vulnerability of the child, and the superior physical strength of an adult, so maybe the whole tableau suggests something that the adult, even if subconsciously, would rather not consider. And maybe it doesn't help that the children in Mann's photographs aren't all that gentle or innocent; witness the tiny violences of childhood (the bloody nose, the scraped knee, the cut requiring stitches), and the evidence of their own desires (a girl nonchalantly gripping a dead weasel by its neck, a boy holding two dried out squirrels, a girl pretending to smoke a cigarette, or a girl upending a board game).

A work of art always says as much about the viewer as it does about the artist.

Art essayist John Berger, talking about the female nude in Western art, "a woman is taught to be aware" and "to be naked is to be oneself, to be nude is to be seen by others and yet not recognized to be one's self. A nude has to be seen as an object to be a nude." He goes on to say "nakedness is created in the eye of the beholder." There is a performative aspect to portraiture: the viewer brings something as well. In some ways, a child being photographed by an adult isn't that unlike a woman, in past centuries, being painted by a man; in each case the artist is in charge of the image of someone with less social position. This doesn't necessarily imply abuse; as Berger reminds us, some nudes are "as personal as love poems."

Then again, only a small percentage of the *Immediate Family* pictures are nudes.

The sisters in *Goodnight Kiss* aren't nude, and *yet*. Mann's photographs are undeniably splendid either way, but if the children weren't occasionally nude would the images lack that disturbance beneath the surface? That jolt, that problem, that *thing*?

To be clear, I don't see child pornography, or exploitation in Mann's pictures. And my "natural environment" theory is put forth in an effort to try and understand what some viewers and critics—*A work of art always says as much about the viewer as it does about the artist*—find so troubling in these photographs since I don't see it myself.

As idyllic as the *Immediate Family* childhood appears, it's still a construct, a distillation and interpretation of childhood. Even Mann's daughter Jessie said when people comment that their childhood must have been "magical" she answers, "It wasn't magical at the time but looking back on it, it was." One can imagine the duality of having memories, and then being given those pictures, those images, those carefully built ideals.

This is my way of saying, while the photographs are, by turns, authentic and staged, they are real in the way that art that resonates is real, which is the artificiality of the work tapping into truth.

6.

Immediate Family, in a very fundamental sense, defined motherhood for me. The series showed children at their most true, that is to say, flawed; it also showed that it was possible to be home with children and make art. And that no subject is inherently sentimental, or banal, or unimportant. Male writers (and artists) aren't often forced to wrestle with the fallout of art when connected to domesticity; they don't have their work labeled as "women's fiction," then quietly dismissed. This series means everything to me; this domestic life; this creative life.

7.

Robert Hughes and Robert Rauschenberg were discussing Rauschenberg's "combine" (a combination of painting and object), *Rebus,* 1955:

ROBERT RAUSCHENBERG (*talking about the color key running through the center of the picture*): The colors are the key of how it [the painting] is to be read, but the whole thing is a fantasy, so.

ROBERT HUGHES: So you establish these kinds of—

RR: You do. These are your experiences.

RH: No, no. You're drawing the pictures, doctor.

RR (*laughing, then getting serious as he answers*): Yes, but you're the one who has all the references, ah, because of your experience.

RH: So you're happy to let people make them up as they go along?

RR: I insist upon it.

*

In an interview with Ethan Hawke, Deborah Soloman asked if he "believes a mother can will her children to grow up into artists?" He answered, "If she abandons them early enough." The other thing he said was that his mother "wanted me to be a novelist. In a way, I am a construction of my mother's imagination."

Does the stay-home mother (Mann, Orkin, Cunningham) "abandon" her children when she becomes the photographer to their models? Do they not become a "construct" of the imagination? Mann frequently talks about her children not as her children, but as models. When you change roles so utterly, do those other relationships cease to exist during the time the mother is inventing, and envisioning?

8.

"I just ran wild for the first seven years of my life . . . then I went to school and didn't take too kindly but then I was eventually civilized." This is Mann on her own upbringing. She ran with a dog pack of a dozen boxers on her family's thirty Virginia acres that were "cleared and planted with rare trees imported from England and Asia." She was frequently nude, sometimes photographed by her father. Her parents were tired of raising kids when she came along and their approach was "benign neglect."

No one, she adds, considered her, with her energetic, loosely supervised, rural upbringing, "trash." This is where social class enters in because, in America, the loosely supervised, happily naked, rural upbringing is admired if it also includes parents who are educated and financially solvent, because then you are closer to some madcap aristocrat than, say, someone yelling at her five kids in a 99 cent store. Mann's mother was "blue-blood New England"; her father "an atheist who practiced compassionate medicine sixty hours a week. Enough of a socialist to

believe that you shouldn't have to pay for it if you couldn't."
(Socialism, too, can be seen as another privilege in this context.)
He was also a master gardener, "renegade Texan," art collector
(Kandinsky in his thirties, Twonbley in his fifties); "an oddball,
a character, an eccentric," who remained a paradox since he felt
"no conflict in the perceived contradiction of being a moralist
and an atheist. He was "courtly," "unassuming," "extravagant in
his vision" and a demon behind the wheel of his sports car.

Her father's chosen Christmas decorations, in place of a
creche, were an "upright log with an erect phallus and scro-
tum," also made of wood and attached. A mannikin of a partial
human torso—the area between the waist and knees—a skele-
ton hand caressing the crotch. For everyday, he graced the dining room table with a "figure-eight white, petrified dog turd."
Three-dimensional "porno" constructions placed in the yard in
honor of the family's extensive garden being chosen for a state
garden tour.

She mentions that she and her brother were pulled out of the
classroom during Bible study. I was in the same circumstances
as a child, though for different reasons, singled out for having parents with a belief system that was clearly in the minority (the minority consisting of me, my brother, and my sister)
and being pulled out of class. Interestingly, Mann's daughter
Jessie notes that while her mother was raised with "no sense
of God and you'll never hear her say anything spiritual or religious" that her art is her "expression of spirituality" and that
"maybe it's the same with *Immediate Family,* a sort of maternal
understanding, a maternal love that is so hard to express that
she took pictures."

It isn't uncommon for artists to be spiritual and non-
believers—it's actually sort of the name of the game. Only art
cuts across religion and region and gender and class and all the
rest to investigate, and express what it means to be human. No
other endeavor in the world—not money, not religion, not sci-

ence—tries harder to get to that place, that essence that all of us can recognize in each other, that nature that we all share. This is not New Age-speak; it's far older, more primal. It's human handprints, across thousands of years, found in an underwater cave. It is urban graffiti, and the Renaissance popes emptying their coffers for art. Art is fundamental to whatever we are. To call *Immediate Family* a prayer is simply too reductive; it is more call-and-response. Mother to child to mother. I know about the difficulty of expressing maternal love.

9.

My family was eccentric, but not in such a splendid, dazzling manner. No noblesse oblige blue blood mother, or the cultural transgressions of the socialist physician father making three-dimensional porno assemblages. The gardens, the dog pack, the nudity. The factual tone in which these details are related, no editorializing, no apology. People with money, whether they're unconventional like the Manns, or rich and dull, rarely apologize. That is one of the things that money buys.

A few of my middle-class family's less lofty peculiarities: My mother refusing to live in a house anyone had lived in before because she was passionately devoted, in every aspect of her life, to the new, the now, and the future. My father, an electrical engineer, endlessly curious about everything except people, was smart and skilled and something of a Renaissance guy but didn't interact much (see where people just puzzled him) and spent the better part of every weekend working in the yard in a waist-high black Speedo bathing suit, very Jeff Chandler, and only because he couldn't do his chores naked, his preferred at-home look.

There had been a fleeting conversation about the family joining a nudist colony, but my mother was strictly a domestic nudist. She was also, unlike almost all the other mothers at my school, a "career woman" who worked in advertising, a field she'd worked since she was seventeen years old and living in New York (she had graduated high school when she was sixteen, even though she had also taken "a year off" because she "didn't feel like going to school"). Her first boyfriend was a Chinese fellow, followed by a Jewish fellow, then two or three Italians. She was Italian American herself and didn't care about much except if the boy liked her. Her male-centricity wasn't passed down to me. She was glamorous to the point that when she wasn't made up, no one recognized her. For three years the woman next door believed that a pair of sisters lived in our house, one pretty and the other plain.

My brother has lived with my mother all but four years of his life. Many people think they're a married couple because of their demeanor and companionship (my mother was widowed at age forty-seven). Once, in an Acting in Commercials class, their teacher gave them an improv that had them seated next to each other on a plane, where my brother was directed to try to pick up my mother (the teacher believed them married). They have weird, good-humored adventures, like spying on a man who spurned their Milanese-born Italian-language teacher (a raging racist, as it turned out), or getting caught in a Class Five hurricane while on a cruise. Getting robbed at gunpoint one night on a deserted downtown Los Angeles street where my mother decided to reason with the robber while screaming at my brother to comply, utterly confusing the gunman. But it's the married part that troubles.

On the last day of sixth grade at my elementary school, my father, a quiet, retiring soul, not at all demonstrative so you had to read him through his actions, gave me a corsage. He pinned the flowers to my shoulder, then had me pose for a picture. (Must I mention that I was the only kid in school wearing a *corsage*? Years later, in the 1980s when my brother went on what is believed to be his only date, my mother had him buy his date a *corsage,* like it's some mysterious family tradition.) I still have the photograph he took with his much-loved Leica, in front of our ranch house with its orange painted roof strewn with a truckload of loose, orange painted rocks, as I stood in the driveway in my favorite dress, with my skinny legs, and the corsage. There's a kind of mystery and poignancy in pictures that parents took of their children in the film era.

The downside of today's constant recording of kids' passages and events is that you (ironically) miss them. You remove yourself from the experience by placing the camera between you; you are no longer a participant, but an observer.

I'm an avid postcard buyer when traveling. I don't collect them, though I did when I was a kid, keeping them filed in a box. The postcards of my childhood weren't all locations, some were animals, objects, or novelties. (I had other collections too.)

I use the travel postcards (the ones I don't send) as records of places I've been, pasting them in my travel journals. My brother-in-law ridiculed this habit, *why don't you just take your own pictures?* even though I *do* take my own pictures, but I take very few because I want to be *in* the place I am visiting, and the camera takes you out of it. If I were a professional photographer, my purpose would be different, but I'm just a tourist and writer who wants to reflect on one or two things when my trip is over. Photographing a vacation moment fixes the moment that you aren't really experiencing; in a sense, the photograph is really offering your *first* experience of that moment, and not a memory.

I photographed a party once in the Caribbean. I hated it. You try to get something out of it through a camera, but at a party I want to be at a party.

—Robert Mapplethorpe

*

Mann's answer to the accusations of oppression, torture, child abuse, sexualization, conquered tribes, sullied innocence, much of which came from a piece, "Nolo Me Tangere: The Family Photographs of Sally Mann" by Noelle Oxenhandler comparing Mann's portraits to the Native American portraits "that manage to preserve that fleeting moment when a conquered people still rest so deeply in their own dignity that they can stare back into the eye of the conquering people with a look that says There is something about me that will never be yours." Oxenhandler mentions the girl swinging from the hayhook, saying it reminds her of a story that she [the writer] read as a child of a little girl being "hung from her wrists in a shower by her parents."

She does ask if it's preferable to have sanitized children's photos, or those that "acknowledge the edge we walk on?"

Here's what Mann says:

"If my children didn't have something better to do, I'm sure they'd love to rebut all the bullshit that comes pouring out of academia about my work . . . but still, Noelle's piece was better than some . . . at least she didn't see repressed memories of incest as my artistic motivation." (One could substitute the word "work" for "mothering skills" and get a handle on Mann's irritation.)

"They [her children] were—and still are—active participants in the art-making that goes on around them all the time. Art is in every aspect of our daily life—in the gardens we have designed around the house, in what we put on our walls, in the pumpkins we cut for Halloween. And any parent knows you can't *force* a child to make art; they have to cooperate, they have to want to be part of the process. When we made these pictures, the kids knew exactly what to do to make an image work: how to look, how to project degrees of intensity or defiance or plaintive, woebegone, Dorothea Lange-like dejection. I didn't pry these pictures from them—they *gave* them to me . . .

no deep psychological manipulations or machinations, just the straightforward, every day telling of a story."

It's a mistake to single out Oxenhandler's essay, especially since it isn't close to being the most vitriolic, yet it is one of the essays that Mann responds to, and the response is interesting because she acknowledges the common parental complaint regarding how difficult it is to get children to do what you want them to do, then uses this as proof that they—kids and mother— were all in this project together. Elsewhere, Jessie Mann has said that her mother simply caught them in the act of being children, while Mann's son, Emmett says that the pictures were thought out. Working with film, as Mann did, demands manipulation, not just in the darkroom, or playing with mechanical or natural light; it can occur in the very moment a photographer crops a picture, changing the emphasis of the image. This is not the same as photographic trickery (another subject entirely). Capturing a perfect picture means so many things must converge: the moment, the eye, the reflexes. To even believe that there is "something" you think you see in the viewfinder is as close to an act of faith as it gets in art. It's harder to understand this photographic belief in an era of digital photography and light rooms and photoshop.

Film is an entirely different proposition, from start (loading it into the camera), to the finish (printing). Imagine making pictures that you cannot see until after what you hoped to capture has passed. In the same way that non-writers believe that all it takes to write a novel or memoir is "knowing the story," non-photographers often think, you see it, you snap it, done.

Of course, Emmett Mann also says that he believed his mother had some kind of "dream" that she was trying to will into reality. And, really, how traditionally parental is *that*?

Mann concludes her rebuttal by offering a Eudora Welty anecdote that concerns a visit to Hollins where she, Welty, says that "the classroom was filling up with all these guys in beards, academic types" who wanted to understand how she "came up with that powerful symbol of the marble cake [given from one character to another], with the feminine and the masculine and the Freudian and the Jungian all mixed together" that had occurred in one of her stories. Her answer—and the one that Mann appropriates for herself when confronted by an intellectual analysis of her own work, "Well, you see, it's a recipe that's been in my family for some time." All of which is a little disingenuous.

Mann's explanation that her children helped make her pictures exposes the artifice, the craft, the skill, the greatness of Mann's work that she makes seem so serendipitous, so effortless, the "corner of her eye" that Ingrid Sischy wrote. Her marvelous "snapshots." This hidden effort bears out Flaubert's message to his mistress, Louise Colet: "One must not think that feeling is everything. Art is nothing without form."

*

"The place is important; the time is summer. It's any summer, but the place is home and here is my family." This is the opening sentence of *Immediate Family.*

*

The first time I thumbed through *Immediate Family,* I was with a writer friend, younger than I by a decade, who fancied herself a socialist. She would go on about politics, injustice, women's rights, capitalism, freedom until it became obvious to the listener how unmistakably uninformed she really was. As with many artists who are radicalized by their own experiences and residency in bohemia, her rants were really only about her; she wanted nothing to stand in the way of her own liberty. She was fitfully employed, frequently broke, and very angry about it.

Everything in this country (meaning being unable to support herself without working jobs she hated) was unfair, though she really meant everything was unfair to her.

The dull jobs aside (who hasn't worked them?), she never lived a life of poverty, or racism. She had two college degrees from good universities, and her "suffering" came across more as petulance than hardship. She liked to selectively borrow from philosophies and belief systems without committing to an entire program.

At dinner one night she badgered J., my husband, about his choice to be monogamous. "How can you allow someone to prevent you from being with other women?" she said. He said it was because he wanted to be with me. That wasn't good enough, as she kept pounding her point that I (sitting right there) had "no right" to tell him what to do, even though I had never told him what to do. I said nothing as she directed this weird criticism at me, through her monogamy argument with J. He sighed, tried to explain again that monogamy was his choice, not some fascist regime that I set up in our household. Still, she insisted that I was "holding him back" from "experiencing other women" and that I should "allow him his freedom because everyone should have their freedom."

For all her radical, free-love socialist views, I was surprised that she turned prudish as the two of us stood, side by side, in a mall bookstore in the progressive city where we both lived, flipping through *Immediate Family* that my friend pronounced "pornographic." I had heard about the pictures, but, as I said, this was my first time seeing them. I didn't agree or disagree with her; I may have uttered a small, noncommittal "hmmm," but, in truth, I was no longer in a mall bookstore; I was somewhere else entirely. *The place is important; the time is summer. It's any summer, but the place is home and here is my family.*

The mall disappeared, I was pitched into another location entirely, with ideas crowding and colliding. I could still hear my friend making it clear that this sort of offensive garbage shouldn't be encouraged, even though I wasn't paying any attention. My friend wasn't a parent, she wasn't a professional writer who spent much of her day trying to figure out the mother/writer equation, who felt that she needed to be everywhere even if she felt sometimes that she was nowhere.

As my friend went on and on, I flipped to *Goodnight Kiss,* an image of young children, sisters, kissing each other on the mouth, the one girl holding the head of the other girl to her. It's beautiful, unmoored and dreamy, and passionate. You just see their heads, no nudity. I could see how this image could rile some people.

But I didn't find these pictures dirty or pornographic—unless I did? Somewhere, deep in my subconsciousness, did I find this work profane? With all the shouting that was going on at the time (and my aggrieved friend), it was hard not to at least entertain the question.

10.

In 2006, when I first began to search the Internet for information on Sally Mann, coming across the Noelle Oxenhandler essay, the following appeared in the margins (and had nothing to do with the essay): Heterosexual porn ("Deep Oral Girls" "Grannies" "Bang Bus"), gay porn ("Bad Puppy" "Soldier of Cock" "Cruise Patrol"), bisexual porn ("Three Pillows" "I Go Both Ways"), women-only porn ("For the Girls"), alt porn ("Nakkid Nerds" "Gothic Amateur"), odd porn ("X-Rated Midgets" "Plushie Sex" "Musical Toy Sex")—along with another lengthy list of articles about Sally Mann. It was very much like being back in Powell's Books with the yellow notice on the shelf in place of *Immediate Family.*

It was nearly impossible, in the early 2000s, no matter how careful you were, not to stumble upon some pornography links when looking for articles on Sally Mann, the woman that in 2001 was named by *Time* magazine as "America's Best Photographer." (Sure, it's hard to call anyone in any field "the best" as if that designation, once bestowed, is unchanging, negating, but I don't think there is anyone working today who surpasses Mann; let's say she's a part of a small, rarified group.) Her work is collected by the Metropolitan Museum of Art, The Museum of Modern Art, The Whitney Museum, the homes of private collectors.

Mann said that when her father gave her first camera (at age seventeen), he told her that the "only subjects worthy of art were love, death and whimsy." Some of the pictures I saw that day with my vocal friend were: a tiny girl asleep among sacks of grain as large as she; another girl sleeping beside an old woman; a boy holding what looks like a pair of barbecued squirrels; a girl casually holding a stuffed weasel by its neck against her naked body; a naked girl lying on her stomach in the grass with more grass sprinkled on her back. A girl smoking a candy cigarette; a topless girl in a necklace of fake pearls and rhinestone earrings; a girl posed next to the arm of an adult still showing the girl's teethmarks; a girl with stitches above her eye; a boy floating on a lake with a blow-up alligator nearby. A sleeping girl under a sheet of see-thru fabric resembling a shroud. A naked girl on a urine-soaked mattress. *Goodnight Kiss.*

There is tension in the juxtaposition of childhood and the decay and death of the lifeless animals, the small injuries; the vaguely Victorian echo of angels and children.

Mann's work is visionary in the sense that it doesn't quite belong in any time or place; it just transcends all that. There is something classic, timeless about the children's portraits. Part of this sense has to do with Mann occasionally using glass plates, or vintage cameras with some damage to the lens, as well as film. This can be seen more clearly in her landscapes. Though it also has to do with the isolation of the rural setting, the board games, the candy cigarettes, playing dress up, and the absence of markers of modernity. There's a hint of peering at the pictures through the wrong end of the time telescope; one can imagine the nostalgia of the images the moment they are printed.

Contact with art isn't benign contact. Our relationship with the painting, the film, the photograph is in play from the moment we stop to look. It's reductive to say that those who see child abuse in Mann's pictures must be harboring some child abuse darkness within themselves. My disgusted friend (shortly thereafter, my ex-friend for reasons unrelated to our difference of opinion about Mann's pictures, well, mostly unrelated) isn't wrong about the distaste she feels for those photographs; there is no reliable right or wrong with art.

I keep coming back to Mann's pictures because the work feels endlessly new to me, alive, shifting, and unfixed. *Immediately Family* is provocative for me, too, but not in the same way as it is for my ex-friend. I welcome the provocation.

*

Lolita had been my favorite novel since I finally read it in its entirety when I was twenty years old. My introduction to the book came via the movie, which was being shown on TV as an "event" sometime during the late 1960s when I was almost thirteen, four years older than the nine-year old Lolita. Watching the movie changed my feelings forever about James Mason— well, more like *established* my feelings about him. Seeing the film led to trying to read the book. I was a pretty good reader, and *Lolita* was by no means the first "adult" book that I had read (*Valley of the Dolls, The Carpetbaggers,* Alfred Hitchcock anthologies, James Thurber). Still, while I could read the words,

I was unable to fully understand the content. This was also true with Thurber and a couple of the Hitchcock stories. It didn't take much to realize that "adult" didn't mean strong language or graphic sex scenes; adult was a sensibility, a state of mind, a variety of sophistication than even I, a fairly bright and precocious kid, couldn't grasp. That is to say, I could grasp that I couldn't grasp it.

I've read *Lolita* in a college class, a few times on my own, and I've taught it. I never tired of the sheer high-wire act of it, the beauty, the deftness, the dazzle of wordplay, the construction, the riffs on America (those road trips!), the elegance, the sacred, the profane, the sly humor, the intelligence, the wink, the tear. In one brilliant sequence, Humbert observes Lolita, her one sneakered foot resting atop the other, standing on a hotel tennis court, as she talks to another child. He admits to himself that the deepest wrong he has committed on this girl was the theft of her childhood, which can never be returned. Irretrievable because who among us can turn back the clock? Does this epiphany cause Humbert to weep into the palms of his own hands? Does he gently drop the curtain, wrestling with the breaking of his own heart at this crime? No! He is inflamed with desire, so much so that he marches out to her, places his hand on the back of her neck, and directs her back to their hotel room.

He loves her. He is obsessed by her. Owned by her. His powerlessness manifests as bullying; his love ruled by jealousy, and fear of losing her. For all the elevation of this book in recent years (when I first began my *Lolita*-loving years, I was hard-pressed to find others who had read it, let alone loved it), it was always a dirty little book. An intellectually playful disturbing dark filthy book. No gathering of all the novel's glories will gloss over this essential truth.

(A digression: As I've aged, I've come to think of *Lolita* as a book about the relationship of art and the artist, and that illusive element of art that the artist is always chasing, desperate, yet unable to possess, until he accepts it, or it drives him mad. There is a very brief chapter where Humbert, a well-educated writer and poet, sits at his typewriter, typing out *Lolita Lolita Lolita* until he reaches the bottom of the page. It's my favorite moment because it illustrates the core dilemma of making art. Humbert spends the entire novel pursuing Lolita; he schemes, he drugs her, he drinks, he bribes, he threatens—anything he can think of to have this one thing. Yet even when he has her in his life, or in his arms, the one thing he knows is that his desire for her is endless, and he can never, no matter how it appears, truly possess her. There is no attainment, no arrival. She is never his. She is always this irreverent, fickle, mercurial child who never really gives herself away (he can only guess what she's thinking); the closest he gets is the illusion of having her, and even then, it's for very short and (for him) happy periods. The momentary satisfaction of artwork. At the end of the novel, he tracks her down, his artist life is nothing without her—she had chosen to devote herself to an insensitive, also perverted playwright/"filmmaker"—and here it should be said, Lolita is not Humbert's muse, she is the essence of Art itself. When he finally finds her she is old, seventeen, years past Humbert's stated "ideal nymphet" age, pasty, and very pregnant with another man's child. What does he do? He *begs* her to come away with him. *Begs* her. The artist is nothing without Art.)

(Another digression: As much as I've loved that book for nearly my entire adult life, as I mentioned, I find, surprisingly, that I *have* grown tired of it in the last few years. The reason is another essay entirely.)

Lolita and *Immediate Family* are only and slightly alike in that I've loved and admired them for decades, though I recognize they trouble some people. Even for me there's something shadowy and disquieting located in the novel and the photo series, but it isn't "child abuse" (the most common charge for both)—the children don't seem entirely without agency—

and *that*, I think, is the problem for people like my ex-friend. These two works induce a bit of moral vertigo because there is something so engaging about the novel, so arresting within the pictures.

11.

The traveling exhibition of *Immediate Family* opened in Philadelphia only months after my first (and only) child was born. Technically, I was a mother, but if parenthood is measured by experience and time, then I was still in a more, or less, "childless" state. I was involved with the care and nurturing, not to mention the loving, of my baby. I adored him. I was wolfishly devoted to him, but I was wrestling with the identity of being a mother. I suppose I was in a period of "becoming"; my kid's transitional years from infant, to toddler, to child were mirroring my own transition to "mother."

My idea of being a parent was more like being an aunt, which is to say, I hadn't had any real drive to be a parent. Ambivalence ruled. I liked the whole aunt idea, or even stepmother, or godmother role. I never felt that a child had to be my child to have a relationship with him or her. Babysitting wasn't for me, even though I did it in my youth and gave it my best. Imagine a scenario where an ill-equipped, Hollywood rom-com guy finds himself having to care for a baby, and that gives a sort of idea of my childcare style. The diaper was never on right, I would read *Crime & Punishment* at bedtime (because it was homework, and the kid wouldn't go to sleep), I had food confusion. Let's just say, I didn't enter the World of Children in an adult (or teen) way and so tended to talk to them in a non-baby way, which I think they kind of liked. And then there were all the babysitting jobs where I accompanied my friends, which is how I discovered the full measure of my ineptitude.

There was anxiety and exhilaration when I learned I was pregnant. I was anxious, you know, in a classic woman artist kind of way, the *how will I get it all done?* The writer part of me, the part of me that's curious about almost everything, was intrigued by being pregnant. So many changes, and all beyond my control. Not to mention how you are seen (no one ever talked about *that*): one day, you're you, that is, until you start to show and then you turn into A Pregnancy. I fucking hated it. I was the same person inside, but now I was a condition. I lost whatever consequence I had as a person, specifically as a woman. It surprised me how dismissive men were, and how interested women were (interest in a pregnancy is different than interest in you).

The core of my apprehension was the fear of being torn financially and emotionally; it was the knowledge that making art or literature is a passionate undertaking and that your kid will most likely be competing with that passion (and that passion with your kid), competing for your time, your attention, and your heart as thoroughly as if your novels were selfish siblings. And you're just scared all the time because the world is exactly how you think it is, only more so. And so many of my friends chose not to have children, so I was pretty much alone.

I'm no sentimentalist. I'm not a hard-case, either. This placed me in a funny area, mom-wise, where I couldn't stand the whole Cult-of-the-Child business that was ramping up in the early 1990s. But I also wasn't taken with the self-involvement of the Bad Mother act. I didn't want all the attention on the child, but I certainly didn't want it all on myself either, you know, the whole, "I'm such a Bad Mother because: *I give my kid sugar,* or *I like wine in the afternoon,* or *I tell them to take it outside*" (as if this is radical; kids are *supposed* to take it outside).

Then, when I had my son, no one in my family took me seriously as a parent. As my mother said, "I never think of you as raising a child as much as I think of you observing one."

Yeah, I'm such a Bad Mother because I refuse to get involved. Except I'm completely involved.

Enter Sally Mann. Her photographic series? I needed to see children and childhood in a way that made sense to me as a mother. It wasn't just the images, it was the making of the pictures, the fluid relationship of parent/child/art, it was the photographer, it was Mann herself. I needed to know that all of this—the range of childhood, the making of art—was possible.

Reynolds Price wrote of Sally Mann ". . . her serene technical brilliance and the clearly communicated eloquence she derives from her subjects, human and otherwise—subjects observed with an ardor that is all but indistinguishable from love."

12.

Mann says, "Over the years I learned not to talk about my work, taking to heart the Robert Doisneau quote that goes something like this: 'If you take pictures, don't speak, don't write, don't analyze yourself, and don't answer any questions."

One of my favorite quotes is from the painter who told an art class that while he enjoyed listening to their theories, they meant as much to him as ornithology does to a bird.

Mann is aware that an audience brings its own personal histories, ideas, sensibilities, prejudices, and world views. How much to take to heart? How much to ignore? If an artist is lucky, people will take the time to think the work through. But what happens when you, the artist, think them wrong? More to the point, can they be wrong?

*

Mann to *New York Magazine*:

"The more I look at the life of the children the more enig-
matic and fraught with danger and loss their lives become. That's
what taking any picture is about. At some point you weigh all
the risks."

"Everyone has all those fears that I have for my children."

"I have a longstanding affection for Nabokov. . . . I love
him, of course. But I found it pretty difficult to read [*Lolita*]
the second time because of what he did to that girl."

13.

Sally Mann has talked about her love for nineteenth-century
cameras with their unwieldy glass plates, and chemicals, their
(for her) desirable flaws and imperfections that have come with
the passing of time. She says of her daughter, Virginia, that
she looked like someone from another century. Motherhood
in Arcadia, the American landscape that contextualizes the
pictures is boundless, idealized, gently illuminated. A radiant
Eden. The settings can call to mind the luminous painting of
Bierstadt or Cole, dreamscapes that presage Surrealism. (Mann
said that she made her way into landscape pictures when she
noticed that she was pulling back from the kids, their figures
becoming smaller as their surroundings took up more of the
frame.)

There's so much tough beauty in these pictures. Mann lays
out a complex, humanist world, both romanticized and real.
Among the nakedness, the injuries, the sleeping, the blood,
the shrouds, the dead animals, the shining sun, the elegant girl
with the candy cigarette, the younger, glamorous girl with the
heart-shaped sunglasses, and the beautiful boy with his collection of bracelets adorning his left wrist, the kiss, there is an
absence of shame. These children who often look directly,

evenly at the lens, are not embarrassed or coy. No matter how intimate or explicit the image, they own it.

Americans seem to think in binary terms about art—you like it, or you don't like it; you get it, or you don't get it; you're a crowd pleaser like the French Impressionists, or you're Francis Bacon—and Mann's work falls nowhere in this system. The children in these pictures are complicated, neither perfect nor sullied. You open a book of Robert Mapplethorpe's work and see one man peeing into the mouth of another man and you say, of course, *Mapplethorpe*. He's allowed—no, *expected*— to bring an edge to his work. He could even make a series of flowers, and still dodge being labeled as cloying or his pictures merely "pretty."

Women have a challenge in that, historically, they've been consigned to the home, and then, when they paint, photograph, or write about the domestic life, no matter how much they abstract the experience, it is dismissed as art without weight, or substance. For anyone who has ever been to a zoo and watched a tiger pace and pace and pace and pace, that should offer some idea of what it means to kill yourself to get into college, then kill yourself to complete that degree, then kill yourself to have that career, only to give it all up. Or to have a need so strong to make art that it competes with everything else in your life. Maybe "domestic art" hasn't been perfected, but maybe the point the critics have been missing when they write off those books (pictures, paintings) is that they are often about a struggle, and maybe part of the struggle is in the making of the book, picture, painting itself.

The hue and cry over Mann's pictures—though it's lessened with time—was so gratifying to me, a woman writer with a child, because it forced the public to see, to really see as if for the first time, that home life, that domesticity, that social sphere as unsettling, and thorny, and as important as any other aspect of human experience. Not a *lesser* experience. Not inconsequential, then kissed off. Flannery O'Connor wrote, "It's well to remember that the serious fiction writer always writes about the world, no matter how limited his particular scene."

14.

If I have a favorite picture from *Immediate Family* it may be *Holding the Weasel, 1989.* I love the girl's grip on the dead weasel. Anyone who has ever seen the unintentionally brutish treatment by a very young child with say, a kitten or a duckling, will recognize this girl's unthinking, yet firm hold on this animal. She glances to the side, her pose of casual confidence, showing neither mercy for the limp weasel, nor cruelty because, you know, life just *is.* I like *Jessie at 5, 1987,* with her rhinestone earrings and pearls, and *The Last Time Emmett Modeled Nude, 1987* (because it was the last time), and the picture of the three kids, taken in 1989, where they look so tough and daring, and young in all the right ways.

I've kept a journal of my son since he was born. It's haphazard, impulsive—I didn't write in it every day because I was, you know, busy raising him. I think about the woman behind the camera who observes her children, transforms them into models, limiting her interaction with them when she becomes the one recording them, interpreting them. I imagine her allowing them to be who they are, and not who you want them to be, to see what happens. Motherhood is all about the open hand, and not the grasping fist that holds on for dear life. You step back from your child because you love him, and maybe because the urge to embrace your child and never let go, is so powerful.

The reality of Mann's art—the setups, the poses, "the straightforward, everyday telling of the story"—is a parable of the artist mother, a way of reconciling those two things, art and children, that come so perilously close to canceling each other out, leaving you, the artist mother, stranded. Maybe if you're an artist, all you think about is beauty.

Sally Mann isn't an easy artist. She did a series, taken at a 2.5-acre forensic facility at the University of Tennessee, called the Body Farm. Corpses (around one hundred are donated a year) are strewn about the grounds, in various poses, and left to decompose in order to study the body in its various post-mortem stages. I can't even look at those photographs because I cannot handle the circumstances, the idea, or the images. She also photographs bones, often of her dead dogs, and, most recently, an ongoing series of her beloved husband, Larry, wasting from muscular dystrophy. The pictures are arresting and heartbreaking. The seeming accessibility of the children's photos is deceptive.

*

When photography began it was a novelty, a way to record people and the world around us. Then, trick photography, a kind of visual sleight of hand, came along, whether for entertainment, or to assuage the grief of a loved one comforted by spirit photography, or *memento mori,* or the cut-and-paste of a dead loved one into a picture. Photography initially imitated painting, using dreamy, slightly blurry effects, while portraying Big Subjects (Bible stories, allegories) often seen in paintings. It didn't take long for photographers to drop all that painterly nonsense and treat it as its own art form (photography was still a record, still a diversion, still journalistic, still portraiture).

It's easy to forget that photography is interpretive—unless the image is wildly abstract or manipulated—because the images are so easy to recognize, and because anyone can snap a photo. Collecting photographs, as one would paintings or sculptures, is relatively recent. Picture taking seems like a level playing field, though crediting the equipment with the final result is like saying a typewriter is as important as the writer. It's hard for some people to understand the eye involved, the inspiration, the quick decisions, the imagined final image, dark (or light) room skill, and the idea of multiple prints prompts a kind of skepticism about a print as an art object. A photograph is valued and devalued at the same time. People can take pictures with their phones, then photoshop them. Sometimes people think a fine picture is a fine picture because someone just happened to take a fine picture.

Our relationship to painting is different; many people walk into a museum with the expectation that a picture might be arcane and baffling. Or maybe they get bored. de Chirico? *Where is everyone?* de Kooning? *What's with the teeth? What does it mean?* Basquiat? *Is that graffiti? What does it mean? See that Mondrian over there? My kid could do that.* Dorothea Tanning? *Why is there a monster at her feet? What does it mean? What does it mean?*

But when they see a photograph, the expectation is the complete opposite of a painting; they absolutely expect to understand it, to find a quick correlation in their world. So, to be presented with a photograph that isn't abstract, that isn't overworked, that looks like children playing on a summer's day, that was taken by their mother, and yet to be made uncomfortable by the images, seems as if it's somehow "breaking the photography contract" by looking, yet not *feeling*, like a picture anyone could (or would) take.

If Mann's work were painted, many people might say, I just don't like it, it's weird, but I don't really get painting anyway. Imagine Balthus's adolescents, say *Therese Dreaming* (1936), depicting a thirteen-year-old girl, gazing out a window in a reverie as she sits with one leg bent, deliberately exposing her white cotton underwear. In *The Guitar Lesson* (1938) a woman sits with a young girl, naked from the waist down, sprawled across her lap. The girl pinches the woman's nipple while the woman strokes the girl's crotch; Robert Hughes called it "one of the few masterpieces among erotic paintings by Western artists in the last fifty years." Balthus's pictures ruffle feathers, but they're paintings. Possibly products of his imagination, not models, not in the room with him while he made the pictures. Paintings invite ambiguity, confusion, refusal. Also, people who enjoy looking at paintings tend to—how shall I say this without sounding the way it sounds?—have more expansive ideas about art. They might let the little things go. But photography, for the reasons I mentioned, is held to a stricter standard, and it may be because the audience is so much broader, perhaps the thinking too literal.

So instead of seeing Mann's children as interpretive works of art, and all that that implies, the literalist, not the person who comes to a museum or galley with limited judgment, wants to know how a mother could take such graphic pictures and still call herself a mother?

15.

There are so many things at work in Mann's children's portraits: the echoing of her own unusual, expressive childhood, of the mother observing her child, of the artist making pictures in her home (the "enormous discrepancies"), of the mother trying to find a way to be a mother *and* a photographer, of the children's willingness to model (to become art themselves), to be surprised, of the pleasure in simply allowing life to unfold and having the mastery to capture evanescence. To understand that if we love, we must love everything, the flaws and the perfection, the blood and the urine, the rhinestones and the roller skates; the disturbing and the pure.

INVENTING THE MALE NUDE

Imogen Cunningham

A Personal Imogen Cunningham Lexicon

CHILDREN

Imogen Cunningham married Roi Partridge in 1915, after an extended correspondence that began with Cunningham's interest in mounting a show of Partridge's etchings. The professional correspondence that began in 1913 soon became love letters; Roi falling in love with Imogen. He had been in Europe with friends since 1910, traveling, studying, and making art, then the letters, then the proposal to Imogen ("You are the ideal woman for me!" he wrote, rhapsodic, "Love and time in Italy!" he wrote of their future lives), who had established her own photography studio in Seattle, offering naturalistic portraits. Eventually forming the photography group *f/64* in the 1920s, along with Ansel Adams, John Paul Edwards, Sonya Noskowiak, Henry Swift, Willard Van Dyke, and Edward Weston. The group had broken with the current photographic traditions of imitating paintings, instead dedicating itself to shooting in natural light, and limiting any sort of photo manipulation, including the cropping of images. Imogen had already moved past painterly pictures of allegorical subjects; her art progressive. Roi said he wanted her for a friend, a companion, and a wife.

The Cunninghams were living in Portland in 1883 when Imogen was born, though she was raised in Seattle (with a brief utopian sojourn on a Washington commune) with an unconventional father (the engine behind the commune idea), and a large, blended family (ten kids, the product of her parents' previous marriages, each parent having been widowed). She was the first of her family to earn a college degree (University of Washington, in chemistry), to win a scholarship to study in Dresden for one year with the foremost photochemist of the time (Professor Doctor Robert Luther), published a paper on a platinum printing, stopped in New York, London, and Paris, returned home and worked for two years in Edward Curtis's studio, eventually opening a portrait studio of her own where she discovered her preference for the natural, untouched picture.

Portland, Washington Commune, Seattle; eccentric, supportive father; university, chemistry degree; New York (meeting Stieglitz and O'Keeffe), London, Paris, Dresden, Dr. Robert Luther, Edward Curtis studio, her own studio, artistic colleagues, published photographs, work shown in Brooklyn, Roi Partridge.

And herein lies the conflict for women who don't have families right away: They can't forget all that life that came before.

When I say there's a conflict, I mean conflict. Not issue, not problem. Many women welcome the change that accompanies the domestic life, though few have figured out how to blend the two lives: parent and artist, old life and new life, erotic romance and familial love. Conflict.

To be brief, Imogen gave up her studio, though not her photography when she became a faculty wife raising three boys. Roi remained a practicing artist, making her an artist married to an artist. She made many nudes of her boys—often taken when outdoors, near rock walls, and waterfalls, in the grass, inside the house. (Decades before Sally Mann.)

She also gardened.

In a letter written to Roi away for a month, sketching, she said that she made a picture of their eldest son posed with a woman: ". . . photographing a mother and child is liable to be either sentimental or absolutely unpictorial but what I wanted to get today was a portrait of Gryff and some of him nude, with a woman in the background." In essence, she gave her son the mother she couldn't be because she was the photographer. Mann, too, had said the act of photographing her children changed the relationship of mother and child, to that of artist and model, illustrating the difficulty in inhabiting the two roles simultaneously.

Like Mann and Orkin—or should I say, Mann and Orkin like Cunningham since she preceded them—Cunningham used her domestically "captive" life to create a larger, more expansive world by photographing their children at home, in their natural (and shared) habitat. (*Anyway, I'm just taking pictures of dog bones. —Sally Mann.*)

BOTANICALS

One of Cunningham's most famous images is *Magnolia Blossom, 1925.* Just one of her resplendent botanicals. The garden just one more thing that she tended while at home, day in, day out. Through the portraits of her children, she offers a kind of self-portrait, a kind of shadow image, or an underdrawing (the flowers and plants work similarly). It's as if she's saying, *Guess what? These guys don't raise themselves. I have to be in attendance at all times, even when we're playing around in the garden, I'm working.* The plants, the kids. The mother figure in the portrait of Gryff is "mothering" Cunningham's son, while his real mother is operating the camera. That room that Virginia Woolf identified as a necessity, regardless of the cost? Yeah, it's empty of children.

Diego Velasquez, court painter to King Philip IV of Spain, painted *Las Meninas* in 1656. The painting has been described as a double portrait, as well as a snapshot of court life, showing a young princess, her ladies, a dwarf, a dog, a courtier, the king and queen (who are likely caught in the act of getting their portraits done), and the court painter, Velasquez. There is buzzy informality to the composition, as well as an unusual perspective that invites a certain amount of interpretation. I saw it, years ago, in Madrid and it was one of the highlights of my life. I think the picture is worth noting for its domesticity, seeming spontaneity, the assembled adults and child (even a relaxing dog!), the mirror reflection, the open, occupied doorway but, most of all, Velasquez' presence in the picture (as if to say, this is my life, my environment, my profession); the need to be included in the place where he lives (and paints).

Maybe Imogen Cunningham, in love with her children, husband, and art, also needed, by proxy, to be seen in the world where she spent so much of her time. As Ruth Orkin said in her seriocomic note to her children, *thank you for keeping me home* since she couldn't have done her *Window* series without them.

A couple of years ago, a writer friend was one of three women on a writers' panel at a literary fair. The audience asked the all-female panel how they got their work done, implying that time and space and solitude was an issue for many of the audience's aspiring authors. All but my friend told the women to rent a hotel room, or apply for a writers' residency, or rent an office. My friend said she could see the women in the audience thinking, *Where will I get the time and the money?* Watching their dreams evaporate knowing they couldn't walk out of their current lives, as much as they might want that Woolfian room devoid of family.

Cunningham's picture of her son isn't complete without a maternal presence, even if it's just another woman, and not herself. She made that picture of her son and another woman in the early years of motherhood and marriage, when she still wrote to Roi to tell him how much she loved him, and how one month would feel like two when apart; before having her second and third children (twins); when she could still have the occasional client, and a darkroom, and a housekeeper.

THE HOUSEKEEPER

This particular housekeeper is crucial in the Imogen-Roi story. Let me amend that statement: any housekeeper is a crucial part of any woman's story. I personally hate housework. I'll do it, but I must admit I've seldom done it as well or as often as J., who was my longtime boyfriend before becoming my husband. J. also cooks (he had been a chef. When our son was a toddler he would always and only search out J. if he was hungry. No fool he.), markets every day, gardens, takes care of the pets, the cars, the bills, went on preschool and elementary school field trips, volunteered in the classroom for years, dealt with the kids our kid brought home on a regular basis, and took care of our son. He is a person of many interests, hobbies and friends (the friends are because he has many interests, among them are other people). He has a wonderful sense of humor that plays nicely with his tendency to reserve judgment. He has traveled, and camped. (Sometimes I traveled with him. I do not camp.) He was a stay-home dad, or house husband, or whatever it was called in the years when these men were rare. When we'd travel to New York, he would be in the park with our son along with all the nannies, none of whom would talk to him. We'd go to parties, and when asked what he did, he experienced a very narrow, and repeated set of responses. The men would say, *You stay home? I would be so bored, doing nothing all day,* before losing interest and wandering off. The women were surprised to find a man who knew their lives, both working inside and outside the home, and warmed to him. He was asked by his family, *When are you going to do something with your life?* To which he would reply, I think I am doing something with my life. *No, no, they'd say, when are you going to get a job?* Maybe I should amend that statement and say he was the one who needed the housekeeper.

I love the story of Imogen's housekeeper because it covers so much female domestic ground. Imogen was still trying to stay connected to photography, either by looking at pictures, or taking the jobs wedged into a life where your profession doesn't come first. At the same time, parenting a toddler, and having a terrible, terrible pregnancy, and married to a man who often went off to sketch for extended periods because of his "need to reconnect with his art," leaving her at home with the "eternal little slavey jobs [that] eat up all my energy so that I have not a pleasant idea in my head."

Those darn little slavey jobs that interrupt every thought.

The truth of creativity is the ongoing need for a fair amount of mental fuck around time; time where you think of nothing, allowing you to see everything, think of everything, be inspired by everything, be curious about everything. It's like being a mental *flaneur.* There is no substitute for this empty/full state that fosters ideas. Without a doubt, children derail that train of thought every time, because you can never *not* think about them (one doesn't have to be an overly involved, hovering parent; it's highly unusual for an artist/mother to fall into that level of over-involvement, since she is often fighting for some form of separation in order to connect to her art ideas).

You have to think about your kids, you're obligated to think about them because they can't think about themselves. You have to remember if they've eaten, or bathed, or gotten enough sleep, or if they're in school, or if school is out, and, holy fuck, *summer.* Holidays and teacher in-service days and those pointless conference days that might last an hour or, when they're in high school, force you to stand in line for five-minute "conferences" with your kid's teachers, except it's more like speed dating than an actual conversation. All you want to hear is, *your kid is fine,* because then you can get back to thinking about your internal world. Those movies that show artists and writers restless for constant stimulation are only showing half of the artist's life. You need experiences, and people, and places (some people like drugs, or drinking, or sex), but the trick is not to let that part of your life eclipse the other, which is where, if you're a writer for example, all you desire is the dullest, most predictable life possible. The best way to access your inner life is not to have to contend with your outer life. Non-writers who live with writers can easily describe what it's like when their writer-partner goes on a kind of autopilot (or as J. says, "When Whitney has left the building"). It can be unpleasant for your partner, this lack of availability, but it doesn't last forever, you'll be back when you have that first draft down.

A kid, unlike an adult, cannot be abandoned in this fashion, which is how they end up crowding out your ideas and your inspiration. A situation that Cunningham described in her letter to Roi about her slavey jobs, adding, "Doesn't this sound sordidly domestic?" Her scattered thoughts a consequence of domesticity.

There is one other small complication which is that you love your son. He is imperfectly perfect. You adore him. You wrap his curls around your fingers, and sigh over his smile. You can't help it. Before my son, M., was born, I panicked thinking I'd never find the time to write. When we moved his crib into my office (our second bedroom that had never been a bedroom but only my office), I felt what I'm sure any number of creative women through the centuries felt when the crib and the changing table and all the other baby accessories crowded out my books and my things in the same way that thoughts of my son would eventually end up crowding the ideas in my head. Never in my life had there been a room dedicated to my writing, and my writer accessories, and I only had it for a handful of months. When our cats made themselves at home on M.'s baby stuff, I felt sure that other mothers-to-be would be frantically brushing off their hair but I only thought, *Live it up while you can, cats.*

Pregnancy often had me saying to myself, *When my life gets back to normal, I'm going to—,* foolishly not realizing that my life was never, ever going back to what it was. And as much as I loved my unborn child, and as good as I felt, I hated being seen as a "pregnancy." It felt awful so much of the time. You're completely de-sexualized (ironic, I know).

How much conversation can be gleaned from folic acid?

People talk to you about your pregnancy, the baby, your plans, their kids; you understand that you are entering Kid World, making you understand that Hell is Other Parents. By the time my kid was in first grade, just talking about public versus private school on the heels of all the discussions about the best daycares, preschools, various hobby classes, baby gyms, swim lessons, tutors, teachers, colleges, summer camps, educational camps, hobbies, interests, various sports, diet, sugar, sleep, play habits, television viewing, books, reading, music lessons gave me a raging headache. Everything was always The Best. The Best this, The Best that. The endless conversations about the behavior of other kids, and their parents, and the little blue pills for ADD and ADHD, and all those "gifted" kids. I offer this short hand: Nine times out of ten, the boys were on the pills and the girls were gifted.

Does it really need to be noted that boys lag two to three years in maturity behind the girls, and girls tend to be more verbal, more eloquent, if you will, and more adept at reading a room, yet we expect boys and girls to be at the same stage of readiness for school? Girls are bright. They graduate high school in greater numbers than boys, and enter and graduate from college in greater numbers. For the past few years, there are more women than men in medical school. And yet, so many parents I met had "gifted girls," something that I'm not sure is even statistically possible. Maybe girls are simply smart?

All those boys on those little colored pills; I think so many of them are just boys. I can't tell you how many parents would say, *You know, when he's in school he just can't concentrate, he gets restless and distracted. But when he's engaged in something that piques his interest, his concentration is total.* Yeah, I wanted to say to them, *thanks for describing me to me.* I do not have ADD. I never had ADD. You know who had ADHD? My brother, who was hell on wheels. If half of these parents grew up in a house with my brother, they would see what's what. It would be unmistakable.

Anyway, all that kid talk gave me headaches, anxiety, and ennui. I thought, *I am on the road to being a shitty parent, and taking my kid for a ride down crap highway with me.* We would be like a mother-son *Easy Rider* duo, except instead of getting killed by rednecks, he would never get into the college of his choice.

Despite all this, I loved being with M., my son. It was more of a fight at times to *want* to write. There were a couple of reasons: one, I liked being with M. and it was easy because he was filling my thoughts anyway and, two, relates to one, which is that it was a struggle to balance his needs and my writing. Some days I gave up entirely and said to myself that I simply wouldn't write that day. It was a relief to succumb. Kids draw on the same love and passion of making art; it's internally competitive.

When I'm writing, and it's going well, everything locks into place so beautifully that it's almost like a drug. I can struggle with the writing, and still get the high. Ideas and possibilities clip along nicely. I can also be happy when I'm not writing. I'm only unhappy when I'm prevented from writing, and/or when it really isn't going well. I don't believe in writing as therapy; I think of it as an art form. An exacting little art form.

This is all a roundabout way of saying that love and conflict can co-exist in the same woman.

Writing isn't the same as photography. Writing is contemplative, while photography is immediate, a thousand spilt-second decisions (film really drives this reality home in the way a memory card cannot). Writing might be voyeuristic but photography can be predatory. My professional photographer friend, CS, recently explained her "relief" at giving up photography because she felt that it had "removed her from actual living." She also said that it wore on her to do something that she considered so "self-involved. It's always about you. What you choose to photograph, and present, is a way of projecting who *you* are on people. You aren't presenting any image but your own."

Because the Cunningham-Partridge's had a housekeeper, a young woman on whom a very pregnant Imogen relied, she didn't have to give up photography altogether. Maybe Roi had envisioned this unconventional, bohemian life for himself and Imogen when the reality was he still took off for more than a month at a time to sketch, leaving behind a pregnant wife still trying to take the occasional photography commission, a toddler, and a household because being progressive clearly had its limits.

So, the hired girl cooked, cleaned, and watched the baby while Imogen spotted prints in her studio. She, the housekeeper, also stole and lit the place on fire three times before the near complete destruction of Imogen's darkroom.

In other words, the theft and arson were forgiven, before the damage to Imogen's studio, because, for the stay-home mom, a criminal housekeeper is better than no housekeeper.

There is no record why this woman was an amateur arsonist, but the third, and terrible fire occurred when Roi was in Northern California, on one of his art jaunts. Consequently, Imogen packed up the kid, hers and Roi's belongings, all the while struggling with her sickening pregnancy, and wrote him a note telling him about the housekeeper and the fire. She wrote that she had to go to her parents in California (which is where Roi was traveling, so they would be closer to Roi) because she desperately needed the help.

Roi wrote back, "I was just starting for Point Lobos with the Burrs. They are picnicking and I'm going to sketch." He continues by saying that she doesn't mention the extent of the damage "but that you should so arbitrarily, capriciously give up our little home seems a great misfortune to me. You have no consideration—as usual—for where I come in," even though she had packed his printing press and prints, while "smashing the majority of her glass-plate negatives to avoid moving them."

He's pissed that his sketching and picnicking with the Burrs was interrupted—not that he offers to help his pregnant wife (who already can't keep up with her domestic and professional life, even with the pyromaniac housekeeper) and their son by coming home, or packing up, or asking how she is, or anything. Does she really not mention her darkroom and glass-plate negatives? And, oh my god, his use of the words *as usual* slays me. And this incident is coming only a couple of years into their marriage. Everything about the housekeeper, the fire, the picnicking Burrs, and Roi's response, pretty much says it all.

*

Many years ago, I wrote a short story where a little girl suspects her married mother is seeing a man who isn't the girl's father. Her suspicions are confirmed when she finds a pair of used teacups in the kitchen sink, late on a Saturday afternoon when the girl had been at a friend's house and the father was out of town on business, the cups signifying an afternoon assignation. The little girl hesitates as she considers the teacups (Should she

tell her father? Say something to her mother?) before smashing them to shards, against each other. In another novel I wrote
about a wronged wife who destroyed as many breakable objects
in her home that she could lay her hands on, illustrating the
complexity of the emotions she couldn't bring herself to voice.

Imogen Cunningham, in her rush to move in the wake of
the final fire, ended up shattering a number of the glass plates in
her studio, the studio that Roi Partridge didn't ask about. I just
don't think it was uncommon for twentieth-century women, in
certain moments, to break their homes to pieces.

MEN WHO AREN'T ROI PARTRIDGE

Imogen had three sons, **Gryffyd, Padriac,** and **Rondal.** By all
accounts, she loved her children, even with "one hand in the
dishpan, the other in the dark room." Gryffyd, her eldest child,
said, "There was nothing that Imogen wasn't interested in," and
that "you felt that she was a friend." Padriac said, "It was very
interesting having Imogen for a mother. She could answer any
question—not highly scientific, but about animals, and plants
and chemistry." He also called her "the center of the home." His
twin brother, Rondal, added, "Her father's attitudes influenced
Imogen, but sometimes in a negative way" and her "liberation"
was a response to "her father's treatment of her mother."

Isaac Burns Cunningham, Imogen's father, was eccentric;
among other things he moved the family (briefly) to a utopian
commune in Washington, and maintained "a small library on
disparate subjects including theosophy, mathematics, vocab-
ulary, farming, plumbing . . . and was known for taking in
abused horses and treating animals with a kindness uncharac-
teristic for the day. He had an Encyclopedia Britannica, and
schooled his favorite child, Imogen, in Shakespeare (hence her
name), and the Bible, though he was not a religious man. He

taught her that no one is entitled to anything, and the importance of work."

He built her first darkroom, then questioned her desire to
be "a dirty photographer."

He was progressive toward Imogen, but not toward his wife,
or women in general.

My own, post-war, Greatest Generation father (b. 1924)
encouraged me to travel "before I had children because you can't
do it after you have them." I know of no other father (though
certainly they must have been around; I just didn't know them)
who understood, by way of that statement, what motherhood
meant for a woman. Of course, he also told me to learn to type
so I'd always have something to fall back on. This was common advice for women of my era. My father was the parent
who got us up, fed, and off to school in the mornings because
my mother also worked, even though he was an electrical engineer with a career of his own. After work, he took us on errands
(usually the hardware store), to various playgrounds, helped
with school projects and other homework.

During the Italian Renaissance, a woman could not be an
artist because she wasn't permitted to apprentice with an established artist. However, she could be "apprenticed" to a father
or husband. The issue then became one of professional opportunities; even if a Renaissance father chose to teach his daughter to paint, one has to ask, *to what end?* Artemisia Gentileschi,
born in 1590 and the first woman accepted by the Accademia di
Arte del Disegno in Florence, is the poster girl for contemporary women when looking at the role of women artists in the
Renaissance. Actually, not just the poster girl but very much *the*
girl. There was no one else.

Imogen wasn't the only twentieth-century woman photographer with a semi-progressive, inventive father who raised her
to do what she liked (nothing in my reading has ever suggested
that these men saw their photographer daughters as surrogate

sons), but often these women resembled the daughters of the Renaissance father training his daughter *to what end?* There were few social opportunities and no norms to support their professional ambitions. Even though women were involved in photography from the beginning (Julia Margaret Cameron, for example, Lallie Charles, for example, Gertrude Kasebier, for example), it was, as Beaumont Hall, former head of the International Museum of Photography at the George Eastman House, as well as being the first director of photography for MoMA, said, "I've never seen a different sensibility in women photographers, but those women had one thing in common—drive." So ambition and sensibility were not the issue. I think Willard Van Dyke, former director of the film department at MoMA, cleared up this matter when he said of Imogen that her "vitriolic personality might have been something of a cover-up . . . when she started out, women were not given the breaks men were given, to put it mildly."

Ansel Adams met Imogen in 1926. Eventually, they, along with a handful of other photographers, including Edward Weston, created *f/64,* a photography group devoted to "natural" photography. They broke from Pictorialism (photography mimicking painting), to wanting to show the "world as it is." When I was living in San Francisco, I saw a photography exhibition at the deYoung that was a recreation of a 1932 deYoung exhibition of the *f/64* group. Adams and Cunningham remained friends throughout their lives, even though Adams said that when Imogen joined *f/64* in 1932, "I'd like to think that that was about the time she really began to realize her creative potential." *Nineteen thirty-two.* She had traveled to Dresden in 1909, wrote a significant photography paper in 1910, had shows in Brooklyn and New York City, had her own photography studio, and in the early part of the century created a scandal with her nudes of Roi, but Adams thinks she wasn't "realizing her creative potential" until 1932.

As a faculty wife, she kept her hand in by taking portraits of the Mills College students—Mills is a women-only institution—where Roi taught art. She entertained the many students and faculty who came to dinner. Then, in 1931, Mills needed a photographer to take pictures for the Mills' School of Science catalogue. Even though Ansel Adams wasn't yet The Ansel Adams, the powers that be at this *women's college,* all of whom knew Cunningham, a working photographer since the first decade of the twentieth century, hired Adams for the job.

(*". . . When she started out, women were not given the breaks men were given, to put it mildly."*)

What else was Cunningham doing in 1931, besides taking pictures of Mills' students? Well, she made a classic photographic series of Martha Graham, a dancer/choreographer said to have influenced modern dance in the same way Picasso influenced modern art. Also, when Imogen was a college student, she had been hired by the science department at the University of Washington to take pictures for their botany department. And after she earned a degree in chemistry, she won a scholarship to spend a year in Germany, studying with the world's best photo-chemist.

If we stop and consider that fucked-up Mills' situation for a moment, one question that immediately comes to mind, followed quickly by *How did Cunningham stay friends with this guy?* is what *was* the point of a women's college where you send this kind of message? Had Adams been more famous, or more experienced (he wasn't; he said he accepted the job because "I needed the money"), or had Cunningham *not* been a faculty wife, or an experienced photographer, or currently taking pictures of the students on her own time, everything would've made more sense. Or maybe if anyone had bothered to read her published 1913 feminist piece, *Photography as a Profession for Women* ("Women are not trying to outdo the men by entering the profession. They are simply trying to do something for themselves"). What, exactly, did the administration at this college think it meant to be a professional woman?

Adams wrote in his 1935 technical book, *Making a Photograph,* where he included a picture by Dorothea Lange that made "his friend" jealous. Imogen, he says, was jealous of Lange's "feeling for the human side and me because of my craftsmanship." In an interview, Imogen expressed admiration for Adam's work, calling it "perfection." He does allow that her *Magnolia Blossom* is "the most beautiful photograph I ever owned." Did he ever buy any other pictures? Did he even buy *Magnolia Blossom?* Showing support for the work of someone in your artistic field where you often feel you are dealing with scarcity, can be tricky since it taps into your own insecurities, envy, jealousy, and competitive sense. Friendship becomes fluid. Until you are in a position to champion someone, you will never understand the ways in which that opportunity is a crossroads.

Keeping in mind that Imogen couldn't easily travel anywhere because of her family responsibilities, how ideal would it be to have a job, like the Mills job, come to you? And the family of five could always use the money. Adams refers to this Mills' business as a "sore point" between them, adding that he didn't realize she considered "Mills as exclusively her domain, so I took the job." They had already known each other *five years* when all this happened, and I don't think she felt entitled to the job because she considered the college "her domain"; I think it was because she was a skilled, experienced professional.

How did Cunningham stay friends with this guy?

When Judy Dater interviewed Ansel Adams for her book on Imogen Cunningham, written after Imogen's passing, Adams says, "I heard people say that Imogen felt competitive with me. But in fact there was very little we competed upon. In the first place, I'm not a portrait photographer, or only a very occasional one . . . she may have felt a little resentment over my more obvious success. I guess I had more shows, more commercial jobs—

but I don't think she wanted those anyway." Look, I know nothing of their friendship; there's no way for me to know since all I have are books, and quotes, and other people's opinions. But I do know that her marriage ended over a "commercial job" with *Vanity Fair*, you know, the ones Adams decided "she didn't want." Few photographers, historically and, I'm guessing, currently, have the luxury of turning down work; almost all of them diversify and, when luck comes along, a job can turn into art (the commissioned portrait, the war photograph, the travel piece). It's distressing to think of Imogen working so hard, for so long, faced with the limitations of where (and when) she can work, and so driven by work (". . . *those women had one thing in common—drive*"), and hearing Adams (her friend) say that he couldn't understand her resentment when he had decided that she didn't really want the assignments, or the money, anyway.

Adams' opinion was that "her blood was three percent acid" but that ultimately "it was a put on" because "deep down she was really very soft, very emotional." Look, it isn't Adam's fault—side note: my father once met the photographer in a state park who was in the company of a very young woman—that he couldn't see the acid in her blood as self-protection, or as frustration, or as anger at being passed over, or dismissed, or having a domestic life that necessarily competed with a creative life. Adams chose to see her as prickly; as the woman who sent him a Hills Brothers can (after he sold an image for use to the company) with a marijuana plant growing inside it. He thought the tears were an indication of "softness" when he had no clue the steel it took to be married to Roi, and be forced to modify your own dreams; to not use your skills, to not have enough room for your art (or even your work), to not even be considered for a job in your field when you are right under their noses. Every damn day.

Edward Weston met Imogen and Roi in 1920. Weston had a wife, four sons, a photography studio in Tropico, California, and a mistress, Margrethe Mather. Mather was a photographer and something of a bohemian's bohemian; her pictures were as unconventional as she was. Their love and artistic collaboration (moderns who influenced each other) lasted for ten years. Weston may be known for his close cropped subjects that abstracted ordinary objects like bell peppers, but he didn't discover his style in isolation. No artist does, because art tends to be inspired by life, while reflecting life, while interpreting life.

In Cunningham's case, Richard Lorenz writes, "Rather than supporting the traditional perception that Edward Weston was her modernist mentor, Cunningham's work of the late 1920s (that marvelous *Magnolia,* the picture that Adams loved) presents a strong case for her position as the most independently sophisticated and experimental photographer at work on the West Coast." At Cunningham's show in Berkeley in 1929, her work was compared to Weston's (also in the exhibition); hers considered the more complex of the two: "Were it not for Cunningham's revelations of what can be created in photography, we might appreciate Weston the more." It is possible to work in the same vein without being identical, as Richard Lorenz points out, "—the core idiosyncrasies of each personality inevitably defined each individual's style: Weston, the perfectionist theoretician; Hagemeyer, the sophisticated romantic; Mather, the illusory aesthete; and Cunningham, the novel and prodigious experimenter."

(Side note: In her book, *Imogen!,* Cunningham writes about a note she received from Weston in 1928: *I went out to the museum today . . . to see the International Salon of Photography. As usual, most of it was rubbish, although several Japanese had fine things, but I had one thrill, and it was your print,* Glacial Lily. *It stopped me at once. I did not note the signature until I exclaimed to myself, 'This is fine!' It is the best thing in the show, Imogen, and if you keep up to that standard, you will be one of a handful of important photographers in America—or anywhere. Thank you for giving me rare pleasure.* . . . Her final remark to Weston's praise, written without rancor, yet infused with the sort of a sigh a woman artist in 1928 may sigh, *Of course, I had been photographing for twenty-five years.* This is not unlike Ansel Adams' comment in 1932 that Imogen was starting to come into her creative potential.)

As a writer, and someone who likes art, and movies and books, I'm wary of a creative hierarchy (the best, the most innovative, the first), because art isn't a hierarchy—it's far more dimensional. Those who make things are influential and influenced; they pull from one place, repurpose, comment on, reshape. All those collages of the first half of the 20th century (John Heartfield's scathing cobbled-together images of Hitler and the Third Reich; Hannah Hoch; Greta Stern's insight into the dreams of the post-war housewife; Juan Gris; Joseph Cornell's three-dimensional assemblages of actresses, ballerinas, birds, the cosmos, and the past. Musicians didn't invent sampling, they just took it into the aural realm). Nineteenth-century Victorian crazy quilts, and memory quilts, with their found patches of velvets and satins, and photo-transfers, beads, and embroidery. Art depends upon what came before, and on everything that surrounds, to make something new. It is, however, a fine line between appropriation and/or theft and making something new. No one worth their salt crosses it.

To bring up Weston in conjunction with Cunningham (or Mather, or Tina Modotti, another photographer/lover/muse of his) isn't to diminish or dismiss his considerable accomplishments; it's to place him firmly among other photographers. To offer a little context. Being inspired by other photographs isn't the same thing as lacking originality; it is really the nature of the beast, as any artist knows. Creative people are always reinventing the wheel; they just don't reproduce the car.

Edward Curtis was the photographer best known for all those serious Native American portraits. When my novel about women photographers, *Eight Girls Taking Pictures* (inspired by real-life women photographers), was published, a biography of Curtis came out around the same time. During a radio interview, I was asked about Edward Curtis. The interviewer asked me if I'd read the Curtis book, then began speaking at length about its (male) author. I said nothing. Curtis has an unflattering cameo in my novel, taken from the life of Cunningham, who worked in his studio for two years, following her year in Dresden. This is what she said of those two years: "Edward Curtis was such a big shot in his own mind that he seldom turned up in the studio and if he did, he never spoke to the help. The man who influenced my life at the time was A. F. Muhr. . . . He was an operator of the Curtis establishment and a gentleman from way back. He was also a fine technician." My final word on Curtis: art is subjective.

But I was annoyed with the interviewer. Radio interviews are carefully timed, and there I was, sharing my time with Curtis— a man I had zero interest in, or connection to—and, even more maddening, the author of the Curtis biography. The interviewer had recently had him on and was now, on my time, rehashing that conversation. I am ever the good girl, letting the radio host talk about someone else's book, which I wouldn't have minded talking about if I'd had any interest in it, or if it had any relevance to my book. Instead I waited. Quietly. Politely.

Alfred Stieglitz is a photographer who practically owned twentieth-century photography, though he began his life as a photographer at the end of the nineteenth century. He studied in Germany (years before Cunningham), had two influential galleries in New York that showed, in addition to photographs, modern art, including that of wife Georgia O'Keeffe (can anyone look at her large, close cropped flowers and not think of photographs?). He founded a movement called Photo-Secession which promoted the idea of photography as fine art. The name alone, *Photo-Secession,* is great. He founded an influential magazine called *Camera Work* (Gertrude Stein's *The Making of Americans*, first appeared in *Camera Work* in August 1912). My favorite photographs of Stieglitz are of O'Keeffe hands, and nudes made when they first started up. They were taken around 1918, causing a bit of a dustup when they were shown. O'Keeffe said husbands sometimes asked Stieglitz about "photographing their wives or girlfriends that way he photographed me," with O'Keeffe thinking they wouldn't be so interested if they knew the circumstances of those (pre-coital or post-coital) pictures.

In a Woman on Paper, Anita Pollitzer recalled Margaret Prosser, the Stieglitz's family housekeeper for forty years, saying of Stieglitz, "He did wonderful street scenes, portraits, railroad tracks and all that before Georgia came. But after Georgia came, he made the clouds, the moon, he even made lightning. He never photographed things like that before."

Cunningham returning from Dresden in 1910, met Stieglitz in New York at his gallery, 291. She idolized him as so many photographers did, but she said of their meeting that he likely wouldn't remember her. It should be said, Cunningham was small of stature, with red hair, and wire-rimmed glasses, adorable in her appearance but definitely not one of the beautiful brunettes that the womanizing Stieglitz preferred. (She also notes how much she loved New York, but "I don't think I was smart enough to think New York needed me." Much of her hesitation at thinking she could make it in New York was her precarious financial state; Imogen was broke.)

Cunningham was correct; Stieglitz didn't remember her, nor was he particularly interested in remembering her. She met him a second time, in 1934, at his other gallery, An American Place. There are many pictures of Imogen's that I adore: *Unmade Bed*, 1957; her flowers and other botanicals from the early and mid-1920s; three of the *Phoenix* photos—*Phoenix on Her Side*, 1968, *Phoenix Recumbent*, 1968, *Navajo Rug*, 1968. I'm moved

by a self-portrait of her naked twenty-three-year-old self, lounging in a field of tall grass outside the University of Washington,
where she earned her degree in 1907. How can you not love
that girl? There is nothing sexual about the picture; it strikes
me as playful and young and hopeful, like someone on the very
edge of discovering just who she might be. I know that girl; I've
been that girl.

I'm even a little attached to her portrait of a decidedly
bitchy-looking Alfred Stieglitz, taken in 1934, with his own camera, in front of O'Keeffe's gorgeous *Black Iris,* presiding over his
little gallery kingdom; his expression one of barely suppressed
(to me) irritation. Cunningham may be established, but she's
still the small, red-haired, bespectacled woman of 1910. Still not
his type. Still someone small and easy to dismiss. After she sent
a print to him, along with the announcement that it was going
to be in *Vanity Fair,* he responded that he liked the picture then
added, "I wish you could've seen my show. It attracted 7,000
people in six weeks. And there wasn't a dissenting voice."

Roi Partridge wooed Imogen Cunningham by mail, from
Europe, where he offered a dream life of "love and time in
Italy!" until the Great War put the *kabosh,* as they said then, on
that. Still, there was love and a marriage and children and a life
together, but one where he went off to work on his art when he
wasn't teaching, and she stayed at home with the children and
the firebug housekeeper. Padriac Partridge said of his mother,
"She was the center of the home. Roi ruled as a stern discipli-
narian. He didn't involve himself with the children."

Padriac also said that they, the children, heard arguments
after bedtime (the couple was not disposed to airing it out in
front of the children). ". . . He [Roi] was raised to have what
he wanted, the way he wanted it . . . he wanted a housewife,
in a sense, and he wasn't getting it. Imogen Cunningham did
her photography in her spare moments, and he assumed these
moments were coming from him. . . ." Rondal said his parents

"never got along a day in their lives." Roi was on one of his trips when she had their first child, and with the second, taxing pregnancy, he left Imogen home with the housekeeper. He said that his uncle told him "get rid of that girl [the housekeeper]— she's a pyromanic! But Imogen was pregnant again—she was apt to be upset when she was pregnant, so we decided it would be better if I went away for a time." I'm sure "we" did decide. *Your wife is pregnant with twins and your housekeeper keeps lighting up the place. You 1) Fire her, or 2) Take a vacation.*

But in the years before all that, there was the working holiday love honeymoon with a pregnant Imogen taking pictures of an unclothed Roi on Mt. Rainier in Washington that created such a stir. Those *outre* photos of her naked husband that, in truth, are more arty than scandalous; it isn't like, say, married Stieglitz's frank, sex-saturated nudes of his mistress, taken three years after Imogen's of Roi. Cunningham's response? "You might say I invented the male nude."

Women in art are often associated with Nature—their elemental natures, their natural beauty, their instincts that go feral if not reined in by societal convention—and here was Cunningham, in 1915, publishing pictures of her nude husband, posed like a fawn, or a bather, or Narcisssus (there was no way for Imogen to know, early in their marriage, how apt her choice of mythological figure). At a distance. Nothing like those pictures of O'Keeffe, so tightly cropped the entire frame is all breasts and pubic hair, with men asking if Stieglitz would consider making portraits of their wives, while the Roi photos were thought to be the transgressive side. Cunningham didn't show the pictures again for decades.

Back at the marriage, post-honeymoon period, where Imogen found herself pregnant again, caring for a toddler and living with an arsonist who finally succeeded in thoroughly damaging Imogen's darkroom, Roi, in a fit of pique, writes to Imogen accusing her of lacking any "consideration" for him. He doesn't even ask her if she's okay, though he does acknowledge that it's the third fire—*the third fire!*—imagine even wanting to keep your family in a house with someone who keeps torching it. Shouldn't he have returned at the news of the *second* fire?

Roi is almost *almost* like a parody of the self-absorbed husband who, in this case, is also a self-absorbed artist.

The Partridges were married almost twenty years, most of which Imogen spent as the aforementioned faculty wife (students and guests to dinner, minding the children, gardening, trying to take a picture or two of whatever or whoever was at hand, keeping house, waving good-bye to Roi when he went on one of his artist walkabouts). In *Ideas Without End,* Richard Lorenz writes that Imogen's "old friend Alan Simms Lee" wrote to her:

> *It is too brutal to say that the two horns of the dilemma that pull you both ways at once—family and art—the youngsters are after all a finer contribution to the community than even your photographs. It is of course less interesting to the general public . . . and hard to sacrifice the artist's need for individual praise from an admiring public but having a family it is difficult as you say to achieve both, at least until the youngsters grow up a bit—you won't be too old then! . . . I think you're rather hard and not quite fair on the achievements of men. Many are very glad to acknowledge the debt they owe to their wives and many do achieve success entailing no sacrifice of others.*

Imogen was married to an artist, and she was an artist. Maybe she made a kind of classic mistake of thinking that two artists, two like-minded souls, could make it in this crazy world. I can't even fathom the effect this letter would have on her, already professionally frustrated and living with Roi, which often sounds rather taxing, and now she's being told her kids are more important than her photographs (she loved her children, but I'm fairly certain no one was saying this to any of her male contemporaries with children), and she needs to be patient because she won't be "too old" (age has often been just so kind to women) to pick up her career, and she should be proud of being the wife of an artist because doing those slavey jobs so someone else can make art is as rewarding as, well, making art.

An Interlude

I'm interrupting myself here to say that I moved with my college boyfriend in our sophomore year. It was the ridiculous mistake of a nineteen-year-old. Here's the problem with youth: If you aren't making poor decisions about drinking, drugs, smoking, or falling in with the wrong crowd, then you make other pretty questionable decisions that fly under the radar because you tell yourself that at least you don't have a problem with drinking, drugs, smoking, or falling in with the wrong crowd. You tell yourself that giving up the university that you love (and that has offered you a full ride) to move across the state to go to a college you hate (except for the library, which is fantastic) is what you wanted to do anyway. And, if you would've had the maturity to know yourself, you would know that you were too young for this domestic life, a life that never held any allure under the best of circumstances, since you aren't even interested in marriage, yet here you are. You want to study a year abroad and maybe never come back. You paint a little, read a lot, and know that art means everything to you (though your curiosity is wider than just art). You haven't even considered the possibility of being a writer yet. You've never met any writers. How did one even become a writer? Nor would you think about yourself because you've thrown in your lot with a guy who knew that he wanted a career in music. His certainty trumps your interests. This guy is the reason you leave one school for another; the reason you give up your ride; the reason you don't apply for a year abroad (he had lived abroad and "wasn't into it"). He also doesn't like your best friend, who doesn't even live near you. The one time she visited, newly returned from India and trying so hard with him, he sulked like a three-year-old. And that friendship went on indefinite hiatus. You are too young to even begin to consider blaming anyone for all of this; instead you convince yourself this is what you want.

The truth is, you haven't allowed yourself to want anything in a long time. You tell yourself that you want what he wants, and he just accepts that you both want the same thing, which is to support his musical aspirations. He is good at what he does; that isn't the issue. He needs to do what he does, he says. You go with him to practices when he starts playing with other people. You listen to his latest songs; you give him his privacy and space to create (this isn't a hardship because you get privacy, too); you spend a miserable winter month in a ski resort where the group is hired to play. It's awful. The kind of awful you can only bear if you are very young. It's the only time in your life you take a Greyhound from one end of the state to the other.

You move again to attend another university, one that you like better than the last but nowhere near as much as the first one, the one you gave up. You don't think anymore about studying abroad. You're always in school or working part-time anyway (he doesn't have to work). Then, a year before graduation, he drops out of college. The college *he* wanted to go to. The college you still attend.

Being a selfish person isn't the same thing as being a bad person (I don't think Roi Partridge was a bad person). I think one difference is that someone can adjust to the selfish person, especially if she believes enough in his art to take on more than she should, including shoving her own dreams in a drawer.

You are tired. Prone to sadness, sometimes crying, even though you are supposed to always be "up" because he has mood swings and you can't be down if he's down, and you can't be down if he's up. You say it's not his fault; it's just how he is. You are confused, and lonely, and you no longer feel like you are living your own life.

Then you fall off your bike, break your wrist, and you can't quite understand his attitude, his sense of "inconvenience" during your six weeks in a hard cast, that is, until years later when you read about Roi and Imogen; specifically about Roi.

End of Interlude

A PAIR OF LETTERS

Letter #1: In 1934, after nineteen years of marriage, three (nearly grown) children, being a wife, trying to take pictures, and supporting Roi's travels, Imogen got a plum offer from *Vanity Fair,* a magazine she liked, except she had to leave two weeks before Roi's teaching term ended. This was non-negotiable since magazines run by a strict calendar. He responded by telling her that if she went without him, they were over.

This is an excerpt from that letter she wrote to him from the train heading to New York:

> *Why in the world would you think it puts you in a ridiculous position for me to go away for a time on a working job. . . . I am sure you are bitter about my methods of working my exit but with your attitude of mind, nothing else was physically possible for me. I begged you too many times for co-operation and permission. . . . I cannot straighten myself out through idleness. . . . The working part only makes the going easier because I will not become involved in debt and it will cost you no actual money. I assure you I do not value myself so highly as a photographer as you seem to think, but neither could I venture in the field unless I had some confi-*

dence in my ability. Only thru putting myself thru it, as it were, can I really think I am really worth anything to you or the family . . . try not to forget that I have always done the essentials, have always been home after school, when the children came, that my work has not been as distracting as most wives' bridge, that I had always had the hope that in place of going down in the scale of worthwhileness and achievement as most hausfraus do that I was going up. . . . I really thought I had the right of an adult to undertake an obligation. I never thought for a moment that a person so liberal in all else would deny me this.

Letter #2: When Sophie Calle, the French artist (photographer, conceptual artist, installation artist) returned to Paris from several years abroad, she decided to "repatriate" by shadowing the city's citizens, noting their habits and conversations, and taking photographs. She also asked her mother to hire a private eye to tail her, Sophie, recording *her* life in detail (writings, photos) "to provide photographic proof of my own existence." She then led the private eye around to places she liked without him knowing it, blurring the line between the observed and the observer. Strangers have been invited to sleep in her bed (she took photographs). There were the "party" projects: in one, she tails a man she met at a party to another country without his knowledge; in another, she invites a man she broke up with without explanation (years later) to come to a party where her reasons for the breakup would be revealed. She records the city where a man stood her up. Her most controversial piece was when she found a man's address book in the street, photocopied it, then proceeded to write twenty-eight articles for a French publication. Each article was an interview with one of his friends from the address book. This man whom she had never met was not happy.

A project called *Last Seen* had Calle traveling to the Isabella Stewart Gardner Museum in Boston to ask the curators, guards, and staff to describe the "five drawings by Degas, one vase, one Napoleonic eagle and six paintings by Rembrandt, Flinck, Manet and Vermeer" stolen on March 18, 1990.

She went to a woman's flat that had been burned and photographed all the charred negatives. (Many of Imogen's glass plate negatives were damaged in the Seattle fire; she ended up smashing a number of the plates rather than move them to California.)

Finally, there is *Take Care of Yourself.* A man with whom Calle was passionately involved for less than a year sent her a breakup email that ended with the words, "Take care of yourself." Calle's response, because she didn't know how to respond, was "to ask 107 women (including two made from wood and one with feathers), chosen for their profession or skills, to interpret this letter. . . . 'Understand it for me. Answer for me. It was a way of taking the time to break up. A way of taking care of myself.'"

The women Calle contacted did straight interpretations, translations (into English, or Latin), wrote a poem, a play, did a cost analysis, talked about diplomacy, parsed out the letter noting the verbs, or nouns, or adjectives. They counted how many times the man used "I." They did interviews. One newspaper editor turned down the letter for publication. The letter was diagrammed, footnoted, reimagined as a drawing of a woman's blouse. A pair of female rabbis argued. It was rewritten as a fairytale. It was song. The reason this art piece is so dynamic is because this is often what women do when a love affair goes south; they talk and analyze and soothe and reassure and "explain." It's all about subtext, even when sometimes there is no subtext, and talking about it makes the sting less sharp. *Why did he say this? Why does he do that? Why? Why? Why?* And once in a while you just wish you could shrug your shoulders and say, *there is no why.*

One of my favorite analyses of the letter came from a lawyer, Caroline Mecary (photographed reading the letter leaning against a radiator next to the window in her office), who cites legal logic and articles of criminal code, and notes things like "2. In the context of the amorous commerce, which you have described to me, it also appears that you have been deceived, as a woman but also in your capacity as a consumer." I won't reprint the letter here, but the short version (and it's only a page long) is that he loved Sophie Calle, even though he had his three "others" and she made it clear that she wanted to be the only one. But, yada yada yada he has anxiety yada yada he thought her love would be enough yada yada yada don't want to lie to you yada yada the others yada I will always miss you (terribly) and the "way you see things" and "your gentleness toward me" yada yada yada we can't be friends, take care of yourself etc. etc. etc. etc.

Lawyer Mecary writes ("X" represents the man):

Reading the letter one observes that:
—X. is egocentric and narcissistic.
—X. is frightened by "disquiet."
—X. is not generous.
—X. refuses all debate.
—X. does not want to lose anything.
—X. thinks only of the prejudice he suffers.
All these elements attest deceit regarding the nature, form, composition and substantive qualities of a man in love.

Upon receiving Imogen's letter (**Letter #1**), Roi filed for divorce.

THE WOMAN WITH THE
MINK SLEEVES

Judy Dater

My Introduction to Judy Dater

American photographer Judy Dater (b. 1941) has a brief and entirely wonderful video, *Memoir,* on her website. It's not even thirty minutes long, yet it's perfect; exactly my kind of thing. In short order, she offers dates (beginning with her birth), coupled with scrapbook pages of snapshots, menus, newspaper clippings, and autobiographical, sometimes cryptic, captions. In 1976, Dater mentions a romantic rendezvous with another man while traveling Tokyo, her unaware husband back at the hotel. In 1977, she describes being a guest at a party where her lover and his wife are also in attendance. Her lover advises her to "act natural," and Dater keeps it together until the wife compliments her dress, adding that her husband (Dater's lover) bought one "just like it for their girls."

In 1976 and 1977, while Dater was in Tokyo, and at the awkward party, respectively, I was living on the peninsula in Newport Beach, part way through college, struggling through the drawn-out ending of a relationship that really needed to end (something I sent on its way when, in a moment of pure anger, I heaved a birthday cake at the person I needed to end it with and a girl he was seeing, only I did it very publicly as they walked the twenty feet to the beach crowded with summer tourists. This behavior was so unlike me that I ended up sending the girl apology flowers, which she promptly ridiculed. I was still very young, and ever my polite, Good Girl self). It was during this time that I went to a local gallery showing Judy Dater's photographs. There were three in particular that I wanted so badly:

1. *Cheri* (1972) is a black-and-white print of a naked woman, full frontal, middle-aged but the really rough middle-age where every year is on display. Her arms are extended as far as they will go, her hands holding a very long framed photograph of hundreds of men in uniform, a full regiment, expanding the idea of the perpetuity of war, violence, and collateral damage. The woman, blonde, looks straight at the lens.

2. *Woman and Daughters, Beverly Hills* (1972) shows a woman, again in the old-school sort of middle-aged way, sitting with her two teenage daughters. One of the daughters looks to be the age that I was in 1972. The reason I loved the picture was because the woman wears a black dress, with a plunging V-neckline, a giant silk flower at the V, and a pair of very large blonde mink sleeves; the sleeves are the detail that had me coveting the photograph.

Gertrude Stein told Hemingway, when he admired her art collection, "You can either buy clothes or buy pictures," she said. "It's that simple. No one who is not very rich can do both." By my senior year of high school, I knew that I wanted to own art. However, my current life barely covered subsistence, so art was out of the question. I did have two photographs that one of my two best friends from high school had given me. She had a Nikon and an enlarger (this was the first enlarger I had ever seen). The pictures were of The Pasadena Playhouse, which she knew had meaning for me, and a window from her travels in Southern Europe with her parents (decades later J. gave me a print of Lee Miller's *Portrait of Space,* the view of the Egyptian desert through the window of a tent). My friend had the photos mounted, and I put them up every time I had a wall to put them on.

Around the time of the Dater show, I had also become friendly with a photographer who lived behind my little beach apartment. He was older than me and dating a girl younger than I. We were friends for a while, and from that friendship I learned not to loan anyone money if I wanted to keep the friendship. It was an unpleasant lesson, and I was reminded of what my parents used to say, which was never loan anything you aren't prepared to give away. I didn't understand what they meant until this particular money-lending situation, though I would add, don't lend any amount you can't afford to lose. It was a large sum for the time—my college money for the entire year, which I needed, augmented by my part-time job and scholarships—and when the note came due, my "friend" began avoiding me, that is, until he went on the offense, getting mean, acting for all the world as if I were hounding him when I hadn't said anything (his repayment was already two months overdue, and I was silent because I didn't want to give him any reason not to pay me back, worried it would provoke some sort of justified retaliation where I was being "unreasonable and greedy"); my school fees were due, and I was too preoccupied panicking than to fight with anyone—but before all that, he had given me one of his prints—of two children (a white girl and a Black boy)—that also went up on my walls, alongside my best friend's pictures. This picture wouldn't have been my first choice had he asked me, but it was a gift, and he was a professional photographer. Even at age twenty, it wouldn't occur to me to ask any of my friends who made art to *give* me anything, and I had no money to buy anything, so it was gifts or nothing.

The very idea of buying art seemed to me not only glamorous, but wildly luxurious.

There I was at the Dater show, lusting after the pictures of the camp follower, and the woman with the mink sleeves, and a third picture, the centerpiece of the show, *Imogen and Twinka, Yosemite* (1974).

3. *Imogen and Twinka, Yosemite,* is not only the most famous Judy Dater photograph, but it's probably the most recognizable portrait of Imogen Cunningham, even if many people don't realize that the elderly model with a Rolleiflex camera around her neck is Cunningham. It is also the first adult full frontal nude that *Life* magazine published (1976). In the picture, Imogen is clothed, head to toe—head scarf, long sleeves, long skirt, stockings, all in dark colors—standing on the left side of a very large tree trunk; her left hand is touching her chin, her expression one of surprise as if she only stumbled upon the other figure in the frame. Twinka Thiebaud, nude, leans against the tree, almost to the other side of it. She is tall, young, a forest nymph, unabashed by her own considerable beauty. One of her legs is bent, her arms are behind her back, her sleek blonde hair is pulled back in a bun, echoing Imogen's own hairstyle without mirroring it. Imogen's hair is as unruly as Twinka's is perfect; she's in profile looking over at Imogen, curious.

Two women. One old, one young. One short, one tall. One clothed, one nude.

The older woman looks at the younger woman, who looks at the older woman. There is a sense from Imogen that she is only now being reminded of how young someone can be; the surprise of youth equal to the surprise of old age.

You can either buy clothes or buy pictures.

I couldn't have what I couldn't have, and there were a few things I wanted at that time of my life—to see Paris and London; have a decent wardrobe; to not have to etch glass for an absentee boss who routinely "forgot" to sign our paychecks; to skip over the ending of my relationship to the place where it was well behind me; to get out of Newport Beach; to go to movies and museums and read—but there was nothing I wanted more, in that moment, than a print of *Imogen and Twinka, Yosemite.*

Instead I got the free postcard of the image that advertised the show and tacked it to my bedroom wall in a beach duplex I shared with two sorority girls, an astoundingly clichéd bitchy gay guy who went back into the closet when his conservative parents visited from central California, and the daughter of a couple who literally walked out of Hungary during the 1956 revolution. This girl also occasionally had sex with strangers from the beach, usually during the day, and once told me that she spent the afternoon masturbating with a carrot. You know, like I asked.

I tacked that postcard to the next bedroom wall, too.

And the next.

And the next.

And the next.

Until it fell apart.

It wasn't as popular an image then as it became, but that wouldn't have mattered to me anyway. Some people disparage cultural popularity, as if by somehow receiving deserved attention, the art (and, by association, the artist) is devalued. Imagine any other profession where finally being able to make a living is cause for disdain. Imogen Cunningham wasn't even awarded a Guggenheim Fellowship until she was pushing ninety, and her pictures earning real income. Success found her just in the nick.

Why do artists, writers, and musicians have to be obscure to the point of poverty to make people who like their work feel good about themselves? What kind of punishing love is *that?*

Most of us have something of the voyager in us, and our world, made so small by globalization and the Internet, combined with relatively inexpensive travel, leaves us so little to discover anymore. Every American child hears stories of explorers, conquistadors, scientific expeditions to islands and jungles. Ponce de Leon's Fountain of Youth. We're told about gold mines, and sunken ships, and trade routes that cross deserts, and continents, and oceans. We're shown the undisturbed footprints left by astronauts in the dusty surface of the moon. Ruins of past civilizations: a buried army of a thousand terra-cotta soldiers in China; the necropolises of Egypt. The Forum in Rome. If you have any imagination at all—and most children's are pretty spectacular—then you wonder, where does all that dreaming go?

For some, this impulse goes into making art. For others, it's discovering art; finding something you love (an artist, a band, an author) can feel more than appreciative, it can feel creative. Fran Lebowitz said the other half of losing so many artists (dancers, actors, photographers, writers, painters) to AIDS was losing so much of the passionate, discerning audience to the disease as well.

Discovery in art can sometimes be the road less traveled. Unfortunately, this impulse can also transform into snobbery of the worst kind, as you wield your singular and enlightened taste. A telling example of the desire to kill the thing you love is wishing against popularity for one's beloved artist/singer/director, even if that beloved artist is having trouble paying the bills.

*

Imogen and Twinka, Yosemite at the beach gallery was my first contact with Judy Dater. My second contact was years later, in 1990. J. and I had just moved back to San Francisco and were invited to a party on Russian Hill. We arrived close to the stipulated time, which is to say, we were early, but I knew the hosts well so it wasn't really a problem. As our host showed me around the house, we ended up in his office where, on the wall, he had a framed print of Dater's camp follower, that tired, old-too-soon blonde who held the photo of all those soldiers. As I expressed my admiration for this picture, my host said, "Judy Dater will be here tonight."

Just hearing this made me nervous. Meeting someone whose work you care about is often a high-wire act where, in my experience, the risk of someone falling, almost isn't worth taking. To make a short story short, Dater arrived with a friend. We were introduced, and she was nice enough as I told her about the show I'd seen in the late 1970s, and how much I loved her work, and how I wished I could've bought something, and how the free postcard of *Imogen and Twinka* had been transported from one inexpensive rental to another. She lost interest when I mentioned the postcard, even when I tried to explain that I just couldn't afford a real print, then turned a bit frosty before abandoning me altogether.

I was shy about meeting her in the first place; I'm not the sort of person who tries to become instant pals with anyone, including the well-known, that is, I wasn't looking to have some elaborate conversation with her that would result in us hanging out all night, making hilarious, knife-edged comments about our fellow guests, then exchanging phone numbers and going on vacations together.

This exchange in no way dampened my ardor for her photograph of Imogen and Twinka, or the lady with the mink sleeves, or the weary, middle-aged woman bearing the visual weight of all those soldiers.

*

My third contact with Judy Dater related to *Imogen and Twinka, Yosemite*. It occurred a year or two after we moved from San Francisco to the city where we now live. J. had gone to a photography gallery that is no longer there, as great as it was, and it was really good. The owner was showing Herman Leonard's pictures of jazz musicians and singers, roughly from the forties and fifties. Billie Holiday, in full performance, all atmosphere with smoke rising in the lights and a plaster cherub floating on the wall behind her. Dexter Gordon, sitting among his fellow musicians, sax resting on his knee, smoking, relaxing in the darkness.

Then there was the "portrait" of Lester Young, just beautiful, evocative, as a series of personal objects. An open instrument case, sheet music spilling out, his signature pork pie hat hung on the corner of the open lid; an empty coke bottle with a lit cigarette balancing on the neck, smoke curling up toward the ceiling. The shadows hitting the objects; Young himself is absent, transformed into the instrument case, the sheet music, the cigarette, the empty Coke bottle. His hat.

This picture, like all of Leonard's pictures, makes you want to be *there,* as if you thought this is what your life would be like, as if all the romance in the world only exists in these discrete, captured jazz moments. It also reminded me of the "portraits" taken by Mann, Orkin, and Cunningham where they too are defined by the people, landscapes, and the things in their lives.

As we wandered the gallery, a very attractive, middle-aged woman with most marvelous cheekbones handed us her card, saying she would be happy to help us. It was Twinka Thiebaud.

I knew exactly three things about Twinka:

1. Her father is artist Wayne Thiebaud.
2. She lived with, took care of, and edited Henry Miller.
3. She was Twinka. Judy Dater's Twinka. Twinka on my walls.

Now I knew a fourth thing: she was living in the same small city where I was living. It was as if having brought her image into so many of my homes, in a number of cities, and a pair of states, that I finally manifested her in the flesh.

We bought a photograph of Clifford Brown and Max Roach, handing our money to Twinka. And everything seemed complete: Southern California (seeing the picture of Imogen and Twinka, 1977), then San Francisco (meeting Judy Dater, 1990), then Portland (meeting Twinka, 1993). My life, this photograph, traveling the thousand miles of coastline together.

*

Currently on my wall: A postcard I picked up at the Norton Simon Museum in Pasadena (where I'm from; I used to play on the little nine-hole course, called Carmelita, every Saturday with my dad and his friend Jim until they tore it up to build the Norton Simon) is a reproduction of a work by Mike Mandel. The tiny portraits of eight photographers, laid out in a grid of nine boxes, are made to look as if they are baseball players on trading cards, mitts and balls and all (the ninth box shows the "reverse" of Ansel Adams's card, complete with his stats). Along with Adams is Manuel Bravo, Imogen Cunningham, and Judy Dater. The picture is called *Untitled (Baseball Photographer Trading Cards), 1975.*

*

Love in the Art World: Part I

Artistic couples are a pretty standard fantasy, art enhanced by an unconventional love affair. Muses and mistresses and lovers. Man Ray and Lee Miller and Kiki. Claude Cahun and Marcel Moore. Weston and Modotti and Mather. Stieglitz and O'Keeffe. Robert Mapplethorpe and Patti Smith. The vision that Roi Partridge offered Imogen Cunningham. No matter how much the Bohemian Class tries to explode the idea of marriage, they all end up married (or "married") anyway, in one way or another.

The short list above is by no means definitive.

When you're young, artistically inclined, and it's the early 1970s, you find yourself searching for love role models. More specifically, and because you're female, you're looking at ways to slip the confines of female expectations. You think about bohemian lives; you are an idealist. You're a feminist; feminism is on the rise, though it isn't there yet. Even the way women were relegated to a combination of mother/wife/mistress by the radical groups that grew out of the 1960s indicated that the New Order was the same as the Old Order, only no one had to buy you dinner first.

Then there's Joni Mitchell, explaining it all to you. Her voice was high, a little thin until her chain smoking finally brought it down to its slightly damaged, far more enjoyable register. She wrote in unexpected tunings about love impossible to sustain that left her brokenhearted and really literate in the retelling. She was all *le dolor exquisite,* so instead of wanting to avoid her experiences, you wanted to embrace them. It *was* better to have loved and lost than never to have loved at all. It was a conjuror's trick; all smoke and mirrors, and none of the women I knew cared.

The Joni Paradox made the listener want to experience the same love, glamorous and aching. She was the perfect voice for the time, extolling romantic freedom, erotic adventure, and art. In her interviews, her arrogance was on par with Gertrude (*There are three geniuses in the world, and I am one*) Stein, with the talent and brilliance to back it up. Mitchell's musical expression went from folk to jazz to world to synth, even if it wasn't always successful, moving through genres before her male contemporaries in her field. Her literate expression was *sui generis* as Dylan's. And she refused to be classified as anything other than a musician, not a *female* musician.

(Side note: In 1991, I was teaching in a weeklong workshop in Los Angeles with an older, very revered, very admired, female activist writer, another famous male writer, and a young, not-famous female writer. The revered writer, who was very likable, had perfected her hole-in-the-stocking, absentminded, wild-haired old lady image. Even so, she brought the young, not-famous writer to angry tears; a bitch move, unkind even though she feigned that distracted writer thing—she was sharp as a tack—because this young girl had nothing but earnestness and youth and an unknown novel, while the famous writer had everything. She said something to the male writer that sounded like a bit more then gentle ribbing, and on our panel when I said that I would prefer to be thought of as "a writer, and not a woman writer," something I stated merely as a preference, and this revered writer, who had been friendly to the point of inviting me to her family cabin for a future visit, snapped that, "I should be happy to be called anything." I had only just published my first novel, and she was a far bigger deal than I, so the audience laughed, and I realized that this wanting to be taken seriously as a writer, and not a woman writer with its whiff of being dismissed, of being told I throw a ball good for a girl, was going to be a bit of a slog, even in 1991, especially if established, politically involved female writers were more than willing to ridicule my simple desire of being called a writer, and not a woman writer.)

There was a book going around when I was in college about "the loves of Joni Mitchell," not written by her, and not complimentary. I remember *Rolling Stone* publishing a chart of her lovers. I don't remember any of her male contemporaries stepping in and saying, let's not think of this woman as a whore, because that was the implication, albeit in a less direct language. Not even the men who recorded her song about Woodstock, which ended up defining Woodstock, spoke up. Her complicated love life as a female artist reduced to an everybody's girlfriend level. The message regarding artistic ambition, accomplishment, and love was, as they say, mixed.

*

The cinematic coupling of male directors and female actors is addressed, briefly, in *From the Journals of Jean Seberg* by Mark Rappaport, a documentary/personal essay of biography, film critique, and feminism, where all the strands of exploratory discourse are never as digressive as they appear. At one point, a discussion begins with Seberg's marriage to a much older (by 34 years), intellectual French writer/filmmaker, Romain Gary, who convinced her to star in a film, *Birds of Peru,* that he wrote and directed. Seberg plays a beautiful, young wife to a much older man; she is also a crazed nymphomaniac. It is not flattering. This leads to *Barbarella,* directed by Jane Fonda's then-husband, Roger Vadim, featuring Fonda nude or in "bondage/hooker style" clothing. Barbarella (Fonda) finally ends up trapped in a contraption meant to orgasm her to death, only she's so sexually durable she short circuits the machine. Vadim also made *And God Created Woman,* with his then-wife, Brigitte Bardot, cementing her sex kitten reputation.

Next Rappaport introduces Vanessa Redgrave in connection with director Tony Richardson, her then-husband who ended the marriage when he became involved with Jeanne Moreau. Moreau, still his lover in real life, is cast in his movie *Mademoiselle* as a prim schoolteacher-sociopathic poisoner. At one point Moreau has a sex scene where her character meets a guy in a field who rips off her dress and makes her crawl around on all fours, barking like a dog. Rappaport links Fonda, Redgrave, and Seberg as contemporaries, actresses, and political activists (Vietnam, the PLO, the Black Panthers and civil rights, respectively) (Moreau, too) to say not only are these roles degrading but what is the deal casting your wife/lover in them? All these movies were made around the mid-1960s, as the second wave of feminism was taking hold. If female artists were more willing to challenge the status quo, why weren't their male artist counterparts equally willing? I mean, if boho couples are such social rebels, so willing to cast aside tradition? And what of someone like me, with her own artistic dreams, thinking if you can't find equality in the arts, then where the fuck are you supposed to find it?

*

No art couple is more non-traditional than Claude Cahun and Marcel Moore, French artist collaborators who modeled for and took pictures of each other. They were lovers, and androgynous, playing with gender and ideas of femininity. And they were sisters. Well, stepsisters.

Lucie Schwob and Suzanne Malherbe (their birth names) met in their teens in Nantes, France, in 1909. Eight years later, their parents married. In one deft stroke the women became family in a manner more enduring than marriage which, of course, wasn't an option.

They settled in Jersey, an island in the Channel Islands, which was Nazi-occupied during the war. Cahun and Moore's response was to turn their art into anti-German propaganda, making no secret of their resistance, which got them arrested in 1944 and sentenced to death. They were separated in prison, each attempting (but not succeeding at) suicide, and eventually released. The Germans had confiscated their property and destroyed most of their art. Cahun's health never recovered and she died in 1954, with Moore taking her own life in 1972.

The art they made is sublime, inventive, challenging, collaborative in every way.

What does it mean when one of the most successful artist couples is two women?

*

What are we hoping to find with these couples? Is it that they reside just on the edge of convention and that maybe we hope to find better ways of being with each other? Are we hoping they'll fail, since they so often announce to the world that the traditional life is not worth living? Maybe it's all part of the conflict America has with artists: enjoying what they produce, be it films, or fashion, or paintings, or architecture, or music— all that high art, and popular art, and practical art—then balk when they need support. This country spends so little on art (in every regard) as if art is optional. Is it because no one believes what artists do is work? Often followed by a *Who do these people think they are?* So, *good* if they fail at their relationships, you who thinks you're too good to be like everyone else. *Good* if you fall apart.

Maybe artists seek each other out because they know that no one is waiting for their art, even if we are so divided by religion and regions and belief systems, that it's the only thing that unites us as it examines what it means to be human. It's the only way we can talk to each other, which is how a militant group destroying antiquities, for example, is silencing everyone. To put it another way: science can cure cancer, and art offers a reason to want cancer cured.

Or even another way, *Art is much less important than life, but what a poor life without it.*

—*Robert Motherwell*

*

Traditional marriage isn't great for women, even now. Looking back, one can chart the sprint for the nunnery or the unconventional union with the unconventional man (same-sex marriages aren't generally considered "traditional") because you knew you couldn't put yourself together in the usual way of many wives. Anais Nin says that she began life wanting to be a muse, and the wife of an artist:

. . . But really I was trying to avoid the final issue—I had to do the job myself. In letters I've received from women, I've found what [Otto] Rank had described as a guilt for creating. It's a very strange illness, and it doesn't strike men—because the culture has demanded of man that he maximize his talents. He is encouraged by the culture to become the great doctor, the great philosopher, the great professor, the great writer. Everything is really planned to push him in that direction. Now, this was not asked of women.

She is writing from the perspective of the mid-1970s, when ambition was still "not asked of women."

Maybe not to have a partner at all makes this artistic life too lonely, where you can feel too unknown.

*

As far back as the nineties, I was saying at book and author luncheons, dinners, library talks, bookstore readings, literary festivals, and on literary panels that the male writers were never asked if they are married, or had kids, or how they juggled family and work. Yet women (including myself) were nearly always asked about marriage and children and juggling. The assumption being that the domestic world held the man's writing at its center, revolving around his work, while the woman had to find time for her writing, domestic concerns being at the center (her real work). This was in 1991, and yet I've heard almost this exact same thing expressed by women writers (and others). Still.

I was often assigned to a "women's panel" at literary events, and never included on a straight writers' panel, which says pretty much everything about how my writing is perceived. Yes,

I've always written about women, but why aren't their stories as important as those of "real writers"? Yes, I made remarks about being stuck in "the women's ghetto," and being subtly dismissed. Yes, I've had men at readings and talks, "dragged along," or so they would tell me, by a wife or girlfriend, then tell me that they can't be expected to read my book, right? since the subject matter has nothing to do with their lives, right? speaking to me as if we have a mutual understanding about why they can't be bothered, as if I didn't spend hours alone, writing, tamping down the usual insecurities that many writers feel, or that I sacrificed nothing, or that I didn't work as hard as I've worked. I've even had some women tell me, *of course, my husband wouldn't be interested in your book,* my book, that coming to my reading is just one more way they indulge the wife. Of course, I'm expected to politely understand that this is my fault for choosing to write about *women* and their tiny little lives.

Here's another thing I sometimes wonder about: why is it if a woman writes graphically about sex and/or drugs, her work is taken more seriously, more on par with a man's? Why are those "domestic" stories thought not to be as rich and as deep, a little like O'Keeffe's painting of a low, dismal-colored barn. And why are "women's stories" all thought to be the same story, to wit, the "mother-daughter-themed" panels, even though I've never written mother-daughter stories.

This not being placed on straight writing panels makes me feel as if I'm thought not to know the first thing about Writing, or really Excavating My Soul like some hard-drinking (smoking, drugging, sport fucking, whatever) male writer. The work doesn't always reflect the effort, which is to say that a book about sex and drugs isn't intrinsically harder to write than a book about a nineteenth-century sea voyage. Every time someone thought of me as "quilty" (my first published novel featuring quilters), I often want to say, yeah, like Clare. Readers often conflate the writer with the material—I get it—but I'm not my material in such an unimaginative way given that my novels are not strictly autobiographical so wouldn't that mean I'm something of A Writer after all?

Years ago, when *The Corrections* was published, a piece about Jonathan Franzen appeared in the *New York Times Magazine* where he talked about working in his room, with headphones on or some such thing, alongside a bottle of booze. The article made it sound like this guy was the Gary Cooper of writers, braving it alone, blocking out everything so he can do this one thing. When I read the Franzen piece my son was very young. A woman writer friend, with a child the same age, called me, steaming. We were so angered by this piece, because all we wished for was a little room, day drinking if we felt like it, and shutting out the daily responsibilities of parenting and other domestic duties. The whole article was like being slapped twice; first, those conditions to write in peace weren't an option, and second, it's a guy writing a domestic novel. Why does it still feel like dancing backward and in heels?

*

Imogen Cunningham photographed Judy Dater in 1972. In the black and white print, Dater is standing outdoors, her hands holding the tips of her long, dark hair, pulling it straight out to the side. She wears eyeliner, maybe lipstick, and a classic button-down shirt. She looks down, as if something has caught her eye, prompting her pretty, sly smile; she appears amused. She looks like a young woman of her era. She looks like she has something to say.

Persephone

In June 2000, Paul Karlstrom interviewed Judy Dater at her Berkeley studio for the Archives of American Art at the Smithsonian, asking her about her interest in nudes. (*"I've done a lot of nudes and there is always a sexual charge.*") She (rightly) responds that the answer is complicated to the point of being nearly unanswerable—who knows why we like what we like, what draws us to one thing and not another, why intellect and emotion and common sense don't always align, where does this creative mess comes from?—but believes her interest has something to do with Thomas Hart Benton's *Persephone* (1939).

In 1989, J. and I went to a retrospective of Thomas Hart Benton at the Los Angeles County Museum of Art. We went there in the middle of day when it was so empty we pretty much had the place to ourselves. As we wandered the galleries, the silence was shattered by an older woman, standing in the center of one of the galleries, announcing in a very loud voice to her much younger, male companion, "This is garbage! Unmitigated garbage!"

I knew of Benton's surprising (to me) role as Jackson Pollock's teacher, which was the main reason we were at the museum. I also knew that he was born in Neosho, Missouri, had lived and studied in New York and Paris. I read that he was "difficult." Robert Hughes called his work "vulgar," saying that "He was a dreadful artist most of the time." Benton was also vociferously homophobic. His idyllic, colorful Midwestern scenes that ran counter to much modern art were derided as "Okie Baroque." Among them was his picture *Susannah and the Elders,* his rural American depiction of the Bible story about lust and lies. In Benton's version, a full-frontal nude Susannah (right down to the pubic hair that created such a hue-and-cry in 1939) is about to dip into a pond, while two elders (men) hide themselves, spying on her. In the far distance at the back is a farmhouse. It's not hard to miss the mix of innocence, menace, and voyeurism, compounded by Benton painting *himself* in to the scene as one of the old, creepy farmers. Benton found the accusations of lewdness and filth "funny as hell."

Persephone (1938), the picture that so influenced Dater, is the visual and spiritual sister of *Susannah,* though Persephone is a character in a story from a completely different, theological system. She was the daughter of Zeus and Demeter, goddess of the harvest, a kind of Mother Earth. Hades, the ruler of the Underworld, happened to drive his chariot up to the earth's surface, whereupon he spied the young maiden, Persephone, kidnapped her, then made her his queen. He loves her (when the gods want to punish, they always seem to make someone love someone, which is in no way a mixed message), and doesn't want to let her go. Demeter, grief stricken, appealed to Zeus, who said if she hasn't eaten anything, Persephone can return to her mother. However, Persephone swallowed six pomegranate seeds, enough to send her back below for six months of the year, thus the seasons came into being.

In Benton's painting, a young woman, naked and exposed, stretches at the base of a tree, in another idealized agricultural setting, sleeping, while yet another old, creepy farmer, a "hillbilly," again resembling Benton, lurks behind the trunk, watching her a little too intently. His cart (read: chariot), has been abandoned on the road. His hunger for this girl is palpable. Again, there is voyeurism, vulnerability, menace. Jesse Benton, the artist's only daughter, said that he made a gift of this painting—sometimes called the Mona Lisa of the Midwest—to her mother.

Persephone, the Queen of the Underworld, in myth and in this painting, is the story of spring and winter (Youth and Age). The painting is also a coupling of styles: Old Master and 1930s pinup girl, a merging of classical art and popular culture. The disquieting aspect of the work, and that echoes in Dater's photograph of Imogen and Twinka, is that of nudity and voyeurism (also Age and Youth, as well as a tree in a natural landscape). The voyeurism in Benton's picture is crude, unmitigated; anyone seeing the painting becomes a voyeur as well, something Benton makes clear.

Ken Burns, in his documentary about Benton, said that the artist took pleasure in the profane *Persephone*. Robert Hughes points out that Benton's relationship with publicity (the loving of it, the courting of it) was on par with Andy Warhol. His notorious nude cost him his job at the Kansas City Institute of Art, and it hung for a time in Billy Rose's Diamond Horseshoe nightclub in New York. None of this harmed his career, since he ended up on the cover of *Time* magazine, using his fame to reject New York and deride gay people.

The painting hangs in Kansas City's Nelson-Atkins Museum, near a photograph taken by Alfred Eisenstadt of a middle-aged artist, painting in his studio, with a young, nude woman as a model. She has her back to the camera, as she reclines on a divan. An older man, studying an unclothed girl.

The artist is Benton, the model is Imogene Bruton, soon to be immortalized and scandalized as Persephone.

Bruton posed for a class at the Art Institute for sixty cents an hour; she was still in her teens. The old man in the picture was picked up at a mission, despite his eventual painted resemblance to Benton. The two models never posed together. It's believed that Bruton posed for financial reasons, perhaps regretting her role as Persephone, since she never discussed nor traded on her image as the Mona Lisa of the Midwest, something almost unheard of in our era of shameless fame. Nor did she sell the charcoal drawing of her likeness that he gave her.

At the time of the Eisenstadt photograph, she asked not to have her identity revealed, out of respect for her family, but Benton went ahead and painted her face anyway.

*

Dater said:

"When I was a kid growing up and I used to love to look at that book [Great American Paintings] and that particular painting [Persephone] really got to me . . . I didn't understand it. I didn't on any, maybe, intellectual level, but it certainly affected me on a kind of emotional or erotic level. And I think I was looking at that since I was, you know, four or five years old. And fascinated by it. And when I started photography that particular image never left me and what was there—the part of it that never left me was the subject, which was this wrinkled up old geezer looking at this gorgeous, young woman naked, and not knowing she was being looked at. This sort of tantalizing, titillating, voyeuristic scene. . . . Which I found fascinating and maybe repelling or repul—not really repulsive in a gross sense but there is something wrong here . . . but totally attractive."

Dater's *Persephone* experience was my *Lolita* experience after I saw the movie version. I hadn't yet read the book (tried to tackle it afterward). The experience of seeing the film when I was not much older than Lolita herself, meant that I could grasp her point of view, seeing Humbert Humbert through young eyes. The movie was like a fever dream, that slightly delirious state where reality and illness warp each other. It took decades before I could somewhat separate James Mason from his role as Humbert (again, to a twelve-year-old girl, he looked really, really *old*), enabling me to watch him without a visceral response of repulsion. And, as Dater notes with regard to *Persephone,* there was attraction, though in my case, the attraction was not sexual, it was more the lure of forbidding. *You don't know what to make of it? It feels dangerous to you? Well then, keep moving toward it.*

This may be a good time to mention that according to the other students in the class with Imogene Bruton, working alongside their teacher, Benton, that Bruton's ribs were showing and she fainted during class. Lizzie Siddal, red-haired darling of the Pre-Raphaelites, became ill while lying in a tub of icy water as Millais painted her as *Ophelia.* Kiki De Montparnasse, most famous as Man Ray's beautiful cello, frequently posed naked in exchange for a meal and a bed. Manet painted Victorine Meurent with the skin pallor of someone who may have ingested arsenic, a popular treatment at the time for syphilis, and posed her in the manner of Titian's *Venus of Urbino.*

(Women and economics are always entangled.)

It wasn't simply Manet's model's skin tone and pose that sparked controversy (though the two aspects did suggested prostitute or courtesan), but it was the lack of idealization; here was a girl, naked, entirely exposed, who was not only stared at, but who stared right back, without any hint of apology (she is not caught off guard by the viewer) or modesty; her gaze meets the gaze of the viewer.

The last thing a voyeur wants is to be looked at.

Having a dark impulse, such a liking to watch, being brought out in the light, is disquieting.

Dater admits that in *Persephone,* "the theme of a nude person being looked at by a clothed person and not knowing they're being looked at" absolutely influenced *Imogen and Twinka, Yosemite, 1974.* The difference between the two master works, Benton's and Dater's, is that her picture is of two women. Where Benton's picture can seem unsavory, *Imogen and Twinka, Yosemite* feels playful, innocent, the voyeuristic tension lessened. Twinka is just a curiosity, you know, something you might stumble upon during a walk in the woods. If the encounter has any weight at all, it's in the juxtaposition of youth and age; Youth literally looking over her shoulder at the approach of Age, with Age nearly shocked by the freshness of Youth. There is a hint of sadness: the small, elderly woman, covered to her neck, her sexuality absent, carries her camera, she watches and records, next to a tall, beautiful girl so at ease in the world she doesn't need clothes. She would never think to carry a camera.

*

Women and Other Visions, or
Love in the Art World: Part II

Dater attended UCLA, transferred to San Francisco State, and somewhere, between her freshman year and graduation, married and divorced. She also met Jack Wellpott, a photographer and professor at San Francisco State, nearly twenty years her senior, who became her colleague, collaborator, and husband. He also became her ex-husband, but that is later, after *Women and Other Visions.*

The mechanics are wonderfully simple: a male photographer and a female photographer take pictures of the exact same women, without identifying the photographer as male or female. Jack Welpott called it a collection of photographs about "womanness."

For me, the project is about sex, unmistakably. And about gender. The "womanness" description I attribute to the era in which these pictures were taken, the attempt to define the "feminine" since the project was done in the 1970s, when the Second Wave of feminism was cresting. The introduction to the book of these pictures is written by an important male photographer with whom, I confess, I'm unfamiliar, Henry Holmes Smith, who writes a bit weirdly about the pictures, that is to say, about women. "Woman is shown here as the crafty wrestler she is." He believes women wear masks; he thinks them "two-faced." He says of the male and female photographers that their pictures "blend," the "two artists work patiently along the way toward correcting our inevitably imperfect vision of women." He writes about Mother Earth and big bodies, breasts and bellies, and taut bodies and the time he walked into the hypogeum, "a sanctuary of the Great Mother at Malta, saying, 'Answer me.'" He even ends with all of us being "horny at the gates of horn." There's a fair amount of pre-Christian mumbo jumbo.

I came of age during the Second Wave of feminism, that is, I'm not speaking as someone who majored in women's studies. There were only a couple of colleges offering the major at that time anyway. This didn't mean that women were silent within their majors; things were transforming and backsliding and lurching along just the same. There was a fair amount of arguing and consciousness raising. It's great that women younger than I, women who weren't there (in the same way that I wasn't there for the Suffragette movement) are interested enough in the history and sociology of women to major in this subject. I was just a feminist with other interests who was already living in a time before it was a history to be studied.

So, let me say as someone who was around then, I can understand how a man talking about wanting to portray a woman's "womanness" might have passed as supportive of women, empowering of women even if it sounds, to me now, like a man who loves the sound of his own voice. And the Smith introduction? I know a woman here in town who is an expert at the insult compliment. You know how it goes, "I heard you were hired by the *New Yorker*. Too bad no one reads magazines anymore." A woman "wears a mask" (a possible insightful observation, women cannot be themselves but must conform to an idea of themselves), making her "two-faced." Duplicitous. Untrustworthy. Hypocritical. But we're "all horny at the gates of horn"? And the mask thing was *so* close.

What comes through here is how much these men reflect their time; they think they're on board with the changes, with feminism, but they simply haven't caught up. This is what that era was like, not the distilled version of almost all history, where the messiness of the timeline and society's struggles are made sleek.

The men's opinions aside, I was immediately drawn to this project when I stumbled upon it. And not just because it's a series that offers multiple viewpoints and portraits of women (the twin pillars of all my books). I like it because, for me, it illustrates an artistic couple, Dater and Welpott, as equals—instead of working independently side-by-side, or artist-muse. Neither is muse. Each is photographer.

But why only female subjects? This is where the feet-dragging of the feminist era shows, though it's more primal than that: what

I saw when I looked at this series was sex and the negotiation of a relationship. I don't know Dater and I never met Welpott, but if art succeeds, it succeeds by allowing for interpretation.

This project reminds me of Sally Mann taking pictures of her children, because she was with them so much, or Imogen Cunningham, also photographing her children and her garden because she was with them so much. Ruth Orkin took pictures of her children, though mostly she took pictures outside her window, of Central Park and the New York City skyline because she was with them so much (the kids and the city), and I like a deeply explored subject. I appreciate that the subjects for these photographs were more *revealed* to the photographers rather than *pursued* by them.

Ruth Orkin said, "Being a photographer is making people look at what I want them to look at." Georgia O'Keeffe said of her enlarged, cropped photographically influenced flowers, "A flower is relatively small. Everyone has many associations with a flower—the idea of flowers . . . nobody sees a flower— really—it's so small. . . . So I said to myself—I'll paint what I see—what the flower is to me but I'll paint it big and they will be surprised into taking time to look at it." Flannery O'Connor writes, "But there's a certain grain of stupidity that the writer of fiction can hardly do without, and this is the quality of having to stare. . . . The longer you look at one object, the more of the world you see in it. . . ." Robert Mapplethorpe began taking his scandalous photos of men after he met Benjamin Green, a pornographic film star, who he said inspired him to "push the envelope" and described him as ". . . the apple of my eye, my unicorn if you will. I could shoot him for hours and hours . . . each print captured the essence of human perfection." Mapplethorpe said of his "degenerate" photographs of fist-fucking, or one man urinating in another man's mouth, or one man inserting his finger into another man's penis that these pictures "inspired him" to "refine his photographs with an emphasis on formal beauty."

In the same way that *Lolita* is brilliant, Mapplethorpe's pictures sometimes touch those stars he reaches for, but *Lolita* is also a dirty, disturbing little book, made more so at times by its brilliance, and Mapplethorpe still has a bullwhip up his ass.

One more digression and I will get to my point. I promise.

Mapplethorpe made pictures of flowers, but he didn't really care for them. He said, "I think flowers have a certain edge. . . . I get something out of flowers that other people don't get. . . . I love the pictures of flowers more than I love real flowers." Flowers troubled him because they were dying; he couldn't save them, so he filmed them, in his formalist style, searching for the same perfection he sought when portraying his human subjects. He said, "If I photograph a flower or a cock, I'm not doing anything different."

John Ashbery writes: "Of course the flower photographs are not what made him [Mapplethorpe] simultaneously famous and unacceptable. . . . But because he is fashionable, because there is tremendous demand behind his work, and because so much of it cannot be shown in public, these presumably innocent photographs have been summoned to stand in for the others. It is impossible to look at them and ignore their context, and they have taken on further ambiguity: They are, in effect, calling attention to the pictures that are hidden from view. Like fig leave for absent genitalia, they point to scandal of what is not there." A comfortable image as a fake narrative; Mapplethorpe's flowers, Cunningham's garden, Orkin's city views are, and aren't, the story.

Can it be said that when Ruth Orkin showed the world her world through her window, she wasn't offering a view of a park and skyline, but a window into her housebound life? Is this what she meant by making people "look at what I want them to look at"?

Why did O'Keeffe want people to really "see" her flowers?

Diane Arbus said, "A photograph is a secret of a secret," yet I feel that the flowers, the garden, the city views aren't secrets as much as they are abstract art, telling you exactly what you are looking at even if it isn't immediately recognizable.

Which is why I get the sense that *Women and Other Visions* is about something other than images about female empowerment, or female beauty.

*

Georgia O'Keeffe wrote of these sex-charged sessions with her then-lover, Alfred Stieglitz, "I was photographed with a kind of heat and excitement and in a way wondered what it was all about." She was twenty-nine. He was old enough to be her father.

"When his photographs of me were first shown, it was in a room at the Anderson Galleries. Several men—after looking around awhile—asked Stieglitz if he would photograph their wives and girlfriends the way he photographed me. He was very amused and laughed about it. If they had known what a close relationship he would need to have to photograph their wives and girlfriends the way he photographed me—I think they wouldn't have been interested."

When he took nudes of Beck Strand and Dorothy Norman, the pictures were expressive, composed, coded. O'Keeffe deciphering everything.

Years ago I read a short story by Andrea Lee from a collection called *Remarkable Women*. This story was about a wife who gives her older husband the gift of a young woman—not a prostitute, exactly, but someone willing to sleep with him. It was their anniversary, or his birthday. You find yourself asking, would I do this for the man I love? And isn't the whole thing something of a "gift of the magi"? Here, honey, I adore you so I'm going to give you a night of sexual abandon, probably a thrilling night of sexual abandon (for obvious reasons) with a girl you hardly know and won't be seeing again because I know how difficult it's been for you to be monogamous, so here's a reward. Then he says, Oh no, just your willingness to do that for me makes me say no. You proved your love and generosity; that your love is greater than your jealousy (insecurity). Just knowing that you would allow me a night of passion with a girl young enough to be my daughter says volumes about how much you love me.

Like the *Gift of the Magi,* no one gets what they want materially; each gets what they want emotionally.

Here are the Dater-Wellpotts, whose own beginning of their love sounded as if they had some, uh, let's call it "marriage overlap." Anyway, so they embark on this project (marrying midway into it) taking pictures of the same women. And the wife, being a photographer herself, knows something about how these images are made (let's call it the Georgia O'Keeffe Model of Photography). Dater says that Welpott's experience was sexual. "I feel like when Jack was doing it [taking pictures of the women], it was sexual seduction and when I was doing it, it was more of a psychological seduction to get them to co-operate with me."

The sessions sound almost like the photographic equivalent of inviting another woman into your marital bed. Because Dater was an artist, a woman, a wife, a lover, I admire her for agreeing to do this at all. I do.

When the book of this project was published—a book that included, by the way, *Imogen and Twinka, Yosemite, 1974*— Jack Welpott wrote a brief introduction, and Henry Holmes, another male photographer (see earlier comments) wrote an even longer introduction. As for Judy Dater, well, her pictures would have to speak for themselves since she wrote nothing.

Welpott wrote:

"For several years Judy Dater and I have been photographing people whom we found fascinating and who, in the same
manner, expressed something about the 'feminine mystique.'
Most were strangers to us. We discovered them in cafes, banks,
shops, and on the street—anywhere we happened to be. We
usually spent several hours with them in their own environment. In every case, the few hours spent with these people were
intense and, at times, progressed to extended friendships."

Really.

"People?" Don't you mean "women"?

A photographer friend, CS, talked about the predatory
nature of taking pictures in the street and how it troubled her.
She doesn't speak for all photographers, but she is addressing
an essential truth of making pictures with a specific intention.
Welpott's passage reads like a couple trolling for a third to, you
know, join them for an "interesting experiment," that is, if
everyone is cool with it, if they all like each other, maybe spend
some time together in a more private location ("several hours in
their own environment"), to see if they all like each other and,
oh, by the way, we're photographers.

None of this makes me love the project any less, and I
think the lack of an introduction by Dater is really a sign of
the times. First, you have to rearrange your own consciousness
since you were raised in the same households that the men were
raised in, with the same values, ideas, and social mores, which
is why these two men (Welpott and Smith) with their introductions say nothing about the women in the project, while
saying everything about themselves. There's even a whiff of
self-congratulations on being so down with the whole "feminine mystique" thing.

It's interesting that each introduction touches on the mysterious, masked nature of women since there was a whole
movement at the turn of the twentieth century that centered
the misogynistic idea that women are ruled by Nature (Nature

and a woman's nature being synonymous), and not intellect. Women are temptresses, desiring to lure men away from a life of the mind, and art, and into a "paradise of erotic materialism." Women were the sexual roadblocks to evolution, spirituality, science, and literature because of their base, essentially, unknowable natures.

In a review of Bram Dykstra's book *Idols of Perversity* about you-know-who and her inability to choose her humanity over her animal "mystique," Joan Palevsky wrote:

> A quick list of descriptive epithets picked from his pages yields an alphabet soup of conventional images: *aggressive, angelic, adamantine, alluring, animal, amorous; brainless, bountiful or bestial; coy, coarse, cool, cute, corrupting, chaste, copulating, childlike, carnal; delicate, devouring, decorous, diabolic, diaphanous, Dionysiac; enchanting, elemental, emancipated, enticing, evil; feline, ferocious, frolicsome, fatuous, frivolous, fervid, flaccid, fertile, flirtatious; graceful; helpless, horrid, hilarious (though nowhere as much as men!); idealized, innocent, impulsive, immature, insatiable, intoxicating, inane; joyous; lesbian, licentious, lewd, libertine, lustful, lubricious, lethal; mysterious, marginalized, meretricious, maternal; nun-like or nymphomaniac; obscure, obsessive; prurient, pure, primal, playful, passive, pliable, predatory, pious, perverse, pensive, promiscuous, pudic, primitive, passionate, placid; robust, raped; sensual, submissive, sphinx-like, spirited, spiritual, seductive, savage, sirens, saintly, sedate; titillating, tubercular, tender, tempting, tedious; virtuous, voluptuous, virginal, vicious, vulnerable, venomous, vacuous, viraginous, victimized, vampirical, voracious; waif, wild, whores.*

Which is really a kind of expansion on the basic theme of what I think both Holmes and Welpott were getting at in their introductions, where they think they are loving women, but really aren't even bothering to understand anything about them. I mean, they're talking about them being sexual, not intellectual, not even emotional, as if this assessment is progress. Part of the women's movement was to free women from sexual judgement. We know in retrospect how well that played out, in some ways creating a different, opposite sexual pressure, when the needle really needed to settle between the two extremes. To put it another way, abortion was legalized in 1973 and for the next forty-two years (and counting), a surprisingly large number of (male) politicians have been trying to wrest choice from women. Rape, particularly on college campuses and in the military, is hardly being dealt with in any sort of meaningful way when it is dealt with at all. It's very hard to hear the light sentences college boys receive—boys who made the choice to sexually assault a girl—using the argument that the boys' lives shouldn't be derailed over "a poor choice." It's so much easier to turn away from the ruin of *her* life.

How does rape work into the fin-de-siècle notion of women and their animal natures? The answer is in the question.

Anyway, as I said, we know how well that sexual revolution turned out.

All this is to say that men really didn't get what sexuality meant to women, or that women weren't the sum of their sexuality ("yeah, thanks for freeing me sexually while keeping my earning power two-thirds less than yours"), even when they were trying to be on a woman's side.

No wonder Dater didn't include her own introduction after reading her interview with Paul Karlstrom. But *Women and Other Visions* is more than an artifact, a dated endeavor; its timelessness lies more in the making of the pictures, the concept for the project, in the conflicts of gender and the arts. It's an elegant, brilliant idea that I'm not convinced would play out so differently in these post-Second Wave of Feminism days.

Except that Dater would have her own introduction.

*

Dater said, "I feel like when Jack was doing it [taking pictures of the women], it was sexual seduction and when I was doing it, it was more of a psychological seduction in order to get them to co-operate with me."

When Welpott, more or less, admitted that her insight was correct, that making the pictures did have a sexual component, her response was one of anger, along with the fact that she had to be present and "protect [her] territory." Dater said it all just sort of came together when they realized that they were taking pictures of the same women anyway, so why not formalize it and see how it ends up?

"Sometimes we'd see them together and we'd agree that we were gonna photograph them but I knew, I mean, I was very aware of Jack's nature. In terms of his relationship with women and his desire for women and maybe I thought this was a safe way to—a safe outlet. 'You can photograph them all you want but I'm gonna be right there with you.'"

So the younger wife arranges for her older husband to have a night of passion, as a gift.

One could sense the sexual something here all along.

I sometimes wonder if a portrait is sometimes about the desire to possess. Maybe that's the difference between male and female photographers (I mean, when they photograph for personal reasons, not because they're commissioned). When Dater was asked if she slept with her male models, she answered, "Well, some of them." She said, "But the thing about it is that every single model I've slept with, I've slept with them all before I photographed them, not after. . . . It's not the result of a session. The session came because I slept with them and I already had a relationship with them and I liked them and I was interested in them. I think probably in every case [I was] in love with them and wanted a picture of them. But there was never a time when I photographed somebody and that led to sex. Ever."

She also says:

"Oh, how, how was it as a woman? Oh, well—okay [participating in the project]. We both photographed the same woman, in the same moment, in the same room, and were photographing them in the nude and sometimes but not often in the nude. So there I am, a young woman working with an older man and we're both looking at the same woman and we're both photographing the same woman and we're getting really different pictures and everything that I said before about my personal experience of working with women, yes, I can acknowledge the sexual charge is there. . . . And Jack's experience of it was—or at least what he would talk about—because who knows what he was really experiencing. . . . It was pretty sexually, much more sexually, charged, much more a man looking at a woman and getting off on it."

In this way, Dater enters into her own *Persephone* situation. A little bit of *Susannah and the Elders*.

Because Welpott was "up front about his sexual desires for these women" she couldn't be sure if anything happened at any other time, when she wasn't in the room. It wasn't that he discussed any of this, she says, "but he certainly let me know."

Cunningham's garden is motherhood. Orkin's park and skyline is the housewife life. Mapplethorpe's flowers are penises. Stieglitz's prismatic portrait of O'Keeffe is the newness of sex.

Women and Other Visions might be about multiple interpretations of women, or it might be infidelity and trying to protect that which cannot be protected.

Eventually, Dater tired of the project, wanted to move on to something else: her idea was for them to recreate the same project, only for each of them to take pictures of the same *men*. Welpott said No.

They divorced a couple of years later.

*

Aarmour Starr, 1972

There are four photographs that I think serve as a contrast between Dater and Welpott:

Welpott portrays Starr in drag in a pair of portraits. In the first, Starr poses theatrically, sporting a blond, page-boy wig, as he drapes himself across the back of a decidedly unglamorous VW Beetle. His dress looks vintage 1940s, with its pattern of small clowns that appear here and there on the black fabric. A black fur shrug across Starr's shoulders. His facial expression is one of awkwardness or discomfort.

In the second image, Starr wears an elaborate, frosted wig, recalling the 1890s, and a gown with huge frilly sleeves, and a skirt made out of a silky fabric studded with small stars. The image is in black and white, but the gown is of a pale color, possibly pink or cream, the color of Starr himself (in fact, he may be shirtless; it's too hard to tell). Starr wears opera-length gloves in the same pale color. His face is slightly turned from the camera, the lower half of it hidden, coquettishly, behind one of the sleeves; a dangling earring catches the light. There is nothing in the background.

Dater's portrait of Starr shows him looking a little like a young Rudolf Nureyev; it's hard to believe that Starr is the same model, in the same place, on the same day. Instead of the cropped Welpott photos, we see all of him as he sits on what looks like a daybed, with a fringed souvenir cowboy scarf tacked to the wall behind him. Next to Starr is a painting of a sobbing Mary embracing the cross of a crucified Jesus, with only his nailed feet to represent Him (the picture is only about Mary's grief); the tiny head of a harlequin, sitting on, or behind, the painting's frame, looking a shade demonic. There is more fringe peeking out from the black tunic Starr wears, along with the sparkling silver hose, his legs drawn up to his chest, staring full face into the lens. He wears lipstick, maybe a touch of eye makeup. The cover on the bed is in a bold, graphic sixties print. He relaxes, shoeless, in a room that looks like it belongs to him.

This is a portrait where we see the central figure in the context of his own life. We see texture, contrast, movement, decoration, someone who belongs in this room, who also orchestrated this room. You are drawn to Starr; his beauty, his charisma. You wonder about him.

In Welpott's *Starr* pictures—two to Dater's single *Starr* photo—you see nothing. You feel bored. Visually, emotionally, even pruriently there is simply nothing for the viewer. No background. No context.

We usually spent several hours with them in their own environment, wrote Welpott in his introduction.

For me, one of the most arresting photographs in the book (taken by Dater) is *Maria and Legend, 1971.* It is equal parts Julia Margaret Cameron and Gertrude Kasebier, like an early history of female photography, along with a touch of a Renaissance oil by way of late sixties Berkeley; the model is undeniably beautiful. Her clothing is vaguely Edwardian and thoroughly contemporary; her child is slightly blurred (as children often are); mother and child hold hands.

It is hard not to stare.

Except the model stares right back. She is Dater's counterculture *Olympia.*

*

In my limited experience of the world I've noticed that there are men who like women, and men who don't like women but who like to *fuck* women so they *think* they like women. I've known a couple of these men in my life. Some of the telltale signs are not listening (and I don't mean the usual selective male hearing), because you, the woman, have nothing to say that they find interesting. Unless you talk about sex. However, they like it when you're attentive, especially if they are trying to entertain you. There are few things more challenging than listening to the guy who is expecting you to laugh and nod and look lively when all you're doing is waiting for them to stop talking at you and maybe, just maybe, ask a question. They don't care for a female sensibility (women tend to be "petty" and "gossip"); and they really, really don't like it if you challenge them, even in the smallest way. I mean in ways where it doesn't even occur to you that you *are* challenging them. The more traditional the male, the greater your chances that he isn't all that interested in hearing from you even on topics that concern you (think the conservative politicians, but not only them). They just know best since you are part of *their* world, like furniture, and they determine the arrangement.

In the *Starr* pictures, Welpott dispenses with the background and just concentrates on the figure, while Dater includes elements of Starr's life. Welpott is telling the viewer who Starr is, while Dater is asking the viewer to discover Starr for herself.

DON'T BE AFRAID TO TRAVEL ALONE

Ruth Orkin

A man and his wife lived next door to the walled garden of a witch who desired a child above all things. When the wife discovered that she was pregnant, she and her husband were elated, that is, until she stopped eating. Her distraught husband brought his wife every savory morsel he could find, hoping to entice her to eat, but to no avail. Then, one day, she caught the scent of a plant called rampion in the witch's garden and she knew that she must have it or she would parish.

The husband was understandably nervous about granting his wife's wish, but he loved her so much that he scaled the wall and stole the lettuce, whereupon his wife made a lovely salad that only increased her hunger. Still refusing to eat anything else, the husband, again under cover of night, returned to the witch's garden for his wife. Again, his wife devoured the salad and longed for more. The third time he stole the rampion, the witch caught him and threatened to kill him.

He begged for mercy, explaining the plight of his wife and their unborn child. The witch then offered him all the rampion his wife could eat in exchange for the baby. "A girl, by the way," said the witch. The husband wept upon hearing that he was having a daughter, and because he understood that she was to be taken away. The witch assured him that he and his wife would have other children.

Having no choice—his immediate death or the eventual death of his wife and unborn daughter—the husband agreed to the witch's terms. His wife feasted on the rampion until the day that she gave birth when, as promised, the witch took the baby.

The couple did have other children, and watched their daughter, Rapunzel, at play in the witch's garden until she turned twelve, when the witch hid her in a tower with no doors and a single window. The witch never cut the girl's hair, so every day, when the witch called *Rapunzel, Rapunzel, let down your hair!* Rapunzel would wind her single, thick braid around a hook so her adopted mother could climb to her adopted daughter.

The rest of the story involves a seductive singing voice, a prince, deception, pregnancy, blindness, a haircut, wandering, reunion, and love. Feminists, psychologists, writers who work with myth, and artists have all had something to say about the girl in the tower.

Out of all the diverse interpretations one thing that seldom comes up is the complexity of love within the story. The husband and wife love each other; the husband risks his life for his wife; the wife sacrifices her child in order that the child may live; the witch loves the girl she imprisons. The prince and Rapunzel love each other. She bears his child, while he bears the scars of the witch's wrath (her anger the result of betrayal of love and trust). And it is the love Rapunzel feels for the prince, driven to tears by his blindness, that restores his sight. There is marital love (the parents), self-sacrificing love (the parents for their child), maternal love (the witch), possessive love (the witch), erotic love (the prince and Rapunzel), before coming full circle to Rapunzel's love for her own child. Love and motherhood push the action, with the story's conflict stemming from a rather specific pregnancy craving.

The tale is claustrophobic. How high is the wall of the witch's garden? How big (or small) was Rapunzel's tower chamber? Even when the reader first "meets" Rapunzel she is in the womb. Her forced innocence, too, feels like another airless room, even after the arrival of the prince who goes to her, in essence the larger world entering her limited world.

*

Ruth Orkin was born September 3, 1921, to Mary Ruby, a silent era screen actress, and Samuel Orkin, sometimes described as a "mechanical wizard," who started a toy company that had a little trouble during the Great Depression. Ruth said she remembered one of his toy boats with flashing telegraph lines, smoke, and firing guns. (Today, boats made by The Orkin Fleet are collectable and quite expensive.)

He imported toys, sold wholesale liquor in partnership with the son of Francis X. Bushman. (I must digress: I spent a fair amount of my childhood visiting a former silent film actress at an entertainment retirement home in Woodland Hills. I would sit in the corner of her small, sunny living room, studying her scrapbooks of that era. For this reason, I have been familiar with Francis X. Bushman, Sr. for my entire life, among other stars of that era, some of whom lived in the retirement home as well and would drop by. You can imagine how useful this information was in the social hierarchy of grade school.) Samuel Orkin worked at Lockheed during the second world war, and invented a process for painting color pictures on plastic. My favorite invention of his, aside from the marvelous toy ships, is his invention of "reproducing paintings in rhinestones"— paintings in rhinestones!—this decades before Damien Hurst ever affixed his first diamond to a human skull.

Ruth received her first camera, a thirty-nine cent Univex, at age ten, followed by her own darkroom at age twelve. Two more cameras at ages fourteen and sixteen, respectively; then, "I could tell those [35mm] cameras could capture a reality that the larger ones could not. I realized that in order for me to really record photographically what I saw, a 35mm camera was absolutely essential! But I had to wait until I was twenty-four years old."

She loved films from the start (this love wound into her destiny). In her youth, she photographed celebrities in lieu of asking for autographs. In 1939, at age seventeen, she hopped on her modest little bicycle and pedaled from Los Angeles to the New York World's Fair. Alone.

I think I have to write that again: *In 1939, at age seventeen, she hopped on her modest little bicycle and pedaled from Los Angeles to the New York World's Fair. Alone.* She made a photographic diary (300 pictures) of her four-month journey.

She worked at MGM studios when she was twenty-one but left when told that, as a woman, she couldn't join the Cinematographer's Union. She took baby pictures. She worked as a nightclub photographer. She was a ship's photographer on a cruise to South America. She became a photojournalist for a handful of major magazines in the 1940s. She took portraits of musicians at Tanglewood (Leonard Bernstein, Isaac Stern, Aaron Copland, Jascha Heifetz). She traveled extensively, working. She photographed Albert Einstein. And Robert Capa. And Ethel Waters, Carson McCullers, and Julie Harris. And Orson Welles. And Lauren Bacall. And Tennessee Williams. And Elia Kazan. Humphrey Bogart, Spencer Tracy, Doris Day, Lucille Ball.

In 1959, Ruth Orkin was named one of "The Top Ten Women Photographers in the US" by the Professional Photographers of America.

Along with her husband, Morris Engel, they made the film *Little Fugitive* (co-written and directed with Raymond Abrashkin), which was nominated for an Oscar. It was part of a trilogy, *Lovers and Lollipops* and *Weddings and Babies.* Orkin was very involved in all the key aspects of making *Little Fugitive,* which Francoise Truffaut said was "the inspiration for New Wave Cinema" for its camera work and naturalistic approach. In *Lovers and Lollipops,* she was on only as a writer. And by *Weddings and Babies,* she wasn't involved at all; she was home with the Engel children, an irony that shouldn't be lost on anyone, given the title of the film. (Even before I learned about her participation, or lack thereof, *Weddings and Babies* was my least favorite.)

*

Ruth Orkin is a photographer that everyone knows, but most people don't know that they know, because they recognize her pictures but not always her name. Her images of street scenes, children playing stickball in the streets of New York, or dealing cards on a stoop, or jumping into the Hudson River. Two elderly ladies in floral print dresses sit at a metal cafe table in a European park. Young New York mothers in swimsuits watch their children on a hot summer day. Three little boys in suspenders and fedoras sit on a suitcase on a sidewalk. Girls walk along, engrossed in the books they're reading.

A young woman, in a black dress and sandals, walks a gauntlet of Italian men on a street in Florence, in the Piazza della Repubblica, on a day in late August in 1951. The large group of idle men are not shy in their "appreciation" of her. This resulting street photograph, *American Girl in Italy, 1951,* is arguably one of the most recognizable photographs in the United States, and one that ended up tacked to the walls in a series of crummy apartments, along with *Imogen and Twinka, Yosemite, 1974.* The crummy apartments? Those were mine. All mine.

American Girl in Italy originally ran in *Cosmopolitan* in 1952. The photo was part of a series about a woman traveling alone.

Ruth Orkin, thirty years old and on her way back from Israel, where she stayed for several months, taking pictures (alone), met a twenty-three-year old American art student who called herself Jinx Allen, staying (alone) at the same hotel as Orkin. They spent the day together, with Orkin photographing Allen (later in life, Allen went by Ninalee Craig) as the subject of a photo essay about—you guessed it—women traveling alone. At some point during the day, Orkin happened to see Allen walking through that gathering of men, and snapped a picture. She asked Allen to do it a second time; that second exposure was the one that became the iconic image of an American girl abroad.

American Girl in Italy is a perfect example of chance and art; skill enhanced by luck. A remarkable photograph is so often the result of a series of exposures, timing, and instinct. Many years ago, I went to an exhibition of Man Ray's photos and films at the International Center for Photography in New York, with proofs marked up with red lines, showing how the picture was to be cropped, or otherwise manipulated.

People are currently astonished by the work of Vivian Meier: How could she take so many successful street photos? How did she get her subjects to ignore her? (Plain, middle-aged women are so ignorable that you would have to be one to fully understand the ease with which you can exist and not exist at the same time.) How, if they are looking into the lens, did she get them to act natural? (I don't think she did. I think they glanced at her, saw the least threatening person, the least substantial person, then turned back to their own lives.)

For anyone paying attention to the story of Vivian Meier, you will recall all the hundreds of rolls of undeveloped film, and all the unprinted negatives. The answer to the question of *how* Meier could get so many good shots lies in those undeveloped rolls and those unprinted negatives, the bulk of which is either no good, or not very good, or not nearly as good as it should be. "Successful art" makes it easy to forget all the tossed-out prints, or multiple novel drafts, or edited movie film, makes it seem so effortless and inevitable. The pentimento of a painting. What the non-artist seldom thinks about is how art is often a series of decisions in a dozen directions. The choices, the adjustments. Art is about order: the organization of form, color, musical notes, dance movement, words on the page. Many people think that artists "make something out of nothing," but it's really more like making something out of everything.

The most naturalistic sounding novel, or play, or movie is artificial; constructed to seem lifted from life. It is not life. I've often been told that I should listen to someone's story, then write it, as if knowing the story is the same as writing the story. As if using a camera obscura means that I can paint like Vermeer. As if there is no discovery with the act of writing.

Or, people will say, "Someday, when I have time, I'm going to sit down and write a book" as if writing only requires one's ass in the chair. It's so flattering to have something that one does for so many illogical, but no less passionate, reasons reduced to sitting around and talking to oneself because you have free time. Okay, there is some lounging and internal conversation happening, not to mention light time-wasting, but not in the way the potential Sunday writer thinks.

So, when talking about the pair of exposures that led to *American Girl in Italy*, it's important to understand the dual nature of random occurrence and the artist's hand.

*

So there I am, young, working my way through college, barely able to cobble together what I need from grants, scholarships and jobs, dreaming, as Dorothy Parker wrote, of having "enough money to keep body and soul apart." Also tacked to my wall (again): a small oval of white cardboard with the Andre Breton quote on it "Beauty will be convulsive or not at all."

It was handed to me when I attended a performance art piece at a small gallery at my university in Orange County in the mid-1970s. Conceptual art was popular at my school (Chris Burden had earned his MFA there). I don't remember too much about the piece, except for a graduate student sort of pitching herself about the floor, in some kind of outfit, then passing out these quotes on cardboard. Breton's was mine. I didn't even know who he was at the time—I just liked the quote. Sometimes, I found myself stifling laughter at performance art, or video art (also popular at the time, along with conceptual art), which I think supports the idea that you must make yourself available to art, and not wait for it to come to you. Even if you are visiting a Los Angeles gallery, staring at an elevated sheet of plywood that someone scribbled on, then left a piece of chicken wire rolled up on top. Even when your art teacher, who is standing next to you talks about the "elegance of the piece." Even when I felt like laughing and wondered if maybe I was supposed to laugh, and couldn't tell bad art from good, or if something was "elegant," but I always, always admired the willingness to make it.

My favorite show at the school gallery had an artist projecting images on the walls that he then traced with paint. The reason I liked it was because it was impossible to own that *exact* picture. If you wanted to buy it, the artist had to go to your house, project the image onto *your* wall, then paint it. Even though the artist used the exact same template as the "purchased" picture from the gallery, it was, by necessity, different. The concept was very appealing to me (here I am, talking about it forty years later), and, as I think about it, maybe it's because there seemed to be a kind of connection to photography, so ambiguous to possess that many people would not think to collect it at all. The idea of multiples, for example, somehow devalues it for them, not to mention the elusive quality of something being the "original."

On my walls, in my small bedroom of the large second floor duplex at the beach that I shared with three roommates (the girl with the parents who walked out of Hungary during the revolution; the sorority girl; the conveniently closeted gay guy whose conservative parents thought I was a whore), I had the Breton quote, a picture postcard of the lower half of a young woman wearing saddle shoes carrying a poorly packed vintage suitcase with clothes dragging and a caption that read *She was often gripped with the desire to be elsewhere;* Judy Dater's *Imogen and Twinka,* and Orkin's *American Girl in Italy, 1951.* I suppose it could be said that these four pieces of paper—one white cardboard with lettering, two postcards I bought, one postcard gallery giveaway—were aspirational for me. At the time though, I just liked them.

I would look at *American Girl,* that young woman (about my age), striding down that Florentine street, her look reminiscent of the Italian photographer-muse-beauty Tina Modotti, with her thick, dark hair pulled back across her ears in a low bun. Her black dress and shawl, looking timeless and vaguely romantic; none of that trussed-up, wasp-waisted 1950s fashion, and her bare legs and sandals seemed less American, less girls in their summer dresses, and more Modotti. The girl carries a horse's feedbag as a purse, and a black sketchbook. (I used to carry a vintage canvas gas mask bag, or a binocular case as purses.)

The very first time I saw this picture, I wanted to be her. Not because of her looks, or the bohemian glamour of her attire, but because she was young, in Italy, and it was easy to imagine that she was in transit between museums, cafes, or maybe just wandering.

Since we are all raised by the previous generation, we are all, in some way, lagging behind our own time (so to speak). My parents were part of the post-war Greatest Generation. I was born smack in the middle of the Baby Boomers who grew up during the sixties, and came of age in the early seventies, placing women like myself in so many places, in terms of female expectations, that it was exactly like being nowhere. This girl seemed like someone who walked away from the 1950s and down an Italian street. She appeared unencumbered.

In a sense, Orkin's American girl's little stroll was not unlike Ibsen's Nora slamming that famous Doll's House door.

There was no idea that created more of an ache in my heart than wanting to be in Europe and being free. Free of marriage or children or parents, even though I didn't yet have a husband or child. Every so often I would see something—a movie, a photo, a painting, a dance, a house, or hear a piece of music— and I would think, *That's what I want my life to be like.* This picture was such a picture, though I thought I might prefer Rome. *That's what I want. That's what I want my life to be like.*

Imagine my surprise when my ex-writer friend, the one who was offended by the *Immediate Family* photos, told me that she had *always* hated *American Girl in Italy.* It was a horror show, she said, just look at the expression of fear on the girl's face as she passes by all those leering men who have nothing better to do than to hang around, intimidating young women. She looks terrified, said my friend, as if she's in danger and too afraid to flee.

Where I saw a stylishly dressed, adventurous girl pushing against the social norms of her time, strolling down a European street, all *La Dolce Vita,* my ex-friend saw a scenario that is just this side of rape.

Orkin wrote in her diary: *Shot Jinx in morn in color—at Arno & Piazza Signoria, then got idea for pic story. Satire on Am. girl alone in Europe.*

As it turned out, the photo wasn't without controversy.

The controversy is found, ironically, in the feminist movement of the 1960s. It is also found in the expression on the model's face, the fifteen men, the way she pulls her shawl closer.

Most problematic of all is the fellow behind her, grabbing his crotch, though this grab has often been airbrushed from the picture. For many women (many of them feminists) the look on the model's face, combined with the crotch grab, is the reason for their dislike of this image, even though Jinx Allen has said that she never felt threatened.

"Some people want to use it as a symbol of harassment of women, but that's what we've been fighting all these years," Craig told *Today News* in 2011 from her home in Toronto. "It's *not* a symbol of harassment. It's a symbol of a woman having an absolutely wonderful time!" Orkin and Allen both attested to all fifteen men being cooperative when Orkin took the second exposure.

Until I began looking for information about this picture I had no idea that anyone other than my ex-friend had this reaction.

In the end, does it matter to the audience what the artist intended? What if you saw *American Girl,* had a negative reaction, and never read anything about it? What if you had my reaction—it is a picture of possibility—and then learned that the girl was alarmed? How much should the artist's intentions matter? Is art more effective when we bring ourselves to it, rather than consulting other sources and opinions, I mean, ultimately does it work better if it's just us and the work? That's the unanswerable question, isn't it?

*

The television show *Mad Men* features a successful, charismatic advertising executive working and living in New York from 1959 to 1970. Insightful, erudite, entertaining and one of the things it does best is to put together a primer on the social placement of women in America. The thing about women that the show gets exactly right is the way in which the second wave of feminism was a stutter-step road trip with many stops and starts, detours, arrivals, even refusals to continue. Young women watching this little bit of history unfold may not realize, when they wonder why the women didn't just assert themselves, is that there wasn't a society to support such actions. Even if you said, *No more,* and struck out on your own, where would you go? What would you do? When looking back at a social movement, it's easy to forget that women had to have the desire for change, and the larger world had to finally accept the change.

Betty Draper was beautiful in the way of Grace Kelly, educated at Bryn Mawr, married young to the handsome, charismatic advertising executive, and frustrated at home with the kids in the suburbs. She had to stand in for all the educated, stay-home moms, and every upper- middle-class wife, even though the stay-home moms were not a monolithic group. Her defining characteristic was misery, as well as holding ever tighter to her tether. This did not make her a beloved character, even though there were small glimmers of light breaking through her facade; tiny moments that kept her from unfortunate caricature.

(Side note: Bryn Mawr was described in Brett Harvey's *The Fifties: A Women's Oral History* as "the one college in the country that never retreated an inch from its rigorous standards for women, dedicated to producing scholars and proud of it." Greek, Latin, a pre-med caliber chemistry course all were needed to graduate.)

At the end of the series, Betty decides to return to school at age thirty-eight and earn a degree in psychology. She's excited about finally attending to her own life—not as a wife, not as a mother of three—but as a student and, eventually, a professional. This dream is cut short—on the first day of school, no less—when she's diagnosed with lung cancer, and told she has six months to live, just when we see her strike out on her own and lightening up a little. This narrative development is almost punishing.

However, Betty gets up the next day, schoolbooks in hand, to continue her classes for a degree she will never complete.

When her husband (her second, the politician) asks, "Why would you do that?" She answers, "Why was I ever doing it?"

I once read that consumption of sedatives and antidepressants by housewives was in the hundreds of thousands in the 1950s, then skyrocketed to the millions mark in the early 1960s, just before Betty Friedan and feminism and the sixties got underway.

I grew up during a time when the surface was shifting while the foundation underneath was still largely untouched, the foundation that would fracture a few years later.

*

In 1995, my husband, our young son, and I attended a retrospective of Ruth Orkin's work at the uptown location of the International Center for Photography. There I saw my American Girl making her well-known walk, as well as Albert Einstein laughing; Montgomery Clift atop a ladder on a movie set, paintbrush in hand; Hitchcock reclining against a floral piece of furniture; Leonard Bernstein, mid-flail, conducting at a rehearsal; a wildly youthful Woody Allen mimicking a pose from a seventeenth-century painting hanging at the Met. Brando dressed as Marc Antony, eyeing his next chess move. Julie Harris sipping tea backstage at the opening of *The Member of the Wedding*, while sharing a sofa with an odd, diminutive Carson McCullers curled into Ethel Waters.

There were New York City street photos of kids playing cards, telling elaborate, dramatized stories, and mothers in swimsuits. Kids and adults are jumping into, walking by, gazing at, or running through water. People waited; on corners, on stoops, in train stations. Orkin said of Penn Station it was "a crystal palace of daylight."

These are scenes of ordinary happiness, commonplace while seeming rare. The remarkable aspect of the juxtaposition of all these subjects—the girl in Italy, the actors, the filmmakers, musicians, scientists, the nameless New Yorkers—is the way Orkin makes their lives seem equally desirable. They are a democracy of contentment.

In my first encounter with *American Girl,* I was single and childless. Years later, as I slowly circled the Orkin exhibit, I was married and a mother; I had my son at roughly the same age that Ruth Orkin had hers (she had her son when she was thirty-eight, and her daughter when she was forty). After all these years, it wasn't *American Girl in Italy* that caught my attention—even though I did feel a fleeting catch of nostalgia for something I never had—it was the discovery of her series *A World Through my Window.* (She later continued the series with *More Pictures from My Window.* Thirty years of photos.) The portraits of the kids and celebrities and even the girl in Italy faded next to the *Window* pictures.

The movie *Smoke* opened just prior to my seeing the Orkin show. In the film, Harvey Keitel portrays the owner of a tobacco shop in Brooklyn. Every morning he stands at the same sidewalk location and snaps a picture. In this way, he can record all the unexpected and variable in everyday life (wonderful, mundane, tragic), in contrast to the unchanging, enforced structure of the circumstances he uses to make his photographs. Chance and order, that artistic linchpin.

Briefly, the *Window* pictures are a series begun by Orkin when she and her family moved into a fifteenth-floor apartment on Central Park West. She set up her cameras and recorded the New York skyline and/or Central Park during the seasons, day and night, through eras and generations. Day after day. Year after year.

I was entirely taken with the concept of a person keeping a visual diary in which she, that is, her image, never once appears, yet the pictures, one after another, say so much about her. Though I had seen the Harvey Keitel version first, it was immediately eclipsed for me by Orkin's, becoming less interesting as it began to resemble what it was: a fictional device in a movie; a plot mechanism related to a fictional tragedy, signifying nothing.

*

It isn't possible to choose my favorite photo among the *Window* pictures because, as with the work of many a novelist, they are all just different views of essentially the same story (the same theme). I could describe some of the pictures: Central Park in the snow, or the moonlight, or with a billow of smoke rising from industrial chimneys filling a red sky; the crowds, the horses; Ruth's tree; parades and parties and protests. Sunlight, shadows, a thousand twinkling lights. Some pictures look noisy, others silent. Some are dense with figures and objects, others empty. There are buildings, other windows, cars.

Orkin said, "Although my movie-making career was over, I couldn't go back to being a photojournalist—I felt that would've been beneath me. You can't make thirty-five hundred people laugh in a movie theater like Loew's Paradise on a Saturday night, and then feel like taking still pictures for a living." She also said that one of the reasons for not continuing movie-making was "because there was no Women's Liberation movement around in the fifties to help educate and back me up." As I said.

The thing is, Orkin did continue to make a sort of ongoing "movie" as she recorded the world outside her window. All those shots, seen together, move and breathe like a film. It's no wonder that this same methodology for telling a multi-character story found its way into the hands of Harvey Keitel in *Smoke*.

Orkin's *Window* series is like Mann's *Family* series is like Cunningham's *Botanicals* in that the images are shadowed by their lives. Judy Dater's marriage, too, was quietly concealed in the *Women* series. Or, the Hermann Leonard photograph of jazz artist Lester Young portrayed by the instrument case, the sheet music, the lit cigarette, the empty Coke bottle. His hat.

I know that as a writer there's the thing I'm writing, and the reason I think I'm writing it, the buried reason that I'm writing it, what my life looks like at the time I'm writing it, and the reason that I'm writing it at *a certain time.* I know that my being a writer has to do with having a parent with a specific world view (she loved stories and glamor, and treated me like an equal, when it suited even if it was a questionable choice, and she made life fun). I had no idea that her world view, so seductive to me as a child, was only masquerading as mainstream when, in fact, through her stories, her disappointments, her little victories, her constant aspirations, her uncensored self, her adolescent romanticism, her secrets, and love of entertainment help me to discover the not-really-welcomed revelation that I would never be fully comfortable in the conventional life. My mother—and my father, albeit in a different manner entirely— only *appeared* conventional, only masqueraded as traditional.

For example, we lived in Pasadena, a bastion of tradition and old money. Private schools and tennis clubs and rose queens and ski trips while a day outing with my family might include driving the local elevated forest, stopping to collect giant rocks, heaving them into the trunk of the car, to place them later in the river of smaller rocks surrounding our house. My sister and I would be trapped in the backseat of the car with our hyperactive brother, who made every drive feel like I was a Samsonite and he was a gorilla.

When we stopped for a picnic, my mother, who loved the outdoors (psyche! my mother *hated* the outdoors) would find a large rock, remove her shirt and sunbathe in her bra, stretch pants, and stilettos, not talking to anyone, as I would silently beg to go home.

Rocks were a theme at our house. In addition to the giant rocks and river rocks, the entire roof of our ranch house was painted orange and covered in small, jagged orange rocks, the color matching the impractical low-pile pale orange carpet inside the house. We also had a rock fireplace that dominated the living room, and no dining room because my mother installed a baby grand piano in there even though no one in our family played piano.

Pasadena has so many historic homes and leafy neighborhoods that I developed an early love of architecture, yet we lived in the only track development in the entire city, a neighborhood so rare most people didn't even know it existed. We moved there in 1959 because my mother refused to live in a house anyone had lived in before.

After we grew up, my brother remained home, eventually spending his days carrying around my mother's giant, very feminine handbags that are often made of gold or pink or turquoise leather resembling ostrich or snake or alligator trimmed with sparkling embellishments. My brother has essentially spent much of his adult life as Eric von Stroheim to her Gloria Swanson, which tells you pretty much everything you need to know (the handbags only part of the story). My parents also converted to a nineteenth-century metaphysical religion founded by a woman whose son tried to have her committed. There were affairs.

Out of all this I learned to keep an open mind. I once wrote, many years ago, that fledging writers should toss aside those writing manuals and concentrate on voyeurism, gossip and eavesdropping, the mainstays of writing. If you are predisposed to being a writer, learning to withhold judgement isn't a challenge because snapping your mind shut is such a bore. Still, you may end up cynical and romantic; you can't help it. Graham Greene said that a writer always has a sliver of ice in his heart, a statement that I think is about having a slight remove from any situation, including being a human being.

Photography and writing are similar in that they can be a service, or an art, or both. The photographer and the writer are accustomed to observing and waiting, though the photographer must act quickly, making split-second decisions, while the writer retires to her room to turn over and over what she sees, and what she thinks about what she sees. It's more interesting to watch a photographer working; a writer is just typing, no matter how fantastic, or far-ranging her interior world. All artists want to locate that telling image, that glimpse, that moment, that insight, that slip of the social mask, that core of the human experience. But for the writer, it's all happening on the inside.

*

Georgia O'Keeffe painted from the small (two rooms, no kitchen) twenty-eighth floor apartment at the Shelton that she (amazingly) shared with Alfred Stieglitz, because he seemed like a lot of person with which to share a room. It was from this vantage point that she painted her wonderful cityscapes—those pictures so disliked by Stieglitz, or so I've read. The couple moved to the Shelton, located on Lexington Avenue, in 1924. "Thirty-four stories high, Arthur Loomis Harmon's revolutionary building was the first skyscraper in New York City to capitalize aesthetically on the new zoning resolution mandating setbacks of one foot of additional air space (and light) for every four feet of height. The attenuated effect caused one lyrical writer to observe that 'the building seems not merely to have a tower, but to be a tower.'"

Benita Eisler, in her double biography of O'Keeffe and Stieglitz, goes on to write that Georgia was never enamored of the city, "its frantic and frenzied human activity—the Shelton was rather perfect for her." Also, "Georgia was even more entranced by the prospect of an aerie loftily—and even quite literally—removed from the pedestrian activities of marketing and house-keeping." The Shelton was a residence hotel, which meant that meals could be taken in a communal dining room. "Skyscraper living was the solution to being *of* the city but not *in* it."

The couple lived in the apartment for twelve years; she made many paintings from that window, some of them other skyscrapers, sometimes a panorama of the East River. I've seen many of these paintings, in many cities. My favorite experience with her city pictures was in Madrid, where I saw *New York City with Moon*, 1925. I also love *The Shelton with Sunspots*, 1926 (a small reproduction taped to my son's nursery wall) and *Radiator Building, Night, New York*, 1927.

I'm crazy for the cityscapes; I love them more than almost anything else she painted. I love that in one of them, she paints the name *Alfred Stieglitz*, lit up on a red sign, to the left of the Radiator Building. I've never been able to decide if it's love, or surrender, that *Alfred Stieglitz*. She always returned to the city for him; he was instrumental in her career, from start to finish; she owed him and he owed her; is the name an honor, a thank you, a valentine, a kiss-off? One writer said it was a "twentieth century tribute," made from one modern to another. She was once asked why she kept coming back to New York after spending months of every year in the Southwest. Her expression seemed to say, *What sort of question is that?* as she answered, "Because my husband was there." When Stieglitz passed, O'Keeffe left the city for good.

There is one oil, *Pink Dish and Green Leaves, 1928* of a bowl on a pedestal set on the windowsill of the rooms at the Shelton, partially obscuring the view of the East River. There is some-thing touching in that arrangement of a pair of leaves against the backdrop of industry; a dreamy Rapunzel-like longing, to leave this tower forever.

*

My office/studio is located on the third floor of my house, which, including the flight of concrete steps up from the well-traveled, urban street where I live in Portland, is four stories high. I have a skylight, and four windows on two walls, and a view of treetops and rooftops. The skylight often resembles a screen tuned to the Weather Channel.

From my window overlooking the street (located immediately to the left of my desk) I have seen rain, snow, sleet and hailstorms, a lunar eclipse, leaves on the trees in the hot colors of autumn, bare branches, then the green lushness of spring. I have witnessed car crashes, arrests, thefts, domestic spats, teens smoking with that timeless mix of furtiveness and bravado. There are all manner of dogs and dog owners; kids and moms and strollers; homeless people; people collecting cans and bottles; the local high school track teams. Cars repeatedly break the speed limit; cars play thumping music; cyclists often carry on loud conversations or sing; cat fights, coyotes, crows with a lot to say, owls, blue jays, robins, many birds I don't know the names of, hummingbirds, pigeons; a million squirrels racing across the skylight, onto branches and tree trunks, and power lines, roofs. Rats, possums, the occasional raccoon, and more pigeons dart in and out of trash cans. Mostly, though, I look out, rather than down, watching the sky.

Outside my other office window, just below, are my neighbors' windows, the distance between our houses so narrow I sometimes wonder if they can hear me.

*

So in 1955 I found the closest thing, a fifteenth floor apartment on Central Park West, just opposite the Sheep Meadow where, as it turn out, you can see everything.

*I hadn't thought of my view as a subject for photography. . . .
Eventually I started taking pictures, not only because it was there
but even more because I was. All the time. At home with the kids.
That's of prime importance when you're shooting scenery—to be
there on a twenty-four hour daily basis.*

*Housewife, scenic photographer. My situation was ideal, I sup-
pose (although I don't remember thinking of it quite that way at
the time). My children, of course, were there on a twenty-four-
hour-a-day basis, so they got photographed too, just like the view.
6:00 a.m. mist/feedings . . . 2:00 p.m. view/playtime . . . 5:00 p.m.
dusk scene/baths . . . 10:00 p.m. night shot/baby asleep.*

*Now that I think about it, I don't see how anyone but a house-
wife could have got all this done.*

—Ruth Orkin, Introduction, *A World Through My Window*

*I want to thank the children for helping me shoot—they helped
me by keeping me home so much.*

—Ruth Orkin, *More Pictures From My Window*

*

When I sold my first book I found myself in the new and for-
tunate position of having time and money, where previously I
would have a little of one (money), or a lot of the other even
though time between jobs is such a waste because you are
exhausted from anxiety and looking for work, and being too
broke to actually do anything. For the first time, I wasn't bot-
toming out at the end of the month. I didn't have credit cards,
so that was good, but I also owned little more than books and
clothes (you can't buy much without credit cards if you don't
have money). I liked being debt-free and I really liked being,
more or less, without many possessions, except the clothes and
books. J., my boyfriend-who-became-my-husband, wanted a
family. In this way, my book "financed" our baby.

I've never understood how people without health insurance and/or money could have kids and sleep at night. It was a mystery, even though I was frequently told, *If you want a baby, you find a way.* Maybe that was part of the problem: I wasn't maternal enough. Babysitting, for example, was all too often a battle between discomfort and boredom, where I was captive in someone else's home for the evening with only a tiny human with needs and no desire to sleep for company. It worried me that I didn't feel compelled to have children. If I'm coming clean, I wasn't that interested in getting married, either. I told my college boyfriend that my ideal marriage would be separate households. For some reason I expected him to agree, a crazy idea considering that our current living together was a better arrangement for him than it was for me.

On the other hand, I had a compulsion to write.

And that worried me a little, too.

My reluctance to wed was, I'm sure, related to my reluctance to start a family. Not that I care one way or another if people have children without marriage. I only knew that if *I* didn't get married, *I* wouldn't be having a child. I don't have any sort of philosophical opposition to marriage or motherhood (nor do I think one must marry to have kids). I wanted to think that I might not be left alone in an experience that I wasn't sure I wanted. I guess with writing on my mind, followed by the twin necessities of time and money, everything seemed positioned in opposition of everything else. Let's call it the Modern Woman's Mystery of How to Have Everything.

The women I admired—artists all—seemed to make all manner of concessions where kids came in, running the gamut of childlessness, to being borderline mothers, though most of them seemed to fall somewhere in the middle. Here's a truism about motherhood: you honestly don't know, or understand, how you feel about kids until you have one, and therein lies the gamble of motherhood. What if your instincts were correct and you aren't mother material? What if you're more selfish than you imagined? What if resentment becomes your daily companion, sitting there, at the breakfast table, right next to your kid who is dining, cluelessly, on Cheerios? How would you live with yourself?

Or, what if you loved this little person beyond all reason? What if something should happen to him? How could your own life possibly continue? Even if nothing happens to him, how do you live, every day, with the fear that something *might* happen? I had a brother who died when he was three; my other, younger brother, the one with the energy of a gorilla trashing a suitcase, was hyperactive (and maybe something else), so things "happening" aren't that farfetched to me. And I'm a novelist; every story is spun out to its dramatic conclusion.

My family was like a game of Which Piece Doesn't Belong, except none of us did, making us five individuals who happened to live under one roof. There was, however, love and goodness and the kind of open-mindedness that is a consequence of being too uninterested in judging others. It's said that people have children to recreate their childhood, or to correct their childhood, but what does it mean when you aren't sure about having kids at all?

My eventual husband, J., and I had the money, and the time, and the kid. We traveled with our son, but not the way we might have traveled, which might have included living outside the country, my enduring dream—if we weren't parents. I was a little stymied by the prospect of a long-term foreign undertaking with a child, *and* trying to be a writer, it would've been a stretch (it isn't easy or simple to expatriate, which is what you're doing if you aren't on some kind of company contract, or in the military; it's expensive and you're on your own, completely), but maybe not impossible, which is why I never feel that our son prevented me from realizing that life. Still, living in Barcelona, for example, might have allowed being a writer to complement being a mother.

Sometimes I really struggled, as I worked in my office, with motherhood. Not, it must be said, with love for my child.

*

One of the things I took away from the *Rapunzel* story is the way she sighed to be a part of the world, wrestling with her remove, and her inchoate longing for—what? She herself wasn't even sure.

Writers need to be in the world, in order to retreat and write about the world. They need the stimulation and variety provided by leaving home. Sometimes the only way they can even write about home is to leave it behind.

Again, Ruth Orkin, in 1939, at seventeen years old, undertook a journey, from Los Angeles to New York on a very basic bicycle. Sometimes she caught a ride, but is hitchhiking alone any less impressive for a seventeen-year-old traveling alone than riding her bike?

She photographed Einstein and Hitchcock and Brando at his most marvelous, her pictures appearing in all the major magazines of her day, in the 1940s.

She traveled Europe, Israel, South America.

She met Jinx Allen at a cheap hotel in Florence, in 1951, on her way back from a photography assignment in Israel featuring the Israeli Philharmonic. She made a classic image of a classic girl, that young American traveling abroad.

She made a movie, in 1953, that was said to influence New Wave cinema.

She was one of the top ten most important women photographers in the US in 1959.

The only advice my father gave me was to "travel before I had children, and to learn to type." Many girls my age were encouraged to learn typing with the idea that you could always be a secretary as a fallback. The traveling advice was less usual.

My father was an electrical engineer. He had graduated from the University of Colorado, Boulder, summa cum laude. He also earned a number of academic "keys," which my mother had made into a charm bracelet when they were first married (I have the bracelet). He was also halfway through earning his masters when he was twenty years old, and the war came along; he was in the Navy but was never sent overseas.

My father was curious about everything: He loved: trains, travel, postcard shows, roadside attractions, sightseeing by car (crisscrossing the USA several times, including dropping off all of us at my grandparents' apartment one summer in the Bronx). Painted, went to art museums, and theater. He liked history and science and Tesla and Nat King Cole.

He wanted to take a train across Canada, considered earning a PhD in computer science when he retired, but became a certified organic farmer in 1982, cultivating twenty acres of Star Ruby and Red Ruby grapefruit in the Rio Grande Valley.

He wanted to build his own house; he had already built almost all our furniture, including wiring our stereo and building the speaker cabinets. I still have some of his smaller wood-working projects. The only time anyone was called in to do anything around our house was when we had a swimming pool dug into the yard, otherwise my dad did everything else, like building us a playhouse, or pouring the concrete for the patio, and making a fire pit; he painted the house (inside and out), hung wallpaper. He was opposed to the First Iraq War (he had passed on by the second war) because, he said, among other things, you have no business being some place unless you at least try to understand the culture. And he didn't talk as much as he listened because he was quiet and not all that interested in himself. He had a Leica and carefully labeled and filed all his slides; a roll of an oil refinery would not only be in a specific order, but he would make a "title" slide, maybe by writing in nearby sand. He kept our dog's rabies tags on a string long after the dog died, even though he wasn't into pets, except he loved that dog. But one of the best things about him was that he never tried to hide the fact that he didn't know what he didn't know—wait, the best thing was that he didn't try to hide the fact that he didn't know what he didn't know *and* asked questions about the thing he didn't know.

In addition to the yard work, and working for major engineering firms, and fixing and building, my father also got us three kids up, every morning, fed us breakfast, and off to school. He did all this just after his morning swim in our unheated pool (often naked because, of course, my parents were domestic nudists). My glamorous mother was busy getting ready for work herself. I knew of no other father, with a career no less, who did so much childcare (including taking us on errands with him, at my mother's request because she needed to "decompress from the office"), while helping around the house. This is how, anachronistically, I was raised. Which is why I could understand how my father could understand the limits that kids put on your life.

My mother was as people-oriented as my father was not. She was vivacious and fun and glamorous. Still is. She was always, always inclusive, which is why we had all kinds of people at her dinners: all ages, races, sexual orientations, religions, nationalities (this was not usual for Pasadena). She dressed stylishly when she was younger, wearing fitted, strapless sundresses with heels to watch me splash in a kiddie pool. Red toreador pants with black braid; beautiful suits, her thick, dark hair held back with a simple velvet ribbon, and thick kohl liner around her eyes under her cat's eye sunglasses. Red lipstick. She painted walls in our house black, and her nails green. This was all before 1960. She went through a wig phase in the late sixties where she switched off with four very different hair styles and colors. I was constantly asked how my mom was managing chemo. The 1980s became the Decade of the Colored Contact Lenses (blue, green, violet, brown); a situation that sounds less unnerving than it is.

Her engagement is purely with other people, while my father leans more toward the inanimate object. Staying at home never suited her personality; it was clear to me from a very early age that we kids were simply not enough. So, she became one of the very few working mothers at my school, and one of the only ones who *chose* to work. A lot of judgement came her way for making that choice, much of it within my earshot. If any-one questioned her parenting (even me), her reply was always, "At least I don't have a martini in one hand and a needle in my arm," as if that is the only possible crossed line. She was a media director in an advertising firm in Los Angeles (though she began in advertising at age seventeen, in New York City, as a secretary) where her desk was situated directly under Lib-erace's swimming pool. She often said things like Nature didn't impress her because it was made by God and since "God can make anything it's no big deal." But skyscrapers and cit-ies thrilled her because they were man-made. When she was made-up, she looked nothing like herself, so much so that, for years, our next-door neighbor thought a pair of sisters lived in our house, one pretty, one plain. Like a fairy tale.

My father loved travel. He loved living outside the coun-try. He chose a profession that would send him all over the world—so many of his fellow engineers lived in London or Bei-rut or China—and was scheduled to move to Rome in 1951, something he was dying to do, and who wouldn't want to be in post-war Rome, in 1951, the year that Ruth Orkin met Jinx Allen and filmed her as *American Girl in Italy*?

Except.

Except, he married my mother, who was rooted to her newly adopted home of Los Angeles (she was born and raised in New York City), and refused to go. My post-war, Greatest Generation father gave up his beloved Rome for a wife and three children and a brand-new ranch house because my mother had that thing about living in any house where someone had lived before. It was an enormous compromise that he never mentioned, even after my mother took up with her also-married boss and left my father. (My post-war parents flipping the script again.) The only advice he ever offered: "Travel before you have children."

*

My dad and I never talked much; mostly we parallel played because we shared more than a few interests. We used to go on architectural and historical house tours together, and to various museums. His correspondence with me mostly took the form of clipped articles about this or that, or newspaper pictures. It took me a long time to appreciate my father because he wasn't warm, or forthcoming, or opinionated, or dynamic in any sense. There was a period, from about age fifteen to twenty-five where I thought he didn't even matter to me.

When I was thirty years old and visiting him for the first time in Houston (where he moved with his second family when I was seventeen), we were driving the six hours to the Rio Grande Valley to check his grapefruit trees and he could take agriculture classes, we passed, in the middle of nowhere, a mansion that looked like something right out of Edward Hopper. I said, "I want a picture," except we couldn't locate any sort of off-ramp to get us anywhere near the place. And so we continued on our way.

Three weeks after I returned to San Francisco (where I lived), I opened an envelope, addressed to me in my dad's handwriting. A close-up photograph of the house fell out of the envelope. No note.

*

In some ways, for some women, it's more challenging to have children later because you can't forget the life you had before. Maybe if you felt that previous life was complete, and motherhood another, welcomed phase, you don't ever lean your chin in the palm of your hand and remember how it felt to be standing in front of a wall of New World gold in a cathedral in Sevilla, or walking the luxuriant gardens of the nearby alcazar. You force yourself to forget the scent of orange blossoms, and the sound of Castilian Spanish. You tell yourself that you never wandered around Paris, or stood on the St. Charles Bridge in Prague before the Berlin Wall came down. *She was often gripped with the desire to be elsewhere.* I often think that the contemporary equivalent of Virginia Woolf's room of one's own is not having to think about the needs and wants of everyone around you, of not having to think of anyone but yourself.

*

I knew my mother wasn't happy being home with her children; she loved working. She loved the energy and buzz of advertising, of office life. We couldn't compete, nor could we admire her in the way she needed to be admired. I was desperate to have her home with me, but nothing I said swayed her. I felt the burden of being a kid from an early age, that is, my mother loved us and she was singular in a way that many mothers I knew were not. She didn't dote on us; she indulged us because it pleased her. If

I wasn't in the mood to go to school, I could hang around the house. By myself.

When I got older and thought about my dad getting us up and fed and off to school, then taking us on errands after dinner. Or to the playground, or the trampoline park. Or doing the laundry, or making things, or doing all those home improvements, and sacrificing the one thing he wanted, which was living around the world like his colleagues with their stories of Beirut and London and Asia. And Rome in 1951. I found myself thinking less about my mother as the stereotypical wife who sighs in the afternoons, her mind dulled by housework, and more about my father and what he waved good-bye.

*

In *Toward the Blue Peninsula, 1952,* a shadow box by Joseph Cornell, the title a nod to Emily Dickinson, another artist in her attic. The box has a simple white-painted interior and a window filled with nothing but blue sky. White metal mesh is obviously cut away from the window, allowing an unobstructed exit into that beautiful blue sky. Whoever, or whatever was once inside has now left.

*

When I was in grade school, my mother began carrying around a small suitcase as a handbag, which meant every time my mother left home she left with a suitcase.

*

As she closed in on age forty, Ruth Orkin became a housewife who took pictures from her apartment window. *But eventually I started taking pictures, not only because it [the scenery] was there*

but even more because I *was. All the time. At home with the kids.*
Though Orkin did take pictures of her two children (fabulous
pictures) they are absent from the collected *Window* series. The
series, too, is a hybrid of visual autobiography and photojour-
nalism, that is to say, we *see* everyone *but* Orkin, her children,
or her husband, her camera turned outward. We do see other
people's children, other people's lives, as well as New York. This
is a large part of the story of Orkin's life, in the same way that
biography is as much about the biographer as it is about the
subject (talking about yourself without talking about yourself).
It's what we don't see that prompted these *Window* pictures:
motherhood, being a professional photographer and filmmaker,
a woman's place in the 1950s until the late 1960s—essentially,
the subtext for the images.

Without her profession, her art, her children, and the
then-social mores, there are no *Window* pictures.

The Janitor Who Paints, 1930 by Palmer Hayden is a picture I
included in a slideshow (using a Kodak Carousel, no less) when
I was on a book tour in the late 1990s. The slides were of images
that inspired my novel, as if to answer the inevitable question,
Where do you get your ideas? *Here,* I could say, clicking slide to
slide, *here, here, here, here.*

Hayden's painting—which everyone should see—shows a
man in a beret, painting at an easel in his basement apartment
while his wife and baby model for him. A cat sleeps at his feet.
The room is modest; exposed pipes, a naked lightbulb, a painting on the wall, a clock, a table, and the edge of a brass head-
board suggests a studio apartment. A mop and a feather duster
hang behind the artist; a large metal trash can takes up much of
the foreground, the lid is his painter's palette.

This painting is important to me, which is why it was
included in the slide show, because I wanted people to see, to
really understand, what it means to make art—the stolen time,
the family, the basement apartment, evidence of a paying job—

this picture is *exactly* like the domestic photographs of Mann, Cunningham, and Orkin. If Cunningham flipped the idea of the female muse by taking pictures of her husband, then Hayden flipped the domestic, female artist scenario as well.

*

The making of Orkin's visual opus was aided by her children as Mann's *Family* series was by hers, except that the Engel children were behind the camera. The *Window* pictures are about the situation in which mother and children find themselves. Orkin wrote in the introduction to her second *Windows* book, *More Pictures From My Window*, "My only complaint is that it [waiting by the window for a shot] can wreak havoc with appointments, phone calls, and other activities, because most scenes and events can't wait until you're ready—they require immediate attention. . . . Those days are behind me, and now, at least, taking care of the 'children' doesn't interrupt my shooting anymore. Instead, they interrupt me with 'Hey, Mom, look at that cloud out the window.' I want to thank the children for helping me shoot the first book—they helped me by keeping me home so much."

There's something touching about the Engel children helping their mother make photographs. Their participation developed, one thinks, an eye for the telling image as they're being instructed to pay attention, to look, to see; they are being artist-trained. It's an evolution of being banished to your New York tower, to gazing out the window at the life below, then finding a way to bring that life into your tower with beauty and nuance. Her thank you to her children illustrates a nice sleight of hand as it expresses obligation and gratitude. And who's to say that Orkin's view of the trees below her window aren't similar to Rapunzel's forest view?

Motherhood, it seems, is responsible for the *Window* series, in the same way that Matisse's convalescence from appendicitis led him to be a painter. Would Frida Kahlo have made all those self-portraits if she hadn't been confined to her bed for long periods, looking into a mirror and not out a window, her sole scenery her face, her body, her emotional landscape?

There is something more fundamental in Ruth Orkin's lengthy project and motherhood and art. The artistic dilemma is this: Solitude is a requirement for making art; to silence the outside world in order to access the inside world. Too much isolation and you lose touch with all the complicated mess of living, and then what do you put into your art? It's a balancing act, where you need enough involvement to keep connected to life, and enough distance to do all the required heavy lifting of world-making. (All of which can be quite taxing for her loved ones.)

If I hadn't been a writer, a wife, and a mother with a very young child when I saw Ruth Orkin's *Window* pictures at the ICP, I might have passed them by. If I didn't have my own creative dilemmas (some of which had nothing to do with having a child), and mother dilemmas, I might not have lingered when taking in her New York views. There would have been no searching for out-of-print copies of *A World Outside My Window*, or *More Pictures From My Window*. I certainly wouldn't have been as moved as I was by a professional photographer mother watching her previous life turn into an exercise in nostalgia (*I used to travel to take pictures*), possibly observing like some modern-day Rapunzel; someone who could become so distracted by a certain slant of light that she could leave the baby "mid-diaper change."

What I think of when I see Orkin's photographs is the story of an intrepid girl whose natural impulses toward experience and art are derailed by marriage and children, then miraculously rerouted back into art. In that fifteen-floor New York apartment with its view of the park and the skyline, Orkin discovered the intersection of maternal love and creative necessity.

I wrote a novel with the word "quilt" in the title. This allowed some people to make assumptions about my book (make assumptions about me). It also meant that my work could be dismissed as "women's fiction." No one read my book and wondered how hard it might have been to write, or the strength of my imagination (Everything in that book is pure invention, by the way. I don't quilt. I didn't live in rural California. And I barely knew my non-quilting grandmothers. For example.) because I'm a woman and when women write domestic fiction it's assumed to be effortless in every regard. Now a man can write a "domestic" novel, or record the minutia of the uneventful weeks of his life and be respected as a writer. No one considers the spine it takes to live the domestic life when you're a professional artist. Mann, Cunningham, Orkin flexing their muscles.

Someone said (it might have been Imogen Cunningham) that men will tell you the only pictures worth taking are on the battlefield. Then they ban you from the battlefield.

Childless Mary Cassatt produced a number of paintings influenced by the flat style of Japanese prints depicting mothers and children. The pictures are lovely. The refined colors, the relationship of mothers and children, so beloved. I like them, I do, but they are a dream, a wish.

Orkin found a way to show a more realistic bond between mother and child, messy and loving, complicated, imperfect with all the grace of Lester Young's hat balancing on an open suitcase of music.

THE SENTIMENTAL PROBLEM
OF TINA MODOTTI

Tina Modotti

A Short Biography of Tina Modotti

Born: 1896 (Undine, Italy)
No longer made pictures after 1931
Died: 1942 (Mexico City, Mexico)

A Nina Simone Quote

*How can you be an artist and not reflect the times? That to me is
the definition of an artist.*

Tina, with a Dorothy Parker Detour

In my youth I would often come across the same soulful photograph of Tina Modotti and wonder *who is she?* She was beautiful and later I found out that she was Italian, small of stature,
went to live with her father and two sisters after they emigrated

to San Francisco (the rest of the large family came over piece-meal). As a silent screen actress she was often cast in "fiery mistress" roles, causing her to cut her career short. She had a number of lovers, one of which was instrumental in getting her to move to Mexico, while still another lover followed *her* to Mexico. She was a famous muse for famous men. She was a Communist (her political, sometimes poor, family was firmly on the side of the proletariat), and a spy, failed political assassin, and rumored murderer. She died mysteriously when she was forty-five years old.

Spy? Rumored killer? Assassin? Mysterious death? Now you have my attention.

My life has been spent looking for women to be, in a sense. For years I made box assemblages, with an ongoing, informal series called "secular saints." They were: Lee Miller, Man Ray, Dorothy Parker, Georgia O'Keeffe, Isadora Duncan, Joseph Cornell, and Madame Yevonde. There's a room on the third floor of my house where these boxes are stored, that is, the ones not sold or, more often, given away. Lee Miller called her inter-ests "jags." These figures are my jags. My earliest jag being Dor-othy Parker.

I read everything by and about Parker starting when I was nineteen. I asked someone I didn't like to drive me to Los Ange-les to see a one-woman play of Parker in the mid-1970s per-formed at theater the size of a living room. Around that same time I saw a Dorothy Parker TV movie, *Woven in a Crazy Plaid.* Years later, I watched *Mrs. Parker and the Vicious Circle,* and *The Ten-Year Lunch.* (Around 2000, a book I'd written ended up with a connection to one of the makers of *Mrs. Parker and the Vicious Circle.*) I listened to her read on the records I bor-rowed from my college's library. I traveled to a great Laguna Beach bookstore, run by a fabulous elderly woman (bookstore and woman now long gone), to purchase a pair of first editions of Robert Benchley. They were cheap because no one in 1977 cared about him. I wanted a friendship like the one he had with Parker, witty and close, eventually sharing an office so small he said, "One less cubic feet of space and it would have constituted adultery."

I was drawn to Parker because she was funny, pale-skinned, small, and dark-haired. I was funny, pale-skinned, small, and dark-haired. She was even a couple of inches shorter than I and I'm short. None of those physical characteristics were even remotely desirable in the Southern California beach towns where I lived (or when I was in high school). People frequently remarked on my unfashionable skin tone, and non-Californians were skeptical that I was a native Californian because of how I looked, and because I spoke quickly, held opinions, and saw the world through a humorous lens.

I've always hated being small. People tend to overlook you since you're the size of a twelve-year-old. Even in college I twice got into the movies as a child. When I was *with my friends.* The cashier just assumed. There is nothing sexy about looking like a kid, except to perverts and even they want the real thing, being perverts.

People pat you on the head. They *lift* you off your feet. They call you munchkin, like you never heard *that* before. They make a big deal *every single time* they pull something off a shelf for you. It turns you into someone muttering under her breath. A lot. So you learn to be funny, a little loud, conversational, and you dress creatively because you are never, ever going to pull off "sexy," and then you discover Dorothy Parker and think, *ah, my people.*

When I read a biography of her (college in the mid-1970s, of course), I learned how difficult she could be, about her love life, her admiration of Hemingway who mistreated her, her drinking (that's really the difficult part), her procrastination, her marginally cared-for dogs, and her politics. Her problematic side paled next to her better side, the side that summed it all up with "I'm just a little Jewish girl trying to be cute," and that humor is a "shield and not a weapon," and her leftist politics (the Spanish Civil War, the Communist Party, anti-fascist groups, making Martin Luther King Jr., whom she had never met, her heir).

This biography also said that she had a small, dark blue star tattoo located either on the underside of her left arm, or her thigh, or her left shoulder blade; there are conflicting stories. I have a ton of freckles on my back (Southern California sun damage) and I used to say that I wanted a small, dark blue star on my left shoulder blade (one of the rumored Parker star locations), among the freckles, in homage, even though it was most likely on her arm.

I talked about that tattoo for decades. In those days basically three types of people had ink: someone who had been in the armed forces, hippie girls, or bikers. So I wasn't sure about going through with it. I came closest, years later, when my best friend and I went to Japan and she said that we "had to get tattoos"—we were in our mid-forties—except it turned out that you needed appointments made months in advance. Then life went on and one day, and for many reasons, I found myself on a rainy Thursday afternoon getting a small, dark blue star—the Dorothy Parker dark blue star—on the inside of my left arm by a French tattoo artist with the professional name of Sailor Roman who specializes in sea and ocean voyage imagery.

If I were to describe the star I would say that it looks like someone who decided to get inked then, once it began, chickened out. It's the opposite of daring, which makes it a kind of perfect symbol of a Good Girl—you're inked, but refined.

All of which brings me to Tina Modotti, another small, pale-skinned, dark-haired girl who also happened to be Italian (I'm half-Italian). I guess you could say I have a type.

Three Defining Aspects of Tina Modotti in No Particular Order

1. Politics. 2. Men. 3. Photography.

An Excerpt from a Letter Written by Tina Modotti to Edward Weston

1. POLITICS

In 1930, Modotti was deported from Mexico. The government put her on a Dutch cargo ship with the final destination of Mussolini's Italy where Tina, a member of the Communist Party, most likely would've been executed. How, you might ask, did she find herself in this situation? She wrote to Edward Weston, her former lover, *I hope, Edward, that you got a good laugh when you heard that I was accused of participating in the plan to shoot Ortiz Rubio [president of Mexico from 1930–1932]— 'Who would've thought it, eh? Such a gentle looking girl and who made such nice photographs of flowers and babies.'*

Modotti came by her politics honestly, beginning with her father's socialist activities, his rumored involvement with anarcho-syndicalism, a movement largely about labor and economic self-determination. When Tina was two years old, her family emigrated to Austria, staying long enough for Tina to learn German, and then relearning Italian (now with a German accent) when the family returned to Italy seven years later. There is a debate about the reason for the move: was it economically motivated, or prompted by politics? In any case, Italians and Slavs found themselves "objects of blatant discrimination—politically organized and racially motivated—more pronounced in Austria than anywhere else in Europe."

Once back in Udine, Italy, Tina began working in a factory at the age of twelve (her education scant) as her father moved with the two eldest daughters to San Francisco, California. They settled in the Italian district of North Beach, where he opened a machine shop (dabbling unsuccessfully and briefly in photography), and remaining politically involved. He was an inventor (making a lightweight bicycle when he was in Austria). He sent money to Italy and brought over the rest of the family as he could afford it; Tina, the third child, came alone in 1913 at age seventeen.

2. MEN

Once, when Modotti, now living in Mexico City in the artistic, political, and ex-pat community, was playing a parlor game where you had to write something about yourself, she wrote: *Tina Modotti—profession—men!*

Ruby La Brie Richey was a French-Canadian American, raised in Oregon who changed his name to Roubaix "Robo" de l'Abrie Richey (something that I personally think says all you need to know about Robo and his own artistic aspirations; his name is like the rhinestone-studded cigarette holder of names and with about as much sex appeal). In 1915, when he was twenty-four, he had married a fifteen-year-old girl (they met when she was fourteen) who, upon arriving in San Francisco, changed *her* name from Viola McClain to Vola Dore. He was an unfaithful husband who expected monogamy from his willing wife. Meanwhile, Tina had been performing in local Italian theater, and modeling nude, the latter which landed her in the midst of a professional and domestic squabble. She met Robo toward the end of 1917.

They ran away together (by now he was divorced) to Hollywood, telling people they first met at the Pan-Pacific International Expo in 1915. "Facts are not always beautiful," Robo liked to say, "and I only wish to be beautiful." Modotti truly loved him.

They moved into the swank Bryson Apartment Hotel, the lobby of which Raymond Chandler wrote "Blue Ali Baba oil jars were dotted around, big enough to keep tigers in." According to Modotti biographer Patricia Albers, "Tina was content to allow Robo to mediate her relationship with the world" and "formed a lifelong habit of using dress symbolically . . . wearing tutus, ballet shoes, harem skirts, sarongs, baubled headbands, bodices, long lace mantillas." Later, Tina would transition from bohemian clothing to traditional Mexican dress to the more austere skirts and blouses as befitted a member of the Communist Party. The theater never really left her. She sewed, acted in silent films, and even made little dolls.

In the meantime, Robo did batik.

Batik in America—and I say this having been a teen and young adult in the 1970s—is the first cousin to macramé and learning that one song on your recorder. This guy couldn't have been more skilled at murdering sexual desire than if he did it for a living—oh, wait—he not only made batik, and wanted everything to be "beautiful," he also *etched*.

So, when Edward Weston came sauntering into Tina's life, with his restlessness and his desire to run off from his wife, four kids, and suburban photography studio where he took the sort of pictures one takes in a suburban photography studio, and his remarkable mistress, Margrethe Mather (more about her shortly), no wonder Tina became his lover within minutes. She fell very hard.

For his part, Weston was impressed by Tina's beauty and her social set, which he described as "a sophisticated group, drawn to me by my photography. . . . They were well-read, worldly, wise, clever in conversation—could garnish with a smattering of French; they were parlor radicals, could sing IWW songs, quote Emma Goldman on free love, they drank, they smoked, and had affairs."

To put it another way, Weston was a modernist, like Tina. Women, and men miserable with convention, are always going to be modernists because the past has nothing to offer but shackles. Weston had no attachment to tradition or the past, whereas Robo "clung tenaciously to an intentional disregard for the spirit of this age." Robo's skills aside, he was really as much aesthete as artist, uninterested perhaps in the sheer scrappiness being an artist requires. A painter might make something beautiful, but there's no elegance in the act of creation because making something out of nothing (or, in some cases, everything) is a type of gut work. The French name change, marrying the small-town girl playing the same name change game, using the French affectations; the strenuously Romantic clothing; the need for his little faux wife Tina to dress it up, too; his affection for the Past and Truth and Beauty; scrubbing off even the vaguest scent of his Oregon roots when he moved to San Francisco, then Los Angeles, each city so wildly different, while Robo remained unchanged by both of them.

Weston knew he was provincial and a closet modernist. He had been living a double life with his mistress and mercurial business partner of ten years, Margrethe Mather, who had changed *her* name from Emma Caroline Youngreen two years after she moved to San Francisco in 1906. It was rumored that the change followed an affair with a physician in another state. A boyishly beautiful lesbian who also liked men, she was a drinker, a sometimes prostitute (it wasn't unusual for Mather to disappear for weeks at a time, only to resurface, a little worse for wear), a daring photographer who used angles and shadow, texture and repeated patterns formed by everyday objects; modernist all the way. When Weston told her that he was going to Mexico with Tina, the couple said their good-byes by spending a week together at the beach.

Mather made a closely cropped photograph of a young male lover in an open kimono, the blue-and-white fabric contrasted by white skin, the balletic pose of the hands; the picture delivering the same erotic kick as an early O'Keeffe portrait by Stieglitz but with something else, something less common, that of a woman photographing a man. She photographed the braid in a woman's hair. She made pictures of her suicidal lesbian lover, and another of a water lily as elegant as Baron De Meyer's 1907 hydrangea in a glass. According to Imogen Cunningham, who had known Edward Weston for years, he was more influenced by Mather than she by him, though they did make a number of prints together in the early 1920s. Though the prints were signed by both photographers (the only time in his career that Weston shared credit with anyone), it was said that some of those dual-signed prints were Mather's alone.

When Tina said she was going to Mexico, Weston announced that he would go with her, their eventual domestic arrangement even more bohemian than many of their compatriots in that Mrs. Weston cooly informed her departing husband that he would be taking their fourteen-year-old son with them. Flora Weston was no fool; having a kid around didn't exactly allow for sexual spontaneity, even her husband did try to convince her that he and Tina were "just friends."

3. PHOTOGRAPHY (ROSES)

There are a couple of Tina Modotti's images that I love, but none more than *Roses, 1924*. The composition is simple: a pile of roses lay on top of each other, crushed crowding the frame. That's it. I love it because it shakes all the sentimentality out of a rose, making it clear that beauty and love are tightly wound into decay and time, but are not more or less valued or desirable for it. This is also a portrait of the New Woman of the early part of the 20th century who rejected marriage, who wanted something else. Like living with a married man and his teen-aged son in Mexico City, where they had a studio and their own bedrooms and an *azotea* (a terrace). This is where Tina learned to take pictures, run a business, and stop dressing in fucking tutus. This is the city where Edward Weston exhibited nudes of Tina his muse, his lover, his studio assistant-protege, pictures that would later take her down, while never affecting his reputation.

Gertrude Stein wrote:

A
ROSE IS A
ROSE IS A
ROSE IS A
ROSE
She is my rose.

Judy Grahn in *Really Reading Gertrude Stein* explains that these lines are about the seeming sameness of one rose to the next, the rose has an existence beyond our clichés about it.

Artist Jay DeFeo made *The Rose* (1958–1966), a massive, massive painting (nearly eleven feet tall and weighing one ton) in a kind of lightish concrete color that darkens at the edges, a play of white with black but not painted the way things are often painted. She used so much thickly applied paint that it ended up sculpted (she often chipped and honed) as well as painted. She worked on it for eight years, only stopping when she had to move from her apartment (a production involving a crate, a crane, moving men, and window removal). *The Rose* eventually stood, hidden behind a false wall at the San Francisco Art Institute for twenty years. It's like nothing I've ever seen (I saw it in 2013, at a Jay DeFeo retrospective in San Francisco, alone in its niche), it's overwhelming and absolutely defies any clichés about a rose.

Ansel Adams, *Rose on Driftwood, 1933.* Georgia O'Keeffe *Abstract White Rose, 1927.* Neither one moves me like Tina's *Roses,* though they work the same color palette, the same cropped aspect. To me, the other pictures, each composed of a single rose, are pretty, but silent.

*

Robo de Richey, who saw in Tina his other half with his let's-dress-up-like-we-live-in-a-seraglio artist couple ideal, the one the former fifteen-year-old Viola (now Vola Dore) was never going to pull off. The Artist Couple, so romanticized, poeticized, admired, desired. No love could ever be as deep and impossible and fated as the love of the Artistic Couple. Even the conflicts are epic; no one ever imagines them arguing about who put the toilet roll on backwards, or what does it take to close a cupboard door? Or who left the honey stuck to the kitchen counter—do artists even *have* kitchens? Don't they live on rarified air? It is so aspirational, the Artistic Couple, that it ends up a collection of everyone's starry-eyed dreams, including Robo and Madame de Richey. That is, until she met Weston and you know what happened? *They* became the Artistic It Couple in 1920s Mexico. The Legend of Edward and Tina. However, they only became the It Couple of Mexico because Robo, who had traveled there first, so loved it that he enthusiastically sent for Tina, but before she could arrive, Robo contracted smallpox and died, transitioning her from fake wife to fake widow. Tina decided to move to Mexico City anyway, and Weston, done with the conventional life, went along for the ride.

Tina as Muse, and a Picture Timeline in Reverse

Navajo Rug, 1968. This photograph by Imogen Cunningham is part of a series she made of nudes featuring a young, blonde woman. The model, slender and sleeping, lies mostly on her side, her figure turned, her shoulders flattened to the floor. Her bent knees, her right forearm resting on her thigh; breasts, hair; face nearly in profile, her body resembles the distant undulating hills of a pastoral landscape, her slumbering figure bisecting the picture. The eponymous rug beneath her on a wooden floor, the pattern of rug and floor perpendicular to each other. The model is bathed in light.

The Virgin Earth, 1926. The pose of the girl in Cunningham's *Navajo Rug* picture—right down to the size and slope of her right breast—is identical to Diego Rivera's figure in *The Virgin Earth* in the murals at the chapel in Chapingo. The model for the mural is Tina Modotti, who had a nearly year-long love affair with Rivera while his wife, Lupe Marin, was pregnant. Though Tina wasn't his only lover, she was the one that broke the marriage. (It's said that Edward Weston was so jealous that Rivera worked only from sketches of Tina and not Tina herself. A sketch does exist but you can't have jealousy and a fractured marriage if you're working strictly from pencil and paper.)

Tina on the Azotea, 1923. Edward Weston, who made pictures of Tina when they were still in California, also made a handful of nudes, taken on the terrace of their rented Mexico City home. In one, the angle of her body, her closed eyes, her face in near profile, the slight droop of her breast is almost exactly like the Tina of Rivera's *The Virgin Earth* (her face obscured by her falling hair), who, in turn, is very much like Cunningham's model in *Navajo Rug.*

Making Tina the muse for Weston, then for Rivera, then for Cunningham; Tina's image spanning the twentieth century from 1923 to 1968, her languorous pose, her dreaming expression.

*

Her biographer, Patricia Albers, wrote, *Tina discovered in Edward's portraits a new scaffolding for her identity. Still young, she fell in love with what she saw of herself in his eyes as much as the human being before her.*

Isn't that what love does to us all?

Men

Edward Weston loved dancing and masquerades and cross-dressing at costume parties. At a Mardi Gras party in 1924, Edward wrote, "She [Tina] smoked my pipe and bound down her breasts, while I wore a pair of cotton ones with pink pointed buttons for nipples. We . . . then appeared on the street, she carrying my Graflex, and I hanging on her arm. . . . I indulged in exaggerations, flaunted my breasts and exposed my pink gartered legs most indecently. . . . Lupe told me that I was *sin verguenza*—without shame . . . ."

What struck me about this incident wasn't that it was one more raucous party (the It Couple of Mexico City held and attended many parties) or that it preceded a night of going place to place (many evenings passed in this way), it was that they were not impersonating just any man and any woman—they were mimicking each other. She became the serious photographer with the camera; he was the woman who grew increasingly sexual, to the point of parody.

The fact was Weston couldn't make the free love leap that Modotti could, he couldn't curb his jealousy (he once slid a small crucifix, a gift from a Tina admirer, in and out of his nose), even when he slept with others, even when his desire for Tina wavered; he wrote in his *Daybooks,* "Next time I'll pick a mistress homely as hell!" He left Mexico after eighteen months with his son (burned his Mexico journals), only to return several months later with a different son. Though everyone was dazzled by the glamour that attached itself to the couple; he was still, in some sense, the Californian provincial.

Artistic Couples, Part #2

Vera Nabokov is pretty much the gold standard of the Artist Wife. If the primary Artist Couple is one where both are artists, then the second type is the one where one half of the couple makes things, while the other half of the couple does everything else. Vera drove Vladimir everywhere, including butterfly expeditions; she recorded his lectures, wrote his letters, edited his work, translated, had their son, was his bodyguard (it was rumored she carried a gun), worked as a secretary, and gave up her own writerly ambitions. She even rescued *Lolita* from the fire. Books have been written about her devotion (what else to call it?). One imagines a vestal virgin.

In the last twenty years there's been a funny sort of little subgenre of literature that I call "Fucking Famous Men." It includes some well-written and well-reviewed books, and some less well-written books. There was the novel about a woman married to Hemingway and a woman who had an affair with Freud (she was his unmarried sister-in-law), and a woman married to Lindbergh and a woman with whom Frank Lloyd Wright fell in love (even a successful male writer got into the Frank Lloyd Wright act with a novel about *four* of Wright's women), and a woman married to Fitzgerald. This type of novel often has titles that include the name of the Famous Man, while the women are unidentified by name and often given a designation like "mistress" or "wife," even if they had some sort of professional accomplishment.

I read a couple of these novels and I have to say that in each case the story really came into focus when the famous man was on the page, or being discussed. Let me be even more clear: these books are meant to be "women's stories," but they're really more like fame-adjacent stories told from the point of view of the loyal lover/wife, not unlike say, the disgruntled dog walker or neighbor who writes a tell-all saying, yeah, he could be such a dick.

(My first attempt at a novel was to write about Isadora Duncan, Georgia O'Keeffe, and Dorothy Parker. This was in 1981 and I got only about twenty pages in, enough to know that I really didn't know what I was doing.

My next attempt was written in 1987, when Georgia O'Keeffe recently died, and Juan Hamilton, O'Keeffe's significantly younger companion found himself in trouble over a codicil that changed the terms of her will, leaving him with everything. But what intrigued me was the rumor that O'Keeffe was convinced she and Hamilton had married and that the codicil she signed was a "marriage license." Hamilton's defense? "I'm already married." The interested public [me] was unaware of a Mrs. Hamilton because there was something so emotionally intimate about the O'Keeffe/Hamilton friendship that it didn't seem to allow time or space for a wife and family.

Now I had my novel: the story of a young woman [based on O'Keeffe] becoming a painter, and the story of another young woman [fictional] with artistic ambitions of her own, married to a man with artistic ambitions of his own involved with the now-older artist who did become a painter, and all the betrayal, jealousy, desire, love, admiration, secrecy. The characters were fictional but much of what they said were quotes I collected from biographies and articles and documentaries. The fictional characters speaking their real-life counterparts' words. Except for the fictional young woman who was, of course, fictional.

This is my way of saying that I completely understand how those novelists would want to write fiction inspired by historical fact, even if mine was man-adjacent to a Famous Woman, who *he* wanted to fuck.)

When Gertrude Stein wrote *The Autobiography of Alice B. Toklas,* she not only achieved the vulgar celebrity she craved but slyly solved the koan of autobiography by disclaiming responsibility for the one being written. Speaking in the voice of her longtime companion, Stein can entirely dispense with the fiction of humility that the conventional autobiographer often struggles every moment to maintain. "I may say that only three times in my life have I met a genius," Stein-as-Toklas writes of their first meeting, "and each time a bell within me rang and I was not mistaken, and I may say in each case it was before there was any general recognition of the quality of genius in them." Stein not only talks about *her* genius while masquerading on the page as Alice but also allows that only *Alice* is perceptive enough to truly know genius. Again, maybe it takes a same-sex couple to strip away the Artist Couple bullshit, call it what it is, and do it brilliantly.

*

How to solve this, then? I mean, besides being a same-sex couple if you aren't so inclined. What does it look like when things are reversed and the woman is the Vladimir Nabokov in need of a Vera? Speaking anecdotally, I know of no woman (myself included) who completely drops out of the daily grind of house and kids, let alone expects her companion to drive her around so she can hunt butterflies. It's not so easy for an ambitious woman in the arts to find the right partner. You have a lot of particular needs, like you need him to be supportive and patient with your career. You need him to stand back when necessary. Or move closer. He has to be flexible enough to understand that the arts are unpredictable and things might go sideways. The country goes into economic distress; a natural disaster or some other state of emergency; your art falls from favor. It's an unpredictable life of always reinventing the wheel.

My college boyfriend was never going to be that guy for me. He expected me to be that guy for him. And, as with many,

many women, I thought I could do it all. I don't mean have a career and a family, no, I thought I could have my life *and* arrange a life where he could hunt butterflies while pursuing his own artistic ambitions. The emotional clash of that situation was impressive, in retrospect, because in the moment it was so crushing.

Then I met J., and I'm fairly sure that no one who knew me thought he was for me. Too many things didn't add up for us at first glance. We had (have) an age difference (before that became common), and an education difference, and we were from opposite sides of the country, and we seemed Just. So. Different. We were (are) different, in some respects, but we get along incredibly well. We had fun almost from the start (he made me laugh), and he was truly decent and kind and kind-hearted (still). He's patient and generous in every way. He reads. Part of his goodness was seeing me as a writer before I ever published a word; this is invaluable to anyone in the arts, this being seen as who you are.

I think the reason there is no male Vera is because, as a woman, you are very well-versed in domestic responsibilities since they are the very ones you often want to avoid. Because you know them as intimately as you do, your empathetic nature prevents you from thoughtlessly dumping all of them onto your mate. You don't stop and say, I'm the one earning, or producing work, or whatever you're doing, so I never have to wash a dish. No, you are more collaborative than that, which is the reason that these relationships are often more equitable than any other couple relationship. You're grateful, not entitled. And, if you find you cannot do it, you look at outside childcare (even if part-time), or a housekeeper (even if twice a month). In this way, women never really leave their upbringing and societal expectations entirely behind.

And there's the money issue. Of course, money is never just money. It's love, power, revenge, independence, apology, nurture; it stands in for so many things that it is both the best and the worst of us. Edward Weston's wife, Flora Chandler, was related to a very wealthy, very important Southern California family (my family's friends bought one of their mansions when we were kids, which is my sole connection to anything Chandler), inheriting enough to allow him to open his photography studio.

In my life it hasn't been uncommon for women I know to provide the financial means (through work, though, not inheritance) for their man to "do what he wants," which is sometimes staying home. It isn't always easy and has come at a sacrifice to the woman still caught on the wheel of work. Then the trouble starts because traditional ideas of "men" and "women" fall apart; the men dig in, the women capitulate, and everyone's resentful.

Then there is the other less traditional guy who really understands this territory, freeing you up to do what you need to do. J. did it for me, decades ago, before the recent spate of stay-home dads, before the collapse of the economy that sort of forced the stay-home dad thing, before people stopped saying unenlightened things about J.'s choices.

The less traditional guy—who is the only kind of guy where you have half a chance of realizing your artistic ambitions—can be a mixed bag. There is a frustration that many women I know have felt with the less traditional guy, often he's someone, seeing the chance to take on the traditional female role, willing to blow out the usual expectations as a chance to do . . . nothing. Or next to nothing. As if staying home is one endless day off from school.

I've known men who identified as "stay-home dads" because they didn't work outside the home. Usually, they cooked dinner and called it domestic work, even as they were dropping their kids off for daycare. Maybe they'd vacuum. But laundry? I don't think so. Baths? Change the beds? Yeah, right. The interesting thing about the home tasks was that these other stay-home dads often cherry-picked their chores, something a stay-home mom wouldn't think of doing (would think she *could* do). It's pretty revealing that these guys felt that so many things were optional, or could be put off until they *wanted* to do them, showing a complete misunderstanding of what women (including the moms who raised them) actually did with their days. That was the state of affairs when J. stayed home, working. Always working.

*

Photography

Estridentistas (strident ones) was a movement that "stressed the urban, the machine and the futuristic but above all, they were masters of the 'statement'—as outrageous, provocative, and as radical as possible. . . . Tina may not have been a 'Estridentista Woman,' but her early photographs were certainly in keeping with their esthetic."

If art is a form of personal expression, as well as a reflection of life (sometimes an influence on life)—Cunningham eschewed artificiality; Mann saw the world, literally, through a historical lens; Judy Dater made portraits—then Modotti was a social documentarian, recording, and, she felt, elevating the lives of the Mexican people. She didn't consider her pictures of her adopted countrymen's lives—working, feeding their children, carrying water, protesting in the street, or even passing out drunk on the sidewalk—"street photography" in the manner of, say, Ruth Orkin who reflected street life; Modotti sought to change, her work pushed against sentimentality, even though her pictures, gritty as they could be, sometimes edged close to that line with a sort of Salt of the Earth admiration. How else to photograph strangers with respect and affection, if you love Mexico, and not worry a little about idealization?

Modotti made pictures of arches, telegraph lines, cane stalks, scaffolding, stairs, wine glasses, all of them man-made goods (as opposed to natural phenomenon), all of them relying on patterns and contrasts of light and shadow. In this way, they sometimes recalled Margrethe Mather's photography with her use of pattern (hair combs, cigarettes, cherries, fans, glass eyes), the objects carefully, tightly arranged and filling the frame of the picture. It would seem that a black-and-white photo of say, cherries organized in a grid on a table would be dull, except when the cherries have stems and their surfaces reflect the light, and the background is typeface; they sit on words, in sepia on sepia tones (*Cherries on Type, 1930*). Then the cherries are remarkable.

Agnes Martin is a twentieth-century painter who also worked in patterns and grids. She was called a Minimalist, though she self-identified as an Abstract Expressionist.

Something that Robert Hughes wrote of Ad Reinhardt's paintings relates to Martin:

> The [Ad Reinhardt] black paintings in their final form after 1960 were all square, five feet by five feet, and filled with the same design: a cross which divided the surface into nine equal squares. So close were their values that you needed to gaze at the canvas for some time before your eyes, as though adjusting to a dark room, could make all this out . . . this almost subliminal trace of light asked for the discipline of looking. Reinhardt's black paintings are among the few works of art that are *entirely* meaningless when reproduced. They are a vindication of art's right to be experienced first hand, because second hand there is nothing to experience.

Agnes Martin's paintings are meaningless when reproduced. The incandescence of the paint, the nuance of the hues, the surprising beauty of her penciled lines and grids, is lost. On the page, her work has no effect, but in person, her work astonishingly moving. You cannot not look. You cannot not feel. I have found myself in tears when standing in front of a Martin painting. I don't even know why, I really don't.

Agnes Martin, Ad Reinhardt, Margrethe Mather all worked within a square and a grid.

Tina Modotti belongs to their group, with her pictures of patterns: telegraph lines, glass doors, stairs.

Tina as Photographer

It's true that Edward Weston, who taught Tina how to take and develop pictures, was instrumental in her career as a photographer. It can also be said that her attention to shadows and shapes and everyday objects influenced his later style, an influence that had begun with Margrethe Mather. Talking about how one artist impacts another is not veiled plagiarism; it's the story of art.

My favorite Tina Modotti pictures:

Roses, 1924. As mentioned, I love how the roses are laid on top of each other, crushed and crowded within the frame. They look like a bouquet that someone thoughtlessly tossed, then forgot, on the kitchen table; the edges of the petals indicate their decay, that neglect that disallows sentimentality. This approach differs from Cunningham's domestically coded plants, or Mapplethorpe's attempt to capture a perfect, uncorrupt moment.

Doors, 1925, shows a series of open glass-paned doors. I live in a one-hundred-year-plus house of numerous multi-paned windows and six glass doors, so when I see this picture, I see home.

But they also remind me of Dorothea Tanning's surrealist painting *Birthday, 1942.* A young woman stands in a room of doors, her hand rests on the doorknob of the door to the room. Beyond that door we see many more doors, old, like in my house, or Tina's picture but without the glass. All the doors are ajar, revealing more doors. The woman gazes at the viewer, the sleeves of her purple blouse deliberately shredded to show her bare arms, the rest of the blouse missing as she stands, stripped to the waist of a skirt made of twigs and silk. A black winged monster, about the size of a house cat, crouches at her feet. I am crazy for this painting.

The Hammer-and-Sickle photographs, late 1920s. A hammer-and-sickle laying on a sombrero; a hammer-and-sickle with a fully loaded bandolier, one with a corn cob, another without a corn cob—these symbols moved and swapped. My favorite is a plain hammer-and-sickle. There is a richness and depth to these prints; they look like the museum pieces they now are, but, of course, were not when they were first made. There is the nostalgia of the black-and-white print, the past is located in the subject. They are devotional images; Modotti was an unapologetic member of the Communist Party, and I'm talking about Stalin's Communist Party, not just Lenin or Trotsky.

These images convey strength and a pledge to stand by the Mexican worker; there is nothing reassuring here; these pictures are not an opening for debate—they are a final statement. There is no romanticized farmer, or woman nursing her baby; no flowers conveying human suffering. Modotti isn't resorting to grace or charm or seduction.

The Curse of the Good Girl

Tina was, in the truest sense, a Good Girl.

(I know a little something about the Good Girl.)

When you mention a Good Girl, everyone immediately has an idea of what it does and does not mean. It doesn't mean being sanctimonious or the class monitor. It's more a matter of being that girl that parents and teachers love, being bookish, often having a sense of humor, often putting the needs of others first, and generally being unobtrusive. The Good Girl rarely commands the room. Her counterpart, the Bad Girl, who isn't "bad" any more than the Good Girl is "good," is often better with boys (or girls) because she's got a kind of cool sexiness (the Good Girl is an acquired taste in the sex department, that is, her appeal isn't as sweeping as the Bad Girl's), sense of adventure, is openly rebellious. She's as good at *No, I'm not doing that* as Good Girls are at *It's okay, I'll do it,* like she's everybody's designated driver. The Bad Girl is the one commanding the room.

Anyway, these are the social archetypes often found in books and movies and sometimes in life (as archetypes often are). The main difference between them is that the Bad Girl is the more predictable of the two; I don't mean that she's boring; quite the contrary, being exciting is pretty much her thing, so when I say she's predictable, I mean she's consistently thrilling, but Good Girl has the power to surprise. She's always that agreeable, sunny girl who one night does something unexpected like picking up a weird hitchhiker on a deserted beach street at 3 a.m. because he pounds on her car window demanding to be given a ride. Or maybe she pretends to be someone famous to get what she wants. Or smokes weed while driving someone else's car with the top down, stopping at an intersection where the only other car is a police car, or thinks heroin is a good idea one ordinary Thursday night (maybe on a Tuesday night, too). The point being, no one ever thinks of her doing anything against the rules because they think she must love rules, allowing her to run off the rails from time to time and get away with it. Anything she does that is counter to what people think is always treated as an anomaly. In this way, she remains private in a world where everyone thinks they know her.

The downside of being a Good Girl is being treated like it's your job in life to be constantly agreeable, apologetic even, and if you aren't then it's like a betrayal to everyone around you.

The sexist hammer comes down a little harder on you because you've neglected to be the adventurous sexy Bad Girl (who can find herself dismissed in other ways).

And, god forbid, you like to talk. You like conversation. No matter how many questions you ask, or how much you listen, or ask to hear someone else's opinion, you are expected to be quiet and, of course, agreeable. Especially if you are small of stature (me), and older (me again).

Related to my lifelong Good Girl persona, there has been a certain male personality that cannot stand me. I started noticing it in college. These men, conventional, traditional, like to be admired; they want an audience. They want to sleep with women, but not listen to them because the female sensibility bores them, angers them, threatens them, confuses them into thinking that if they like sleeping with women they must like women. Misogyny resides in that space between sexual attraction to women and wishing they'd never speak.

When I was younger and could sense their displeasure, I would dance faster to try to mediate the situation. Sometimes this only made things worse. I couldn't make a joke, or say anything without being dismissed, or perceived as "challenging" them (even when I wasn't). This type of man doesn't listen, instead makes unfunny jokes about how much I talk—entirely different from objecting to *what* I'm saying—only that I'm saying anything at all. They want me to stop making "noise," as if they believe me to be a sound without thought or feelings. I eventually became my own walking litmus test to measure how much men like women (and trust me, it *is* possible for a man not to like me for other reasons—it just isn't as usual—or to be indifferent. I'm talking about something else here. There are other women who know *exactly* what I'm talking about). For example, if you are a man and you are reading this (and who am I kidding?) and you've ever wondered where you fall on the

Traditional Male Continuum, come spend an afternoon with me and you'll know.

*

Blue is considered Joni Mitchell's soulful masterpiece. *Court and Spark* was her most commercially successful "breakthrough" record. The album that never wears itself out (for me) is *The Hissing of Summer Lawns,* the less successful 1975 follow-up to *Court and Spark,* even though its topical (re: feminist) theme risked dating itself. I don't know if it's a testament to Mitchell's talent or our sluggish-to-change society that has kept this record's themes current.

(Note: Even the most radical organizations of the sixties were riddled with sexism; paradoxically, it was those disco party seventies that were pivotal to many marginalized people, bringing about some of the change that the sixties failed to complete.)

Don't Interrupt the Sorrow makes it clear why *The Hissing of Summer Lawns* is still relevant. In this song, with the usual Mitchell markers of longing, impossible romance, and inner conflict, a new element is added when the woman singing is ordered, twice, to "be polite" as the man speaking reminds her that "we walked on the moon." Since there were no female astronauts then (no women walking on the moon), he's telling her that "we" do things that matter and it's your obligation to defer and not get all cheeky. *(Men tell you that the only important pictures are taken on the battlefield, then they ban you from the battlefield.)*

He calls her "liberation doll"—a descriptor that is so deeply 1975, so sharply belittling within its time. Today it might annoy but never anger. Not like then.

Few things in my life have irritated me more than being told to smile by passing men as I would go about my business during the day, though it doesn't happen as often as it did in my youth. I don't have a single woman friend who hasn't experienced this presumptuous command, or been told how much prettier she'd look if she smiled. There were times I wanted to just stop and say, maybe my father just died, or I'm having a bad day, or fuck you.

Manners are important. They mean we care about the social comfort of others. They are a form of consideration and empathy; they also allow us to be private in public. But enforced politeness is a form of oppression. Show me a woman placed on a pedestal and I'll show you a prisoner.

Tina Modotti was, in many respects, a polite revolutionary. A Good Girl in red, if you will. She was often described as thoughtful, gracious, generous, and charming. She used an empathetic approach with her portrait subjects, to put them at ease, and got away with her unambiguous visual political "statements" because, as she wrote to Weston, from her American holding cell during her deportation to Mussolini's Italy, that she was the "gentle looking girl who made such nice photographs of flowers and babies." This amused comment of the Good Girl (her humor on display) where the true meaning of her work (flowers and babies) is misunderstood because no one can quite believe that this pretty woman, a hair under five feet tall, and soft spoken, gracious, and polite is as radically Red as she is (the element of the unexpected in the Good Girl), because if you can't trust a Good Girl, who can you trust?

*

Politics

All too often, Modotti was buffeted between art and politics, acquiescence and ambition. Politics and immigration that were a part of her life from the age of two years old, when her family went to Austria to work.

If Robo tried to invent a costume-y artsy counterpart in Modotti, Weston saw Tina clearly enough to provide a "scaffolding for her true identity"; with Weston Modotti no longer dressed in tutus, or pretended to be married, or even wanted to pretend to be married. She developed an unapologetic, progressive persona that both attracted Weston and drove him away because he couldn't handle either the free-lovism or the politics.

Weston tired of Tina's work with the Communist newspaper *El Machete,* her increasing involvement with and subsequent membership in the Communist Party (1927). After Weston (and during Weston and before Weston) there were other men, usually Communists (Diego Rivera, for example, Xavier Guerrro), with the final man in her life being Vittorio Vidali, another Communist Party member. But in between Weston and Vidali was Julio Antonio Mella, the love of her life, though when Weston left for good she did write to him *You are that to me, Edward—no matter what others mean to me you are that—*. Though Weston and Mella were different, they influenced her life to take different directions, but only Vidali completely rewrote her.

Vidali "paint[ed] a picture of Modotti as an unquestioning Party worker" and began "shaping the Modotti biography from the moment she died." With Weston it was art; with Mella politics.

There it is: Men and politics. The Tina Axis.

*

I cannot—as you once proposed to me 'solve the problem of my life by losing myself in the problem of art'—not only can I not do that but I often feel that the problem of life hinders my problem of art.
　　　　　—As Tina Modotti once wrote to Edward Weston,
　　　　　　　　　　　　　　　　after they were over

*

Vittorio Vidali went by many names (Enea Sormenti, Jacobo Hurwitz Zender, Carlos Contreras, "Comandante Carlos") as suited his career as a Communist Party organizer and agitator but mostly the aliases were useful in his career as a Party assassin. It was said that he murdered between sixty and one hundred people.

He grew up in grinding poverty (is there any other kind?), forty-five miles from the Italian town where Tina was born. Though Modotti and Vidali lived in Italy and the United States (where he spent time going from factory to mill, from Chicago to the east coast) at the same time, they didn't meet until Mexico.

Mexico City of the 1920s was a post-Revolution city with its own enclave of expatriates, painters, photographers, idealists, writers, radicals, which is a way of saying it wasn't all that different from 1920s Paris, or 1920s Harlem, or 1920s Greenwich Village. Each place had its own colony of artists and radicals among everyone else, who were just living and working, but the romance lies in those artists and radicals.

In Mexico Tina ("Tinisima") went from being a beautiful model, photographer, and muse with the non-political Weston to embracing Communism and a more austere existence. She also wanted to "simplify life, in particular with men." Patricia Albers writes, "Her comrades were about 600, many foreigners, an impoverished, scrappy, self-important, and starry-eyed lot. Like most of them, barely conversant in Marxist theory, Tina has less interest in familiarizing herself with Marx and Lenin than in observing the Communist codes of etiquette. . . ." It was as if the actress in her never quite disappeared.

Tina and Weston's house had always been a gathering place, but now the crowd was more political. Tina, that scandalous woman, stopped modeling (often nude); her photography shifted from art for art's sake, saying she now saw people with a "class eye. . . . I look upon people now not in terms of race or

types but in terms of class. I look upon social changes and phe-
nomena not in terms of human nature or of spiritual factors
but in terms of economics." She wrote translations and dressed
in the west's version of modesty attire (the straight skirts, the
black stockings), which really just underscored how, even with
her fellow Communists, she was still a second-class citizen. She
could be a full-fledged member, and still be treated as nothing
more than an office worker. This wasn't the reason that Weston
wasn't having any of it (one wishes it was because she was seen
as a tireless secretary); he just didn't care for the party line and,
I'm guessing, he had a sense of humor.

*

When I was an undergraduate with a messy academic situation that included one private college (very progressive, freshman year), one state school (party school, sophomore year),
and one public university (academically demanding, junior,
etc.); many majors (many interests), and placed on academic
probation (two years and one quarter), culminating in a letter
explaining I was to meet with the assistant dean where we could
"discuss expulsion," I was introduced to the ideas of Antonio
Gramsci. Gramsci was an Italian Neo-Marxist who spent half
of the 1920s and much of the 1930s (until his death in 1937)
in an Italian prison. In brief, he talked about dominant class
hegemony using culture to maintain power or, to put it another
way, the ruling class creates a consciousness in the non-ruling
class where the non-ruling class believes it can rise to join the
ruling class and so is invested in preserving that class instead of
taking it down.

    You can see the appeal for someone growing up in capital-
ist America, raised on the idea of class mobility without ever
fully believing it. The great thing about a capitalist democracy
is that everything is evident: the privilege, and the inequalities,

along with the possibility of change. Class, we're told, is fluid, unfixed. Except it isn't, exactly.

It doesn't take a lot for many writers and artists to lean left. It's the empathy, the outsider observer sensibility. It's the desire (or a need) to make art (in essence, to make a world). Much of your life is spent getting by: cobbling jobs together, working on spec or being underpaid. It's a life of hustling because there is no reliable professional ladder for the thing you want. You're like one of those third-rate criminals in a B-movie always looking for that one final, lucrative score so you can breathe.

The luxury of money is simple. It isn't about what you can wear or eat or drive. It isn't about good schools or having a house bigger than anyone needs. It's not about travel. It's not about power or superiority. All those things can factor in, of course, but they aren't the main thing.

The luxury of money is never having to think about money.

Gramsci's ideas (which I have simplified here, I know) impressed me enough to devote my senior thesis to a critique of higher education in California (when I had so recently been on the Whitney Otto California College Tour) by way of Gramsci. I wasn't a Marxist exactly though I was interested in social justice (something I shared with my hero, Dorothy Parker), and I did spend three months of tenth grade with my desk situated next to a poster of Lenin, developing a bit of a thing for him, and I was also working my way through school, tired and broke and just had nothing to lose even if I wanted to become fully radicalized (I didn't). I was more like one of those parlor socialists in the Modotti set where you like the theories but it's all too much work.

Still, that didn't stop my roommate's (one of the sorority girls) slightly older boyfriend who dressed in a suit and tie and looked like a cross between a Mormon missionary on a bike and a snake in toupee, from calling me "that little pinko." Not only did The Boyfriend dress like the fifties—and we lived at the beach on Balboa peninsula where a bathing suit cover-up was something you wore because you had to go out to dinner with the parents—he was also a mind-game-playing oppressor to my roommate who, inexplicably, was in love with him, even when he acted like our duplex was an off-site McCarthy hearing. This guy was such a garden variety jerk that being called the worst name he could think of, the retro "little pinko," really felt like a compliment.

The Boyfriend worked for a health food restaurant/market concern headquartered in Boston (he had been sent out by the folks in Boston), and was also a member of a "philosophical" group that included an ex-girlfriend and her brother (who also worked for the same health food company) founded by a man whose name began with a G. The "philosophical" group was basically a pyramid scheme where you were invited by existing members and asked to sign up for a series of classes taught in someone's living room. You then advanced to more and more classes (more and more fees), refining your understanding of the world view of G. where he believed the perfect society was one solely run by insurance companies. There were endless discussions about Ayn Rand's *Atlas Shrugged* and how it was degrading to people to *give* them anything. Even people born without arms, for example, or who are bipolar, or elderly, or children. Helping people—*ugh, what an insult.* Like it was only respectful to step over someone lying in the street.

Mostly, The Boyfriend tortured my roommate because she wasn't Dagny Taggart, the blonde Randian goddess of *Atlas Shrugged* and constantly reminded her that she wasn't Dagny Taggart. Once, he returned from a trip, saying he spied his "perfect woman" in the airport, with her "shining helmet of blonde hair," exactly like Dagny, then "strongly suggested" that my roommate lie in a bath of icy water, then afterward lie very still so they could have sex. Another time he had her beg, "like a dog," she said, for M&Ms because he was "helping her lose weight." She was a tall, ex-dancer who wasn't fat, but she wasn't anorexic like Dagny, and The Boyfriend's skeletal ex-girlfriend.

When The Boyfriend broke up with my roommate he "strongly suggested" that she become roommates with the skinny ex-girlfriend whom I had met but I couldn't tell you what she was like since she was too starved to possess a personality. Everyone in this small crowd of G. followers were really thin because in Rand's anti-pleasure world no one ate anything but the minimum required to keep up your strength to have faux-hate sex. It was like they were all incarcerated but without the jail cells (the thin part, not the sex part).

Now I had already read Ayn Rand in high school, *We the Living* (because my best friend read it. I liked it because it was a romance set against the backdrop of the Russian revolution! And because I was 15 years old), and *The Fountainhead* when I was in college, another book I really liked because it was supposedly inspired by Frank Lloyd Wright and I was always into architecture (I had wanted to major in it in college, and had taken a series of Saturday classes with Whitney Smith in high school—there were only three of us in the class—but went on to have every other major instead) and it had a lot of speechifying. Ayn Rand can be a convincing writer, and I was young but even in my youth I could see the heartless impracticality of Rand's "virtues of selfishness." Also, all of Rand's "love scenes" are undeniably rapey.

I think you're supposed to grow out of Rand very quickly, unlike my roommate's emotionally challenged friends. I ended up as a guest at one of their meetings, a couple of years later in Marin County after we had all moved to San Francisco. It was like a Tupperware party where everyone talked about charity like it was barely distinguishable from animal porn and, of course, that idealized New World order, insurance companies.

This period of my life was also a couple of years after my immersion in Dorothy Parker, that "little Jewish girl trying to be cute." She was involved with civil liberties, racial equality, the Spanish Civil War, anti-fascist groups, and the Communist Party, involvements that landed her on the Hollywood Blacklist. She was never happy in California (my home state), even if she and her husband made money hand-over-fist writing screenplays in Hollywood. She was unhappy in that way that an astute, sharp-witted writer who loved New York and drank too much could be unhappy, making her misery, I'm sure, dangerous to be around.

My enduring fantasy was to be a screenwriter on a movie lot, with a tiny garden-level office with steel-paned windows that cranked open to allow in the fragrance of eucalyptus and jasmine while dreaming of the novel I would one day write. I wanted to sell-out in that tortured, wistful way of someone who should've been doing "better things." I wanted to live in the Garden of Allah. (It's now Chase Bank. I visited it when I was in college; they had a diorama of the original hotel that had such guests as Orson Welles, Ernest Hemingway, Dorothy Parker, Fitzgerald. My old friend Francis X. Bushman was present in 1959 when it was razed.)

I didn't care that Parker's assessment of Hollywood was "a block-long limo with a gloved, jeweled hand sticking out of the rear window holding a bagel with one bite taken out of it." It was Joni Mitchell again, only the personal heartache was replaced with professional heartache; Parker's intellect kicking at the traces, and I wanted to experience that romanticized (by me) frustration, too.

*

It takes so little to move to the left, or to find socialism mildly attractive if you're a woman turning from tradition. But for Modotti to increase her commitment, it took a man. In 1928 she met Julio Antonio Mella (birth name Nicanor MacPartland), a Cuban revolutionary and founder of the Cuban Communist Party, seven years her junior (she was thirty-two). The attraction was instantaneous. He was the Cuban-born son of an English mother and a Dominican father who was married to someone else.

Mella and Modotti were beautiful and in love and sexy and revolutionary. Once again she was the adored half of a glamorous It Couple. Once again, he was married, with a child (his family had returned to Cuba; Cuba unsafe for him, and he was in love with Tina); once again Tina brushed off convention.

Her portrait of Mella, close on his profile where he looks as noble and as unreachable as a royalty. His work shirt is opened at the throat, the picture stops just below his handsome shoulders, he gazes off into the distance, his thoughts on the glorious Marxist future. All around him is only sky. Iconic, heroic, like Korda's Che.

She made a picture of Mella sleeping.

She made a picture of his typewriter, a partially typed page rolled onto the platen. The title of the photo is *La Technica*. (Side note: The early twentieth-century artist Francis Picabia made drawings of machines that represented his friends.)

Maybe she gave up art for art's sake, but she hadn't given up on love. Clearly.

Here's another image: *Distributing Arms,* the Diego Rivera mural that shows Frida Kahlo, the central figure, dressed in a red shirt with a star (she too was a Communist), black skirt, holding a rifle. The lower right-hand corner tells a less political story.

Tina is dressed in a red shirt and black skirt, black stockings, and holding a bandolier, heavy with bullets. She looks up at the man next to her, wearing overalls and a fedora. She loves him; her upturned face telegraphing that love. But there, over the man's shoulder, is a second man, wearing a black hat, watches; he only has eyes for Tina.

The (adored) first man is Julio Antonio Mella, the second is Vittorio Vidali, assassin.

Diego Rivera, former lover of Tina Modotti, painted a crowded mural that featured his future wife, Frida Kahlo, but in the corner of his red star, hammer-and-sickle, armed-to-the-teeth extravaganza of violent revolution is this love triangle. Not a true triangle since Mella and Modotti were lovers, while Vidali longs for her. Modotti, furious enough over the depiction to end her friendship with Rivera. Later, when Diego was kicked out of the Party, she said that he was nothing more than a traitor who deserved to go.

*

Here's another image:

Tina and Mella are walking, her arm threaded through his, down a deserted street at ten o'clock at night on January 10, 1929. The air is cold. Then there is gunfire and Mella drops to the pavement, cries out that he is dying for the revolution, that the head of the Cuban government, General Machado is behind it. This might be true, or it might just as easily be a man named Jose Magrinat (another name Mella called out) or maybe someone sent by the fractured Communist Party (Mella likes Trotsky, who will be axed to death in Mexico in 1940). Two shots penetrate Mella's stomach and thorax. He breaks his arm. Vittoria Vidali, Party operative, in love with Tina, is a cat emerging from the shadows to help his fallen comrade. A distraught Tina on her knees in the street doesn't register the sudden appearance of Vidali; she is a mess at the hospital, unable to connect with anything, or anyone, around her. Diego Rivera and two friends stay with her during the two-hour operation that did nothing to save Mella.

Jose Magrinat, the man Mella named, an assassin later murdered in Cuba.

Tina answers her door the next morning, sleepless, disheveled, her clothing caked with blood. The press runs the nudes that Edward Weston had taken of Tina and they write about "The Sentimental Problem of Tina Modotti" calling her "passionate," implying a love triangle gone wrong saying she is a part of a murder plot. The police ransack her home, finding more of Weston's photographs (nudes), love letters, diaries—all of which they read before sending them to the newspapers.

She is arrested for the murder of Julio Antonio Mella, love of her life. They ignore her weeping on her knees by his side in the street. They treat her later shock as if it's calm. They think she's too calm.

The interrogation lasts hours, days, five full days—that picture she took of him sleeping? *Tina Modotti imagines Julio Antonio Mella dead.* The police want to know why she gave a false name that night. *Tina Modotti calls herself Rose Smith Saltarini, a teacher of English from San Francisco.* The police demand to know how Tina's arm could be through Mella's, so close, yet she wasn't shot herself? They walk her back to the crime scene, *I don't know, I felt gun smoke on my cheek.* People at Mella's funeral said she looked "old, like someone no one would want." Tina Modotti, they said, a Stalinist, wouldn't be above suspicion in killing a Trotskyite like Mella, she was a temptress, a tiger, a whore, her silent film roles come to life! Look at those photographs! Naked. Shameless. Scandalous. Isn't the victim married? What about Vidali? He's a killer. Isn't he in love with her? Isn't he?

They don't ask.

*

Mella's death became the center of Tina's life. She gave up photography at a time when she was much sought-after, including being offered a paid museum job (she wouldn't compromise her principles for a government position); her political commitment deepened, even if the Party was now the Party of Stalin. Instead of her former free, expansive, sweetly bohemian self, she became a kind of Party Puritan, checking her own behavior as if she were both matron and prisoner. Supporting the Party, being deported for the Party, spying for the Party, using an alias in the Spanish war zone for the Party all became a kind of honoring of the dead, as if loving the party was the same as loving Mella.

She said of the weeklong interrogation that it "didn't matter" that "whatever doesn't kill me makes me stronger." (Two years later, exiled from Mexico, broke and miserable in Berlin, hating the gray cold, unable to take pictures, she wrote to Weston that whatever didn't kill her only killed her.)

*

The Mexican government was never very enamored of the Communists; the foreign ones were particularly vulnerable since they could be deported. Tina Modotti, a small woman pushing middle age without a history of violence and by all accounts a good soul, was now accused of trying to assassinate the president. And just in time since Mussolini in 1930 was very interested in having her extradited, which is how she came to be a passenger on a shabby cargo ship ultimately bound for Italy.

Modotti loved Mexico, but she was resigned. Good Girls can handle resignation. Even if she faced certain death ("dangerous Communist") upon her arrival in Italy.

Except she never arrived in Italy because there was another passenger who happened to be on that same ship that wasn't even a passenger ship: Vittorio Vidali. When Tina arrived in Rotterdam, she simply disappeared.

Her deportation/flight from the authorities was the beginning of her fifteen-year "political marriage" to Vittorio Vidali, no longer content to be the man in Rivera's mural who only watches, waiting, and who mysteriously appeared under a streetlight as Julio Mella lay bleeding to death, and who only happened to find himself on the same beat-up Dutch cargo ship with its single prisoner, Tina Modotti. Men and art and politics, that is to say, the story of Tina Modotti's life. I like her pictures because they feel like they are the only place where she isn't being told who she is (a muse, a model, a comrade, or, in the case of Vidali, *mine*).

She was her radical father's daugher, then Robo's artsy dream doll, then Weston's partner in art and life and freedom; then Mella who loved the radical in her; then the covetous Vidali who waited until she died to tell the world who he decided she was. The costumes (Robo), the photographs (Weston), the written biography (Vidali). In some ways she is an example of thinking that love must be connected to your life's work, whether it's art or politics; the artistic couple gone a little mad. The Good Girl who too often tries to please, to be helpful, to be polite.

When she died, at the age of forty-five, slumped over in the back of a taxicab in Mexico City (having quietly returned to the place she loved best), subdued, her beauty no longer bright, her generous heart having simply stopped. A small photo of Julio Antonio Mella in her pocket.

A WAR OF MY OWN

Lee Miller

It's possible to start with World War II even though, in many respects, it is the end of Lee Miller's story. What I mean to say is that Lee Miller, born Elizabeth Miller in Poughkeepsie, New York, on April 23, 1907, had a life that sounds like a dream of a fabulist. Though she lived to age seventy, the Lee Miller that has influenced me was the Miller of everything up to and during the war years. Then she turned forty and became a mother.

Lee gave birth to her first and only child, divorcing her first husband (they had lived apart for years), to marry her second, the father of her child (why is it that a traditional heart can still beat in the wildest girl?). She became Lady Penrose, mistress of Farley Farm, an art-rich home, where she drank, became a cook with a Surrealist touch, and hostess to friends like Man Ray, Picasso, and Saul Steinberg, to name a few. There. That's the brief history her post-forty years.

I first noticed Lee Miller in Man Ray's photographs. It wasn't just that she was beautiful—and she is beautiful—it was also that she had that sort of look that allowed the viewer to *imagine* her. Because of that quality, every encounter made me see her a little differently than I did the time before, as if her image was always in some kind of motion. In a sense, that's the very thing that makes her image (for me) a work of art, that feeling of never being quite finished with what I'm seeing, the mystery of which deepens every time I run across it. Of all the men who made art inspired by her (and when I call her a work of art, I mean that her charisma wasn't wholly dependent on these various artists)—Picasso, Cocteau, Cornell, Man Ray—Man Ray was the most successful because he worked *with* her instead of purely interpreting her; his portraits feel collaborative.

For years I was drawn to her image. I didn't know who she was because my interest in her pre-dated *The Lives of Lee Miller,* her first biography (written by Antony Penrose), wasn't even published until 1985 (and I didn't read until well into the 1990s). For this reason it was still more years before I learned that she was a photographer in her own right. For me, as with all those famous fashion photographers who shot her for *Vogue* and other magazines during the years she was a professional model, and for Conde Nast himself, who rescued her from falling into a New York street when she was nineteen years old (thus beginning her modeling career), my interest in her began with her face.

Meet the Bad Girl

What else did I love in Lee Miller? I loved that she was sort of the quintessential Bad Girl. Tina Modotti, so similar in some ways, was more like the Good Girl to Lee Miller's Bad Girl—these women will always be twinned for me, even when one was small and dark and the other tall and golden, these fairy-tale girls. Recall the urge toward adventure and freedom in each woman with the difference that Modotti was often driven by a sense of service to others (the politics, maybe her penance for her sense of adventure and sexual freedom?), while Miller seemed completely, wonderfully, and gloriously about herself. She didn't take the things she wanted by promising to take on things she didn't want (penance), nor did she apologize. She wasn't one to surprise: she was always who she was, even though she said to her husband, Roland Penrose, in 1947, about to become a mother for the first (and only) time and anxious about surviving labor, *I kept saying to everyone, "I didn't waste a minute of my life—I had a wonderful time"* even though she added, . . . *if I had it to do over again I'd be even more free with my ideas, with my body and with my affections.*

It's hard for me, by turns phobic (flying, electricity, small spaces, including those fucking tiny houses), and neurotic, with just the slightest perfume of hypochondria, to imagine Lee Miller, who has captivated me for much of my adult life for her willingness to live her life all in, talking about the need to be freer with any part of herself.

For anyone who has read anything of Miller's extraordinary life—a novelist's dream—it would be easy to understand how jaw dropping a statement this is, it feels like the only possible response is, *get the fuck out of here.*

How could a classic Good Girl like me not fall for someone like Lee Miller. And fall I did, making novels and articles and box assemblages.

*

The War & the Past

When Lee Miller hitched a ride on a troop plane from England, she had been living in London with Roland Penrose, the man who was to eventually become her husband, and David Scherman, a twenty-five-year-old *Life* photographer. Soon he was coming around to the Miller-Penrose household, sleeping with Lee (monogamy wasn't part of the Penrose/Miller arrangement). At the time Lee was still married to her first husband, Aziz Eloui Bey, an Egyptian businessman who was living in Cairo, a good man who financially supported her despite their separation and her living arrangements. Whenever Lee left Roland she encouraged him to find someone to sleep with until her return; she was never interested in monogamy either for herself or for her lovers. It's worth noting that the Surrealists, Lee's friends, had a lot to say about sexuality, and their view of women appears to encourage sexual freedom in women, but the reality only sometimes supported this philosophy.

This was a problem for someone like Man Ray, whose love for Lee caused him to lose control, prowling the Parisian streets with a gun, then taking a self-portrait (*Suicide, 1932*) with a cigarette in his mouth, as he sits at a table with a noose around his neck, a bottle of poison, and a pistol aimed at his head. Lee really did believe in everyone following their own sexual interests and was notoriously free of jealousy. I'm guessing that a fair number of Surrealists weren't faced with their own double-standard because they were often involved with women who were unlike Lee, so how would they know if they, too, might find themselves one day running around Paris with a gun?

The men that Lee married, Aziz Eloui Bey (husband #1), gave her no-strings-attached money, even when she was off with other men, while Roland Penrose (husband #2) gave Lee a pair of solid gold handcuffs, a Surrealist gift, which she loved. Man Ray gave her a career and an introduction to his rarified art world (and his adoration), but he couldn't abide her independence. Even friendship wasn't possible until a few years after she left him; then they remained devoted to each other for the rest of his life.

Penrose had artistic aspirations. Lee, by age thirty-four, had been painted by Picasso six times, filmed by Cocteau, photographed by Man Ray numerous times. Joseph Cornell made

Lee Miller collages and boxes. What artist doesn't love a muse, even a little?

She had been a muse beginning in childhood with her father taking pictures of her, then a sought-after fashion model in New York, a Surrealist sweetheart, a Surrealist photographer, then a photojournalist, with a brief, accidental stint as a war photographer.

After taking pictures during the London Blitz (which didn't frighten her as much as one would think), and of land girls, and in local field hospitals, usually for British *Vogue,* all the while dying to get across to the Continent, she finally made it the last days of the war. When she landed in San Malo, Brittany, on August 13, 1944, she assumed, as everyone else did, that the Allies were "mopping up." What she found instead was a full-blown battle between the Germans and the Allies. Which she photographed. Which is how she became a combat photographer, by sheer serendipity, at a time when women weren't allowed to be combat photographers (*they tell you that the important pictures are taken on the battlefield, then ban you from the battlefield*). Miller wrote of her experience in San Malo, "I returned to the CA (Civil Affairs) villa and organized that I should stay in San Malo. . . . I was the only photographer for miles around and now I owned a private war."

Once in France Miller traveled with David Scherman, both of them taking pictures—he for *Life,* she for *British Vogue*—and wrote dispatches. Later, after they spent time together in the final days of the war, Scherman observed that in London Lee was "fastidious" about food and fashion, but ". . . in the excitement—joy—of battle, all this went out the window. For about a year, with occasional exceptions, she looked like an unwashed, unmade bed, dressed in o.d. fatigues, and dirty G. I. boots. . . . She thrived. . . ."

In her beloved Paris, she visited friends, some broken by the war.

She reports how, when she and Scherman were attached to an outfit of American soldiers, liberating parts of Europe, she "ground her heel in a dead, detached hand, and I cursed the Germans for the sordid, ugly destruction they had conjured up in this beautiful town." She runs. She slips on blood. *Christ, it was awful.*

Displaced children, people living in the street, French women collaborators with shaved heads, death, and smells of death. She saw the death camps, and piles of skeletal bodies heaped or spilling from open box cars. She took pictures of a group suicide of a high-ranking Nazi official's family, he and his wife and daughter, peacefully arranged in his study. Her foot once broke through the surface of a hillock she had scrambled up (to get a better picture), revealing the mass grave underneath. The brutality was shocking, and she recorded it, sending it to her editor at *British Vogue* with the headline "Believe it."

"She had done some work of which she was proud," writes biographer Carolyn Burke, "'but,' she [Lee] confessed, 'I got in over my head. I could never get the stench of Dachau out of my nostrils.'"

Lee took pictures that even the men wouldn't take, partly because of the lost physical distance between camera and subject. David Scherman said that Lee took pictures he couldn't take.

No telescopic lens meant coming in close.

I think about that a lot.

In Munich, Lee took a nap on Eva Braun's bed in her small villa. The furnishings were "strictly department store like everything in the Nazi regime: impersonal . . . average." A pair of exercise rings dangled from the ceiling in the upstairs hall. She wondered "which collector would capture the large brass globe of the world which opened . . . that once held the glasses and bottle for toasting . . . '*Morgen Die Ganze Welt*' . . . 'Tomorrow the World.'"

The pair also found their way into Hitler's pristine, featureless apartment with its "mediocre art"; Scherman photographing Miller as she washed off the dirt of Dachau in Hitler's bathtub. While staying in this apartment that "lacked grace and charm and intimacy" they learned of Hitler's death. She remained unforgiving of all things German (language, people, culture) for the rest of her life.

*

How did this beautiful woman, this Surrealist muse, who lived so many different lives by age forty find World War II as the place where felt most at home, following American troops for the next year as they advanced across Europe? It could be argued that her exterior reality finally matched up with her restless, sometimes ravaged, interior self.

*

Fathers & Nudity

Little Elizabeth Miller was raised in very comfortable circumstances in her native New York, the middle child, and only girl, of Florence and Theodore Miller. Her father was an executive with a firm based in Sweden, where he frequently traveled. The children grew up on an enormous farm, a kind of Eden, where they camped and built train engines that ran on a small track; rode the skis that their father made for them based on a pair he brought back from Sweden (a new thing for Poughkeepsie). Her father was an inventor and amateur photographer; his preferred equipment was a stereoscopic camera that developed prints to be viewed in three-dimensions, using a hand-held device.

Theodore Miller was progressive with regard to his daughter, though Florence Miller wished Elizabeth would be more feminine, maybe a ribbon or two in her hair? (In one of those unexpected reversals, Lee's older brother John liked the feminine clothing that his sister did not.) Father and daughter were close, sympathetic, sharing interests.

When I had my son, I was asked, more than once, if I would allow him to play with dolls. I shrugged, answered, if he wants to, I guess, even though I had never enjoyed playing with dolls myself. As far as my kid went, I didn't get the point of imposing a gender-reversed interest in the name of feminism.

So when we were asked about things like giving our son dolls, for example, we would just say, you know, instead of buying him dolls, we thought we'd have his dad stay home while I work. This was our joke, our way of life. You can give your kids all the contra-gender-roles books and toys you like, but if you live traditionally, that's the lesson they're really getting. More to the point, your kids are who they are. In other words, you can't just wish or buy gender equality into existence, you have to live it.

My mother, born in 1926, was raised in a traditional Italian home with a very indulgent father, and a very frustrated mother who didn't get along with her daughter since her daughter, my mother, made it clear that she "wasn't going to be a hausfrau," as if her mother, my grandmother, ever had a choice. My mother graduated high school two years early, went to work in advertising in New York, forcing the Bronx out of her voice before she was twenty. My mother, always glamorous, loved the business world, loved people, and loved being an aunt.

Then she moved to Los Angeles, met my father, an electrical engineer newly returned from three years in Saudi Arabia, and began her life as a glamorous stay-home wife and mother in the Valley (moving to Pasadena after I was born). Here is a typical photograph:

My mother, in her Burbank backyard with two other mothers—they in their capri pants and camp shirts, no makeup—

my Italian mother in black eyeliner and red lipstick, large gold hoop earrings, wearing a strapless, fitted sundress with a full skirt and black pumps, a choker at her throat, as they watched their kids splash around in the kiddie pool. She also painted one of the rooms in her house black (and her fingernails green), with the rest of the house all dramatic graphics and colors. In other pictures, she wears toreador pants with braid along the seams, and movie star sunglasses. A beautifully tailored suit. The New York girl learned to drive (though she did have an accident during her first driving test), cook, and clean. I will give this to my mother: she tried. She tried to be absorbed in her home, and in her wife role. She tied her thick, dark hair back in velvet ribbons, still dressed like she cared. Gold and silver at her throat and wrists and ankle. She socialized with the neighbor women, and had them over to "luncheon" (she was surprised they brought their kids along—I have no idea where she thought the kids would be, in the middle of the day at lunch time).

By the time we moved to Pasadena, and my sister (the fourth and last child) was born, my mother found a job at an ad agency in Los Angeles where her desk was directly beneath Liberace's swimming pool (he had an apartment on the top floor of their office building). It drove her crazy to be home.

It made me miserable not to have my mother home. I adored her because she was glamorous and fun and a great storyteller. We had many, many babysitters—some live-in, some daily—male, female, young, old, foreign-born from various countries (Denmark, Guatemala), white, African American, Latinx. Sometimes an additional housekeeper. My father, a man ahead of his time, spent evenings and weekends taking us places and caring for us; I have many more memories of him as a parent (getting us up the morning, getting us off to school) than I do of my mother, even though both parents worked.

Once, when driving with our son who was about six at the time, he asked me if a male friend of ours was coming over to the house. I said, No, he has to work. Our son gave me a sly smile, like he knows he's being played with, and said, going along with the joke he thinks he's getting, "Boys don't work." (That he didn't see everything J. did as "work" at that time is another story.) That's when I knew, as surely as my mother influenced my artistic life choices (with her glamour, her stories, her unmet aspirations, her discontent), that our kid had been pulled out of the mainstream.

I wrote a novel where a Renaissance girl lives with her artist father who falls into apprenticing her because she has a natural gift, and they live alone, and he is a retiring sort, and she wants to be a painter, like her father. He teaches her everything he knows, even though they're both aware that, as a woman, she will most likely never earn commissions, or have a patron. When this realization fully comes to her, and knowing her only life choice is marriage (or religion), she cries, asking, *Why anyone would marry someone who can make a triptych but cannot make a home?* Then adds, *Your instruction has ruined me.*

*

My mother's restlessness at being home and her choice to work elsewhere, even though my family didn't need the money; my son being raised by his father while I worked elsewhere (he is now pursuing a career in music and writing). My mother stepped outside the mainstream at a time when it wasn't common, especially if you didn't have a college degree and only wanted to be in business. Then I came along, then my son. Advertising, writing, music; our legacy.

Being outside the mainstream is the very short, simple answer to How One Becomes an Artist; that is to say, one doesn't become an artist or writer in order *to move* into the fringe. Look on the edge of any social map to find: *You are here.*

So, how did a beautiful, privileged white girl like Lee Miller become radicalized enough to feel most alive in a cataclysmic event like World War II, running *toward* it instead of *from* it?

*

At night—caresses. He begs me to undress and lie at his side. His caressing suppleness and mine, the feelings which run from head to toes—vibrations of all the senses, a thousand new vibrations . . . a new union, a unison of delicacies, subtleties, exaltations. . . . We sat up until two or three, talking. "What a tragedy that I find you and cannot marry you." It was he who was preoccupied with enchanting me. It was he who talked, who was anxious, who displayed all his seductions. It was I who was being courted, magnificently. . . . Endless stories about women. Exploits. Teaching me at the same time the last expertness in love—the games, the subtleties, new caresses. I had at moments the feeling that here was Don Juan indeed, Don Juan who had possessed more than a thousand women, and I was lying there learning from him, and he was telling me how much talent I had, how amazing an amorous sensibility, how beautifully tuned and responsive I was. . . ."You walk like a courtesan from Greece. You seem to offer your sex when you walk."

—Anais Nin, *Incest*

*

Voyager is a 1991 film, adapted from a novel by Max Frisch called *Homo Faber*. The time is 1957. An American engineer, played by Sam Shepard, is returning from a job in South America. On his flight home to New York, his plane develops engine trouble and crash lands, gently, no one hurt, in Mexico. A series of coincidences follow. On his first night home in New York (leaving his married mistress in his apartment), he ends up impulsively boarding an ocean liner bound for Europe (he is due on another engineering project in Italy, and must leave in a couple of weeks anyway).

On the ship he meets twenty-year-old Julie Delpy, who is planning to hitchhike to Greece to meet up with her college professor mother.

Julie and Sam quickly become friends; there is something each is drawn to in the other. They say good-bye when they arrive in port, but then run into each other again at the Louvre. Sam, concerned about her hitchhiking across Europe alone, makes the decision to rent a car and drive Julie to Greece. They are friends, they are familial with each other (given their age difference), they are attracted to each other, and partway into the road trip, Julie comes to Sam's room and they begin an affair. He feels something for her, some correctness (and she for him) that he hasn't felt since college, when the love of his life broke up with him and married someone else.

Of course, because the story leans heavily on Fate, and ends in Greece, and we learn more about Sam's broken college relationship (the love of his life got pregnant, then told him she got an abortion), we figure out before he does (but altogether too late) that he's been sleeping with his own daughter. The movie ends tragically, as it must.

My question when I saw it: Was he drawn to this girl, both comfortable with, and excited by, because of her genetic connection to the lost love of his life, or was he compelled by some vague recognition of self, his own genetic material, now hidden in plain sight?

It could be argued that the movie, being fiction, relies on "poetic incest," like Oedipus, for example; incest elevated. And there is a poetic component to the story of Anaïs Nin and her "lost" father, though there is an equally strong psychological argument, something along the lines of rewriting her abandonment, the thrill of being desired by the man who couldn't leave fast enough, a sense of control with the new situation, not to mention the erotic charge of engaging in the same taboo of Egyptian pharaohs and Greek gods, and also, you know, just being bad.

*

One of the things that interested me about the female photographers in this book is the nature of the relationships with their respective fathers. The elemental, timeless connection that seems outside of age and gender. My own father was curious about nearly everything, except people. He could build or wire anything. He painted pictures. He read. Took dance lessons at the urging of my mother. Gave me 3,000-year-old bead he found on an archeological dig in the Middle East; he also unearthed a rather plain jar that he donated to a museum. He was a train buff, which included sometimes playing a record of train sounds (why yes, it was just as entertaining as it sounds). He traveled, graduated college summa cum laude, and was halfway finished with his masters when he was twenty years old. I have a collection of keys from academic fraternities that my mother had made into a charm bracelet (he also gave my mother, in 1952, a 14-karat gold anklet—a slender snake chain with a charm of a heart and a key. I have that, too). He was a nudist, loved the desert, and became a certified organic farmer in the early 1980s, before it was fashionable. In 1960 he invested in a Las Vegas company that imported strings of the most whimsical Italian-made Christmas lights. He even invested in some wacky ceramics factory in Mexico that manufactured those hideous cats with the uplifted paw that were sold to Chinese restaurants. He contemplated working toward a PhD in computer science when he retired from Bechtel (one of a handful of firms where he worked in his lifetime, changing companies because he was scouted). He liked the theater. We toured historical homes. We went to art museums. We didn't interact as much as we parallel played. He was good with money. I don't know where the cats and Chinese restaurants came from.

*

"No one knows for sure who raped seven-year-old Elizabeth Miller; she was staying with family friends in Brooklyn and was left alone one day with either a brother-in-law or a nephew." Some say he was a sailor on leave.

The incident was further complicated by the gonorrhea she contracted. Lee's mother had been a trained nurse so the treatment fell to her. For the better part of a year, Lee's little body took "antiseptic sitz baths followed by the 'irrigation' of the bladder with a solution of potassium permanganate (the ominous-sounding equipment included a glass catheter, douche can, and rubber tubing), after which the patient was douched with a mixture of boric acid, carbolic acid, and several oils . . . the cervix had to be probed twice a week with a cotton-wool swab to remove secretions, then daubed with a solution of 'picric acid in glycerine.'"

Oh, and everything she touched was routinely sanitized.

The heart breaks.

*

"I don't feel toward you as if you were my daughter."
"I don't feel as if you were my father."
"What a tragedy. I have met the woman of my life, the ideal, and it is my daughter! I am in love with my own daughter."
—Anais Nin, *Incest*

*

Lee's father, in the spirit of getting his daughter to dissociate herself from the terrible event, told her that sex and love were different, entirely separate things. Just before her eighth birthday, he had her pose naked in the April snow as she tried not to shiver. As Carolyn Burke points out about Theodore Miller's "blend of therapy and Art," the snow photo was "inspired by Paul Chabas's *September Morn* (Theodore's was titled *December Morn*), a painting of a nubile nude emerging from a pool that provoked a national scandal when it was shown in New York the year before."

Lee's parents took her to a Manhattan psychiatrist who further encouraged this chasm between sex and love, the physical from the heart. In later years, Lee's genuine lack of sexual jealousy and possessiveness—often encouraging her lovers to take other, temporary lovers, if she was to be away for an extended period, and sleeping with whomever she liked, even if she was in a relationship (even if she was home)—drove men to distraction; a case of "be careful what you wish for" as some male fantasies go. Man Ray made *Object to Be Destroyed*, a sort of "ready-made" assemblage. He took a metronome and a cut-out photograph of Lee's eye with this message on the reverse: *Cut out the eye from a photograph of one who has been loved but is seen no more. Attach the eye to the pendulum of a metronome and regulate the weight to suit the tempo desired. Keep going to the limit of endurance. With a hammer well-aimed, try to destroy the whole at a single blow.* Man Ray intended to take a hammer to it (love as object), transforming it from assemblage to performance piece, but mostly he wanted to take a hammer to his faithless, but always honest about it, mistress.

It doesn't matter how spiritual the love, the message is always carried by the body. It can be expressed in the voice, the glance, the fingertips, in the love letter, the sonnet; it can be in the thoughtful gesture, the favor, the care for someone. And, naturally, through sex. The body is always integral to love. *I keep saying to everyone, "I didn't waste a minute of my life—I had a wonderful time," but I know myself now that if I had it to do over again I'd be even more free with my ideas, with my body and my affections.*

What prompted this sentiment? Was it that, despite all her adventures and abandon, nothing outside of her ever lined up properly with how she felt inside? The separation of sex and love? Just a fantasy, a wish. Unless it came true, and this is what it looked, and felt, like?

Maybe it was impending motherhood, since she said this just before giving birth. Male artists may live with their heads in the clouds, but women artists are realists when it comes to the home; it is the source of so much anxiety.

*

For all the men in Lee's life, her brother Erik noted, "He [her father] was the only man she could feel comfortable with and really love."

*

Consider the stereoscopic camera that Lee's father so loved. He continued to take nudes of his daughter well into her adulthood, including, but not limited to, front-facing nudes of her when she was in high school, and sometimes of her teenage friends, too. The camera's prints rendered the subject (Lee, his daughter, no longer a child, his muse of sorts) in 3-D, as if she was sitting there, small enough to hold in the palm of one's hand. There she is, posed with her hands behind her back as if she is bound at the wrists.

*

Nudity

When I was in college I enrolled in art history courses because I knew nothing and I wanted to know something. Art was my favorite subject in school, even though I was a mediocre art-ist at best, which wasn't all that troubling. Even though I was the Student of a Thousand Majors, I never majored in Art His-tory (my degree is in History), though I took a number of art history classes so go figure. The only thing I can say is that it wasn't the first time I held back from something I loved.

One of my classes included John Berger's program *Ways of Seeing*. I've never forgotten it. His episode on women in art ended with a casual discussion among 1972 era woman talking about women, and how they're seen. One woman said that she never sees herself as she is—she's always inside the mirror—unless she catches herself by chance, like in a shop window. But here is a lit-tle of what Berger had to say (I imagine Lee as her father's model through her childhood, youth, and young womanhood):

"A woman is always accompanied by an image of herself."

"To be naked is to be in disguise . . . to be on display is to have the surface of one's own skin turned into a dis-guise which cannot be removed."

"A picture is made to appeal to his sexuality—it has nothing to do with her sexuality."

"To be naked is to be oneself, to be nude is to be seen by others and yet not recognized as oneself. A nude has to be seen as an object in order to be nude."

"You paint a naked woman because you enjoy looking at her—then you put a mirror in her hand and call it vanity, thus morally condemning the woman you have depicted for your own pleasure."

It's no wonder Lee could transition so easily from being her father's subject, to fashion model, to Surrealist model.

*

Billie with Glass, 1971 by Ruth Bernhard is a black and white photo showing a naked woman, the picture cropped just below her breasts. She holds a square piece of glass over her face, just above her mouth, one hand on each side, elbows extended. Her face is made small by the glass. Because her mouth and top of her head are not refracted through the glass, the effect is that of two faces, as if the glass isn't just clear, but a mirror.

*

In my youth I was twice asked to pose nude in order to be sketched. The first time the request came from a small co-ed group, the members worked as graphic designers. They got together regularly in each other's living rooms for informal sketching sessions.

The second time I was asked by my roommate with the parents who walked out of post-revolution Budapest. She was taking an art class and wanted practice drawing from a live model. I refused the group request (I did pose, but clothed), and said yes to the second request, partly because my roommate reciprocated by modeling for me. The first situation made me feel that I would never forget that I was naked, while the second situation made me feel as if I was nude instead of naked.

*

Romaine Brooks, an American painter born in Rome in 1874, and a lesbian, made a series of nudes, which led to "groundbreaking the self-portrait of 1924"—her portraits are among my favorites—"[using] pictorial traditions that destabilize the categories of masculinity and femininity."

*

The War & the Past

After the war, Lee was reluctant to return to her former London life, or with Roland Penrose, the man with whom she shared that life. She was deflated at the thought of photographing shoes for *British Vogue,* unable to settle into the fashion work she had made before the war; her colleagues found her "unapproachable, as if the war and its aftermath had created a wall around her."

David Scherman, her lover and traveling companion was eager to separate from her, impatient with their restless, aimless post-war Europe wandering. He wanted her to go back to Roland before there was no going back. She was thirty-nine years old and in a more or less constant state of anger and agitation, having difficulty adjusting to the end of the war. Her looks were blown, as Scherman wrote to his brother, "She is getting old and with it fat, and she won't face up to it."

She returned to London where she lived with a kind of nervy joy, finding herself the lady of the house (literally, she become Lady Penrose when she married again), in the English countryside, with a garden, and house guests, and a baby. She drank to excess, burst into tirades, and complained of depression to Dr. Goldman. "There's nothing wrong with you," he is said to have replied, "and we cannot keep the world permanently at war just to provide you with entertainment," as if she wasn't her own razed village.

*

If you grew up in Southern California during the sixties and seventies, particularly if you spent any time at all in the beach communities (or lived there, as I did from time to time), you understood that the standard for beauty was blonde and tan. I was dark-haired with a pale complexion sometimes referred to as "butt white," which, of course, only makes sense if one has tan lines, which I did not. I was very self-conscious. I was, and am, just under 5'2", something that helped the situation not at all. And I spoke quickly, with enthusiasm, often about books or other things I cared about. Caring about a life of the mind while living at the beach on the Balboa Peninsula pegged me as The Smart Girl, which tells you how low the bar was set. It wasn't that I thought blondes were stupid; it was more that if you were blonde, your job was done.

For example, the girl across the street who lived in her parents' beach house was blonde, buxom, long legs, sunny personality, desirable even if she had nothing to say—and it should be said that having nothing to say isn't really a hinderance if you spend time with people who have no interest in listening—the quintessential California girl. It was like she had been built to specification: blonde, rich, going to the University of Southern California.

It wasn't as if I couldn't see the attraction, whether male or female, even if I wasn't attracted. Too much time spent in a blonde world left me jaded *and* secretly wishing to be blonde and tan. Lee Miller was blonde. It was very confusing.

That boyish side-parted blonde hair, the heavy-lidded, ice-blue eyes, a figure that is more delicate from the waist up, a little heavier in the hip and legs; sexy without effort. Her allure wasn't in her clothes, or makeup; there was something knowing about her, that indefinable *something*. My oldest friend, S., had it, too. Lee fell just short of perfection; she was perfectly imperfect. (*A great painting comes together, just barely.* Picasso.) It was rumored a glass manufacturer made champagne glasses to the dimensions of her breasts.

One of my favorite paintings is by Man Ray, who wanted to be a painter more than he ever wanted to be a photographer, another reminder that talent is a gift, is called *Observatory Time – The Lovers, 1936.* Miller's red lip-sticked closed lips float in a cloudy sky, above a stark landscape of hills. Even though the content is realistic, the work is mysterious, curious. Then, because he was a genius photographer, he placed a sofa beneath the large (eight feet by three feet) painting, and posed a clothed model on the sofa; she lies mostly on her side, her right arm reaching up to Lee's lips.

A second photograph shows the same sofa, a naked model beneath the painting, also lying on her side, the profile of her figure echoing the rise and fall of Lee's mouth. At her feet is a table with a chess board, the pieces arranged as if for a game to begin (Man Ray and Marcel Duchamp, chess opponents; I seem to remember reading that Duchamp rated people on a scale from one-to-ten, with Man Ray as the sole person in his life who earned a ten).

There is a third print, where the nude model sits in profile (sofa, table, chess game, Lee's lips), her knees pulled up to allow her to wrap her arms around them as she buries her face.

Two more Man Ray objects, made in 1936, are the classic Venus torsos; Man Ray wrapping each one in a web of rope, suggesting a kind of corset, the body contained and eroticized within a web of rope.

*

Number of novels I've written influenced by Lee Miller: 5. Box assemblages: 6.

*

Favorite Lee picture: *Exploding Hand, 1930*. A woman's hand reaches for the glass door of a jewelry store that has been scratched so many times by diamond rings it looks like an explosion. (I'm crazy for Meret Oppenhiem, she of the fur-covered teacup, who also made a "diamond" ring set with a sugar cube.)

*

It's believed that Anais Nin's incestuous relationship with her father was encouraged by a therapist. The idea was that she should seduce, then abandon him.

*

This from Man Ray's private notebook, a word game: INCEST IS NICEST.

*

Alfred Stieglitz was married (unhappily) with a grown daughter when he started up with Georgia O'Keeffe. He made photographs of O'Keeffe's hands, breasts, torso. Her face. Her unbuttoned shirt, camisole, little black straw boater. She often looked as if she had just been roused from a post-coital nap. "I was photographed with a kind of heat and excitement and in a way I wondered what it was all about." O'Keeffe was 29; he was 52. Old enough to be her father.

In 1927, Dorothy Norman, a young, dark-haired woman (Stieglitz's type) came into his gallery and they began an affair that lasted until his death in 1946. He took nudes of *her,* some were exhibited alongside pictures of O'Keeffe, the one person who knew, precisely, the circumstances under which such pictures would be taken. When Norman met Stieglitz she was 22 and he was 64. Old enough to be her grandfather.

*

I once read something very dark about Man Ray, involving sex, and a little girl, himself in his teens. If I seem vague it's because, if what I read is true, then I can't comfortably love his work anymore.

*

There is a perennial interest in The Why of Creativity. *Why* do we need to know? *What* good will it do? *Who* will care?

A short answer to the *why* of art could be found in Surrealism as a response to World War I. The world hadn't seen an event so cataclysmic, so *nightmarish*—horses blown to pieces, their limbs hanging in trees. Gas masks that made the soldiers appear robotic and alien; gasses that destroyed the organs; machines that flew and sprayed bullets. Try being a part of *that* and wonder if you can tell the difference between waking life and dreams.

America doesn't love art, despite turning out art and artists, musicians, and writers, and actors, and filmmakers (the culture has a similar issue with intellectualism). When the United States invaded Iraq, the national museum was looted while the oil fields remained secure in case, you know, anyone doubted what America considered valuable. I only wish that choice wasn't representative but I promise you that it is.

*

Disturbing Letters is a short story by Lee Miller about a young, privileged girl, the daughter of a judge, who is receiving a series of letters commenting on her attire and behavior (the letter writer finds both too sexy, too *declasse*). She eventually discovers that the letter writer is none other than her father, the judge.

*

Fathers & Nudity

When Lee Miller was living with Man Ray (she was in her early twenties, he was 17 years older and smitten. They could be seen walking the streets of Montparnasse—she young, tall, blonde; he short, dark—attached to each other by a gold chain) her father came through Paris on one of his many business trips. He and Man Ray got on very well (they shared a passion for photography, and those other troublesome things that I don't want to think about).

Here's a Man Ray photograph that has often given me pause: Theodore Miller, in suit, tie, and round eyeglasses, looks into the lens, his hands folded on Lee's lap as she curls up on his lap, her beautiful face in profile, eyes closed, her head tucked up under his chin. She wears a modest dress, with a feminine pattern; demure. In this picture, Theodore is so at ease, so comfortable and familiar with the figure of his grown daughter, who leans so close into him it's hard to believe they aren't recently reunited lovers, or some sort of modern Pieta (Michelangelo of Montparnasse). The way she melts into him reminds me of someone who has missed someone so much that all she can do is breathe, *you're here.*

Not to forget that Lee's older lover is taking the picture. The picture intimate; the act voyeuristic.

Another picture, this one taken by Theodore Miller. When Theodore traveled though Paris, Lee accompanied him to

Stockholm, where they had adjoining hotel rooms—I'm assuming—her father photographing her naked and posed, in a bathtub. I wonder whose bathtub? Which room? I'm reminded of the road trip in *Voyager* where Sam Shepherd and Julie Delpy have separate rooms, not that it mattered.

After Sweden Lee and Theodore stopped in Hamburg, definitely sharing a room, purchasing a Mainbocher gown for her.

Back in Paris, around the time of the father-daughter Pieta portrait, Man Ray and Theodore took a series of nudes of Lee with two other models, and with one other model that is, according to Carolyn Burke, "in a position that stops just short of lesbian sex." Pictures of Lee in her bed in "the most contorted poses—she arches back over the bed or lies with her legs up the wall, pubic region exposed."

Do I believe, as Lee's brother claimed, that Theodore Miller was the only man she ever truly loved and trusted? *Yes* (you can see it in Man Ray's dual portrait). Do I think that their relationship was unusual, carelessly crisscrossing every line ever drawn? *Yes*. But I also have to say this: Theodore Miller was also the agent of her escape, attempting to emotionally rescue her from her rape, funding her interests, her travels, her studies. Maybe the reason she always came back to him was because he always let her go.

*

War & the Past

World War I broke many people, some of them artists. More than seven million horses died in the war as well. I trip on that number because I know the horses weren't alone, and because of the horses, those beautiful animals, themselves. The painter, Henry de Groux, said the war, along with being "truly opulent in its excess of horror," was "like a machine functioning in the void." German artist and socialist Kathe Kollwitz (one of the first art books I ever bought was a book of her prints) lost two sons in the war. She made war pictures, and said, "I have repeatedly attempted to give form to the war. I could never grasp it."

The Disasters of War by Francisco Goya is a series of eighty-two prints done between 1810 and 1820. They were published thirty-five years after his death in 1828. His own title for them was *Fatal consequences of Spain's bloody war with Bonaparte, and other emphatic caprices.* Goya was a court painter who walked the edge, as so many court painters did, between showing his subjects honestly, and showing them as they wanted to be shown. This need to glorify could extend to paintings about the righteousness of war, and heroism, ideas that Goya rejects in *The Disasters of War.* The plates run the gamut of the effect of the war on individuals, as well as famine, atrocities, degradation, and the humiliation that comes from being occupied. The images are graphic; dismemberment, torsos impaled on tree branches, rapes, pile and piles and piles of bodies. Like a series of photographs.

Picasso's *Guernica* (1937) hung in the Museum of Modern Art until 1981, after being shown in Paris. Picasso didn't want the painting returned to Spain until democracy returned as well. I never had a chance to see it when it was in New York, though I did get to see it in Spain in the 1990s, at the Museo Reina Sofia. It wasn't crowded, there was no rush or jostling for position. The painting does not disappoint; for me it was that nexus of wish and fulfillment.

An art history professor, Philip Leider, introduced me to *Guernica* in a class he taught on Picasso. Mr. Leider was probably in his mid-forties (I'm guessing. Early fifties?) when I took his class, a man who already had another career before this one (he was the founding editor of *ArtForum,* which he left in 1971), without any art history degrees (he did have a law degree). He was an enormously popular teacher. When he explained, in his

New York accent, that he got interested in art because he and friends would agree to "meet underneath the *Guernica*," when convening in the city, I realized that museum art wasn't outside the realm of ordinary life—it was part of ordinary life, so that when I finally saw the painting in person, I also saw those boys from the boroughs.

*

Philip Leider's lectures were these sort of energetic, highly opinionated, animated affairs; he didn't just show slides of the work, he included a variety of seemingly disparate connections, as he paced in the dark, occasionally stopping at the lectern to read something. When he was teaching Picasso, he put up a photograph he had taken of a student he saw on campus because she resembled Marie-Therese Walter and, suddenly, that girl that Picasso took up with, painted, had a child by, came to life in this contemporary college girl, which in turn, brought Picasso and his work to life. But Leider also brought in historical events, commentary, quotes from the artist, or other artists, or cultural critics; he didn't just build context, he built a narrative; and that narrative made it clear what he loved (and I always loved what he loved because he loved it and that made me love it, too), and that art was a living thing. It was changing, and human, and beautiful, or shallow, and facile, or the artists were beautiful or shallow or casually cruel (Picasso, for example), but art mattered. The importance of art was inextricably wound into everything human. I have never been in anyone's home where there wasn't at least one art-related thing, even if it was some crummy, sentimental landscape. It kills me when people dismiss art, or cut it from schools in favor of something "important."

I often think of Philip Leider, pausing in the middle of one of his Beat-inflected, perfectly articulated lectures, stopping to look at a slide on the giant screen hung behind him, really look at the work, as if he was seeing it new, in the way loving someone can just happen to you all over again, even if you spend every day with them. It was like a tiny stutter, a moment of wonder, the littlest fermata.

Here's the last thing I'll say about Mr. Leider: he didn't approach his subject with irony, so his emotional connection to the work that he showed was in no way mitigated. He never catered to the students, nor was he unkind or disdainful. You knew that he was a paid professional, doing his job with the integrity of someone who actually cares about the job they're doing, and no matter how cool, how ageless his demeanor, he maintained a student-teacher distance, because that was the deal. During breaks, he went outside and smoked a cigarette (smoking was allowed inside the auditorium as well), alone; I never once saw him socialize with a student, and we all were so taken with him, so it wasn't indifference or dislike that kept us away. It was The Deal. Hollywood loves one type of teacher, you know, passionate, wise, either *Dead Poets Society* (posh school) or *Stand and Deliver* (inner city school), always awakening the dormant scholar in each student, lifting every class to a new awareness through questionable pedagogical methods. These teachers say, or do, things you really can't say, or do, to students if you hope to keep your job (or your liberty). I've taught college-age students (and older), on and off, for twenty-five years, so I know a little about being in the classroom. What I liked about Mr. Leider was his professionalism; all his emotion went into his subject, not into us.

*

Miller photographs: A living head beneath a glass bell; the glass door of a jewelry store so scarred by the diamond rings of customers, every hand that reached out looked to be exploding; a tiny, solarized piano; patterns in the sand on the Sahara Desert; a picture frame in a torn screen that looks out on the vast nothing of the Egyptian landscape. Those pictures of Dachau? The bodies, the beatings, the suicide with the perfect white teeth, the shaved heads of female collaborators. Bathing in Hitler's bathroom during the hours that he and Eva Braun are killing themselves, the phones still live in his Munich apartment? How can your dreams even begin to deliver that?

*

There is economy of language and poetry in Miller's war pieces for *British Vogue*. The weather: *Tonight was brilliantly, bitterly cold. The day had been icy and the blue shadows of the broken world clutched at the sunlight,* or *It was a gray day. Far off, storms lurked and prowled, looking for a place to settle. . . .*

She wrote about going into German homes where the monograms on the linen and silver didn't match the names on the mailboxes. A lesser writer would use the word "looted."

Maybe Holtzwihr never was a pretty town. I'll never know . . . the ruined church, the smoldering houses and the newly-laid shell fire stank. . . . Jebsheim must have been one of the prettiest towns in Alsace. It stank too. The journalistic and the lyrical, the simplicity of describing a ruined village, *maybe it was never pretty. I'll never know.* She is there and not there; she is at the crossroads of a life and a casualty of war; when she describes the viability, personality and death of the town, she is talking about people.

She wrote little novels: *On the window seat was a set of photo albums, dating from a long time ago when a pair of babies was baptized in long, flossy dresses on a cushion. I don't know which child it was, the right or the left, but he grew up. He had holidays in pretty scenery, he met docile looking girls, he went to University, and he got married himself to a buxom dame who produced a child for him in about 1933. The book progresses and there are a lot*

*of professional pictures of banquets where people are dressed in uni-
forms and there are snapshots of his several children, by now in little uniforms of a madchen schule. They are quite young and blond
and climb on his knees and wear his Nazi party hat in his next to
last pictures. There are photos of him in the Wehrmacht: the conquering hero in front of the national monuments to Europe's freedom, and there the pictures stop. Pretty little baby he was.*

She brings the war down to a personal level, taking a rank-
ing Nazi officer from baptism, through his life, his marriage,
his children, his death, then exploding that life to represent the
war. The deftness of the Nazi party hat as part of a celebration
and the innocent play of a parent and child. Miller explains
nothing; she never steps on her own meaning.

*

*It is difficult for a woman to define her feelings in a language which
is chiefly made by men to express theirs.*
—Thomas Hardy, *Far From the Madding Crowd* (1874)

*

*She's having a tough time, largely through her own making, and
sooner or later she is going to break to pieces like a bum novel.*
—David Scherman, photojournalist, writing to his brother
about Lee Miller

*

Hemingway was eighteen years old when he was seriously
injured in the Great War. He was also decorated, in love with
an older woman, got engaged, got left, and returned home; he
was not yet twenty years old. But love and war had imprinted
him, and the rest of his life was spent restlessly moving from

place to place, woman to woman, conflict to conflict (the Spanish Civil war, World War II, China in 1941, accompanying Martha Gellhorn). Along the way he had a series of accidents, three children, a Nobel Prize and pretty much alienated anyone who ever loved him. At age sixty-one, he committed suicide.

There are a handful of men associated with war-related books: Stephen Crane, Michael Herr (whom I once met in London when my agent and I were on our way to meet my publishers for lunch, and he insisted we stop at a pub for a quick drink; he was that sort of man, lovely in so many ways, who often needed a quick drink. Michael Herr was already having his quick drink. Before lunch); Tim O'Brien, Tobias Wolff, Erich Maria Remarque, Joseph Heller, Kurt Vonnegut, Norman Mailer, Graham Greene, Dalton Trumbo and, of course, Ernest Hemingway, who kept a small leather bag with "charms" among them a ring set with bullet fragments, and a piece of shrapnel.

The world breaks everyone and afterward many are strong in the broken places. But those that will not break it kills. It kills the very good and the very gentle and the very brave impartially. If you are none of these things you can be sure it will kill you too but there will be no special hurry.

—E. Hemingway

Age, Beauty, and Falling Behind

Georgia O'Keeffe once said that she was "one of the few artists, maybe the only one, who is willing to talk about my work as pretty." Hunter Drohojowska-Philip wrote that O'Keeffe "comprehended the subversive possibilities in choosing the 'feminine imagery of flowers.'" She understood that "pretty was derided for its association with female creativity. Her response was not to discard prettiness but to cast off the masculine assumption that categorized prettiness as inferior. O'Keeffe ascertained that the only true manner by which women could make art as equals was to make art differently, and according to their own sensibilities, experiences and contexts."

For example, write what you think of as a serious novel with the word "quilt" in the title and see what happens. If "women's fiction" or "chick flick" didn't carry a whiff of dismissal, there would be no problem with these designations. (*The men tell you that the only pictures worth taking are on the battlefield, then they ban you from the battlefield.*) Substitute "chick flick" or "women's fiction" for any, say, ethnicity, connected to what you will or won't read, or see, and hear how it sounds—because that's *exactly* how it sounds.

My ceramist friend, Joan Takayama-Ogawa, who is collected by museums and individuals and shown in galleries, has struggled with her work being called decorative, or pretty, even though it is both. "Decorative" may be the language, but the message is about the Japanese American experience; it's about internment camps, and the injustice and violence, and theft suffered by Japanese Americans in this country. Even if the piece is a whimsical teapot, it's still about Hiroshima and Nagasaki. "Decorative" becomes code.

Kehinde Wiley's paintings with backgrounds that resemble wallpaper, and contemporary African American figures who reference classical figures in historical European art, are beautiful.

Gertrude Stein said that beauty comes with rapture. Andre Breton said that it will be convulsive.

To put it another way, *Beautiful is a term that rarely can be applied to painting anymore . . . but in Rothko's case, 'beautiful' is not inappropriate. . . . The beauty of the work has nothing to do with its bite. . . . Beauty tends to be misleading; to disguise—not express—the real content, as Mozart's tragic passion is obscured for some people by his elegance.*

—Elaine de Koonig, 1958

Georgia O'Keeffe said of painting a shanty, "I can paint one of those dismal-colored paintings like the men. I think just for fun I will try—all low-toned and dreary with a tree beside the door." When it was shown she said, "The men seemed to approve of it. They seemed to think that maybe I was beginning to paint." She also said, "I found I could say things with color and shapes that I couldn't say any other way—things I had no words for." Most people crave approval, artists most of all because their very livelihood depends on it (and that's the least of it), so for her to write about color and voice, then to say that her work was thought to be better when using dark, muted colors, it all just becomes another way of asking a woman to be softer, quieter.

There are photographs of Lee Miller in her late teens, early twenties, taken by the leading fashion photographers (Arnold Genthe, Edward Steichen, George Hoyningen-Huene, Horst), and *the* art photographer of the era, Man Ray (who really immortalized her most thoroughly). There are her self-portraits, bringing to light the role Miller played in her own image, even when she wasn't the one tripping the shutter. There are her father's portraits, which are nothing short of arresting, affectionate, disturbing. Flipping through those early pictures—fashion, art, nude studies—you think, *beautiful, beautiful, beautiful, beautiful, beautiful.*

Beauty is a woman's problem, wait, let me rephrase that, beauty in women is a societal problem, because women aren't allowed to age. (*She is getting old and with it fat, and she won't face up to it.*) Who can deny the relief when an actress still "looks good," and the discomfort when she hasn't "held up." Aging in America is treated like a moral failing, as if it were a choice and you chose excess instead of denial. We don't like to factor in genetic luck (or bad luck). If the plastic surgery is bad, it's somehow the fault of the woman, and not the surgeon. Lee Miller had a late-in-life facelift (and it was the surgeon's fault).

Just imagine how hard that fade must be when you were painted, photographed, and filmed by everyone who mattered? What is it like when you were defined by your face and figure and your allure?

In the film *The Object of Beauty,* a young woman who cannot hear steals a tiny Henry Moore statue belonging to guests in the London hotel where she works. When asked why she did it she said, "Because it spoke and I heard it."

Robert Motherwell said of artist Joseph Cornell, *"He forces you to use the word 'beautiful.' What more do you want?"*

Gertrude Stein said, *"We are always the same age inside."*

Now You See Her (1994) is the story of a woman turning forty and literally disappearing. I chose forty because of all the mythology that surrounds it; it's The Big Milestone, even if today Fifty is the New Forty. I am now many years past forty and I have some sense of what it's like to be a Woman of a Certain Age. I color my hair because if I let it go gray I immediately gain five years, and I cannot stand the judgment of five more years on my age. The suppleness of my mind is nothing next to my late middle age, my Defining Characteristic. When I wrote *Now You See Her* I wasn't yet forty and was often thought to be younger than my age anyway, but I had already seen how women "disappear" in America when they get older. Part of the problem are those handful of aging women that everyone thinks are "still sexy," like Helen Mirren, or Gloria Steinem, or some aging supermodel who's kept her figure (the impossible standard never goes away). I was interviewed on the radio in Seattle where the interviewer, a man, explained to me how the premise of my book was "completely false because Ann-Margret was fifty and she was a fox." The whole interview was about how I was wrong, culminating with the comment that he "hadn't actually had the time to read my book, but he read the flap copy." These celebrities are held up to women as aspirational in the same way "self-made men" are held up to everyone as examples of being able to make it in America.

Lip service is routinely paid to "inner beauty." As if anyone really cares. No, as if anyone would actually take the time to talk to you, to get to know you, to see who you are on the inside, unless you already command the room. Instead, you enter room after room after room, knowing that you will be ignored or dismissed unless you somehow catch someone's attention. There will be assumptions made about you—"older women are bitchy and impatient" when really you've just grown tired of asking your server for a glass of water for the fifth time. I am not bitchy, even when I'm being overlooked, but I fully understand why some older women do get impatient. I don't know why, but I thought that things would be different for my generation than they were for my mother. You aren't a person; you're a collection of preconceived ideas. You have to make your own peace with it, you really do.

I wasn't a great beauty in my youth, but I was cute enough. In a way, that was a blessing because I knew, as I aged, I wouldn't have as much to lose. I wouldn't feel it as acutely as someone like Lee.

This is from the *New York Times,* September 3, 2000, "An Art World Figure Reemerges, Unrepentant": an interview with my old teacher, Philip Leider, where he succinctly explains what it means to be in the center, then on the periphery. He's talking about culture and art, but it could be about Lee Miller.

Falling Behind turns out to be a stage in one's career as real as the stages of Paying Your Dues, Getting In, Being on Top of Things, the nice period of Instant Comprehension when you don't need anyone to tell you what's going on, then a kind of Unconscious Withdrawal, then a kind of Conscious Withdrawing, with snarling and anger and the certainty that everything has turned to nonsense. And then, if you're still alive, there's Falling Behind.

Miller's life was such a thrilling tale of privilege; an unusual relationship with her father that is ambiguous, defying pure condemnation, while supporting her many jags, as she called her burning interests that would flare and fade. Europe, Conde Nast, modeling, Man Ray, solarization, muse/photographer/actress. Opened her own successful photography studio in Manhattan with her younger brother, Erik; impulsively married a rich Egyptian businessman she knew in Paris, expatriated to Cairo, taking trips into the desert; then roamed the Balkans with the man she would eventually marry and have a child with, who would also give her a title but before that, she photographed and wrote about WWII, then settled into comfort in the English countryside, then became a "surrealist" cook. She also lost her looks by her mid-thirties, was a heavy smoker and alcoholic, dying at the age of seventy.

Yet the life she seemed to be looking for, and the one she couldn't leave once she was in it, was a war. It was a violent, chaotic locale, recognizable in that the aftermath didn't seem like an aftermath, but just more of the same for her. As everything wound down, and her fellow soldiers were impatient to return home, Lee kept traveling: to Vienna (more chaos, a *Third Man* world of several foreign occupations, and corruption); to Eastern Europe, broke, wandering, avoiding the thinly veiled ultimatums of the man she would eventually marry because she already was home among the elegant ruins.

(When Lee learned she was pregnant while on a photography assignment in post-war Europe, she wrote to Roland, her artist lover, that she was happy about the baby, then added "There is only one thing. MY WORK ROOM IS NOT GOING TO BE A NURSERY. How about your studio?")

The war made, then ended her career as a writer and photojournalist, since she was incapable of making the transition into fashion or advertising photography. Audrey Withers, her *British Vogue* editor, who had supported her war correspondence, said,

"Lee came into her own during the war. It had an extraordinary effect on her. Afterwards, nothing came up to it. She was not meant to be married, have children, or live in the country. She thought she wanted security but when she had it, she wasn't happy. She couldn't write."

And now we're full circle to the artist-wife-mother conflict. Instead of embracing her body of work, and her experiences, she simply put them all away. For her, that life—those lives— were over by age forty, when she married and had a child. She wasn't much of a mother. It must have seemed like someone else's life, the way it does when you settle into domesticity later, after. Maybe it was age. Her son said that his mother drank because she had undiagnosed post-traumatic stress syndrome from her war experiences, but I often thought she found a home in the war, that it was more comfort than cause, because of what happened to her as a child in that Brooklyn apartment. In the end, even the war turned out to be more than she bargained for (those camps), and she did go to pieces like a bum novel.

All she ever said was, "I used to take a few photographs."

BE ORIGINAL OR DIE!

Madame Yevonde

There is a very cool, very hip jewelry store in my little city. Everyone knows this store which also sells some household items, large and small, and artwork, but it is predominantly a jewelry store. It's tasteful in that cool, hip way.

One day at the market I ran into the owner, who offered to come over to my house to look at some shadow box assemblages that I had been making for the last ten years. I didn't want to say yes because I wasn't planning to show them to anyone, but also this guy isn't the nicest guy. Then I thought maybe it would do me good to have someone who knew me as a "close acquaintance," the way you know people whose places you frequent, so I took a deep breath and said okay.

We weren't complete strangers. I was hesitant, and I had not asked him over, was nervous to have him over. His sole purpose in coming to my home was to look at the shadow boxes. I had no expectations of receiving praise; the best I hoped for was some constructive criticism, and even then, I wasn't quite ready for that conversation. I'm not an artist and the boxes were something I did for myself and gave to friends, or sometimes sold, though I had recently had an art show (and in 2014, had one of my boxes on display, in its own case, at the Portland Art Museum—which is another story).

After walking into the dining room of my 115-year-old bungalow (my shadow boxes are kept on the third floor, not in the dining room nor on display) he folded his arms, and began shaking his head, then decided that he couldn't wait another minute to comment on the paint color. Imagine that someone has just been served a meal of rancid meat with a side of spinach so old it has liquified in the crisper, followed by a chaser of spoiled milk and you'll have some idea of his reaction to the color of the narrow section of wall between the ceiling and the wainscoting. My self-invited guest just kept circling the room, shaking his head with his bad spinach expression and saying, "Oh, no. No. No. No."—as he kept glancing around my fairly modest dining room in disgust—"No." Then ordered me to have it repainted a shade of brown. Immediately.

I was reminded of Georgia O'Keeffe's painting of the shanty, "low-toned, dismal-colored" and "dreary" that "the men," as she called her fellow artists, praised, saying her decision to abstain from color meant that she was "finally beginning to paint."

My guest told me that he and his wife were in the process of building their own home, which I knew without asking, was going to be some kind of mid-century modern (everyone with means was currently in the midcentury modern mode). I'm pretty sure the walls would be white (where painted), maybe a nice neutral grass wallpaper, and possibly tasteful wood paneling on a single accent wall somewhere. Not that there would be too many walls since having unbroken expanses of glass is practically required. Everything would be minimalist, you know, *clean*.

A few years ago, at a mid-century exhibition, the Los Angeles County Museum of Art recreated the Eames's living room, dining room—basically the entire, smallish downstairs. There was shit everywhere. Everywhere! Books, toys, folk art, vases, candlesticks—stuff, lots of stuff—not like hoarding but more like the 1975 home of a Berkeley professor and his photographer wife who live in a modest, but beautiful mid-century in Palo Alto and like to collect travel souvenirs—masks, kilims, carvings, throws, and are really into Aboriginal art. It was that house.

The dining room color that this man found so abhorrent was a mid-range lavender made by Crayola and called, I believe Easter Egg, or some such thing. I'm not a fan of purple, or lavender, unless it's in small doses, if at all. Our dining room is mostly wainscoting and box beams that are painted the dusty silvery green of drought-resistant plants because I'm not enamored of forest green, so it isn't a strong green as much as natural green. I wanted the accent color to be a washed-out shade of rose, except our painter talked me into letting him decide the other color since it would cover such a small space (the same small space that had so offended my guest). So, I said okay. It looks fine. It works in its weird way. So we left it.

*

In his book of essays *Chromophobia,* David Batchelor tells of going to a very nice late-nineteenth/early-twentieth-century home in an affluent English neighborhood. Despite the traditional facade of the exterior, the interior was an expanse of white. "This was assertive silence, emphatic blankness, the kind of ostentatious emptiness that only the very wealthy and the utterly sophisticated could afford. It was strategic emptiness, but it was also accusatory." We have all seen this home in movies, and in magazines; many of us have been in this home at some point, or aspired to it. It never leaves us indifferent, even if it's just to wonder *who cleans it?* How do they keep it clean? What about red wine (the notion that color could damage a home)?

Batchelor goes on to say:

. . . A very paradoxical, inside-out world, a world where open was also closed, simplicity was also complication, and clarity was also confusion. It was a world that didn't readily admit the existence of other worlds. Or it did so grudgingly and resentfully, and absolutely without compassion. In particular, *it was a world that would remind you, there and then, in an instant, of everything you were not, everything you had failed to become, everything you had not got around to doing, everything you might as well never bother to get around to doing because everything was made to seem somehow beyond your reach* [italics are mine], as when you look through the wrong end of the telescope. . . . There is a kind of white that is more than white, and this was that kind of white.

*

I first became aware of the photography of Madame Yevonde in 1990 when J. and I were in London. Every so often we would happen upon a poster promoting her exhibition at the National Portrait Gallery. The poster showed a cropped portrait from Madame Yevonde's *Goddess* series—an aristocratic woman, not a professional model, muse, or lover—done up as Medusa, and what a Medusa! Her beautiful face, powdered a deathly pale, her lips prefiguring the goth fashion in a shade of berry so dark it looked black. Her made-up eyes, that were a deep blue-purple. In her hair and wrapped around her slender throat were a series of rubber snakes, in browns, yellows, and black diamond patterns, whose eyes and scales studded with tiny rhinestones that caught the light. The background was a wall of sparkling, shimmery pink. The model was so arresting, and the presentation so deliberately artificial, a true balance of allure and danger, that I thought, as I stood in an overheated tube station, looking again at this poster, that I would give up seeing anything else in London if I could see this one show. I had never heard of Madame Yevonde and, as I would soon learn, no one I met, even at American art colleges, had either.

*

Why did I fall so hard for Madame Yevonde?

I could say that it was my life at the time, which felt perfect to me. I was on an extended six-week vacation in Europe that followed a quick visit to New York to meet my agent for the second time, then on to England to meet my foreign rights agent (something I didn't even know existed until a few weeks before) for the first time.

And I was with J., who is such a great traveling companion (an obvious metaphor for our life together). We weren't yet married or parents. And you're walking down a London high street, or coming upon a Madame Yevonde poster in the tube, and you look around, stopping to mark the moment, and at the person beside you and you're young and unencumbered and you just sold your first novel for decent money and you're done with your MFA from a really good university and you really like your new New York agent and her husband becomes one of your favorite people and her office is in a high rise overlooking Central Park and your foreign rights agent has this great name, and a fantastic office in the basement of his Knightsbridge house (and on your way to a four-hour lunch with your editor and publisher, respectively, in a good Italian restaurant you both stop at a pub where you meet Michael Herr, day drinking, and so you both have a drink with him) and rights are being sold and for the first time you aren't broke and there's movie interest and the *New York Times* calls and wants you to write a culture piece (which you don't write because you're new to this world and you get inexplicably tongue-tied, but the written version) and you're going to Paris tomorrow and J. is the best person you could have in your life because he's sweet and generous and really funny and you aren't exactly alike but then again so incredibly well-suited that you can't believe your great good luck and you remember the part in the movie *New York, New York* (a not-perfect film) where Robert De Niro's jazz artist musician talks about trying to find the "major chord" in life and you know exactly what he means because without looking for it, it played for you, and you think, *This is what it's like to have everything I've ever wanted,* because your real life, the one you often imagined, has begun and in about a week you and J. will be staying in this borderline crummy place near the Louvre, run by this gay man who is brusque but a nice person and doesn't punish you for being American, and you will be sitting in the Luxembourg Gardens, not sightseeing or acting like you have to do something every three minutes because you're in Paris, you will be reading, and J. will be reading, and you will also people watch and make comments and laugh your ass off because you have a similar sense of humor, then decide about dinner, which is a limited decision because you're on a tight budget and after Paris you pick up a car and go on an extended European road trip bringing to mind *Two for the Road* but only the happy parts.

Music, movies, plays, photographs, dance, opera, paintings, books are never separate from moments in my life; it all happens concurrently. Even my foreign agent's London office was the same sort of below street studio Yevonde herself had decades before. It was in this sweet spot of my life that I was introduced to Madame Yevonde's work.

Introducing Madame Yevonde, Part 1

Yevonde Cumbers, later Middleton, was an English photographer who did much of her best-known work between the wars, when she embraced color using a camera called the Vivex Color System Model A with a Taylor-Hobson Aviar 14.5 lens. This was no lightweight camera coming in at twelve pounds. She would expose three plates at once. She used flood lights, colored cellophanes, paper, and filters. All of which created pictures so sharp and so color saturated that they made even the most straightforward portrait seem surreal.

Much of Yevonde's best color work—the goddesses, the celebrity and society portraits, the advertisements—was made between the wars, though it wouldn't look out of place today with the playful props and incongruous elements of composition (the Venus de Milo statue with a virginal blue ribbon in her hair and red lipstick; a bust of Caesar wearing a gas mask; Nefertiti and an electric iron, and those were just the advertising prints).

JOAN MAUDE, 1932 (PORTRAIT)

Joan Maude, with her red hair, red lips, red wrap over her shoulders against a red background. Red on red on red on red. David LaChapelle made a picture in 1992 of actress Sheryl Lee (Joan Maude, too, was an actress). In it, Lee has red hair, a short, red silk kimono, red nails. Red lips.

THE EARL AND COUNTESS MOUNTBATTEN OF BURMA AT KING GEORGE'S CORONATION, 1937

The Earl and Countess Mountbatten of Burma (Yevonde called him "the number one pin-up boy of his time") posed at the coronation of King George VI, 1937. The regalia is astonishing (cape, glitter, tassels, massive medals, smaller medals, medals worn around the neck on chains the width of a woman's wrist;

gold braid, bows. And that's just *him*. It overtaxes the brain). She wears a formal gown, more sparkle and jewels on the head, on the wrists, the opera-length gloves; the couple stands before a backdrop of white drapes, studded in gold stars. It is a royal fantasy, pomp-and-circumstance taken to the extreme; you get the sense that these royals are entirely ignorant that the photographer has pushed the portrait beyond commemoration and into some crazy princess fantasy of a little girl.

(Feel free to take a deep breath here. I would love to simply reproduce her photographs instead of describing them because they really must be seen but permissions have gotten tighter and fees higher, a state of affairs that has no place good to go. Especially since art has always influenced art. Imagine not having the collage works of the twentieth century and you can see the problem. But that's another story.)

THE GODDESS SERIES

For me, Madame Yevonde *is* her *Goddess* series, since it was the goddesses that first caught my attention. Twenty-four prints of aristocratic English women dressed up as various Roman and Greek goddesses and muses. Europa caresses the stuffed head of a bull, festooned with flowers. Andromeda is chained to a rock in a pale sea green Fortuny gown that cost $5000 during the Great Depression. Minerva wears a soldier's helmet, her stuffed owl nearby, and holds a large handgun because she's the goddess of wisdom and war. Venus in silk and pearls, while Diana is posed amid laurel leaves in *her* pearls. Arethusa has shining green ribbons of metal wound into her hair, standing on end as if she is underwater; she gazes downward at a passing parade of small glass fish. Ariadne wears a sarong and *her* pearls in her hair, brandishing a length of gold thread and a sword. Ceres is dressed in a column-style gold gown trimmed in golden flowers, gold feathers frame her head, standing before gold drapery, a golden cornucopia in her hands, spilling to the floor with golden fruit. And, of course, the spectacular Medusa with her violet-blue eyes and rhinestone-studded rubber snakes.

There is no attempt to disguise the markers of modernity, or even the interwar period (the makeup and hairs styles are very 1930s). These women look exactly like what they are: aristocrats playing dress-up. The whole effect is intoxicating; the colors, the whimsy, the awareness.

NIOBE, 1935 (AND MAN RAY)

Lady Dolly Campbell is *Niobe, 1935,* a goddess referencing Man Ray's portrait, *Larmes, 1930:* the tilt of head, the close-up of the face, the cropping of the image, the tears down the cheeks. Yevonde's interpretation is not even the more stylized of the two images. Then again, Man Ray is still a Surrealist. Each eyelash of Man Ray's model is adorned at the tip with a tiny mascara sphere; the tears themselves are droplets of glass. Yevonde's Niobe is genuinely crying, the tears are uncontrolled and copious.

ELIZABETH (LISA) MAUGHAM, LADY GLENDEVON, 1936

A young woman wears a simple, sleeveless floral-print dress with a low neckline, and a string of pearls. Her lips are painted red, though her makeup is otherwise conservative. The dress, the pearls, the tasteful makeup looks like money. She gazes, with her chin resting in one hand, studying a gigantic globe that is barely visible at the edge of the frame. Who knows what she is thinking? Behind her, the empty, ombre sky goes from a yellowish shade at the bottom of the picture, becoming light blue then dark blue. White cut-out stars of various shapes and sizes hang in the sky; the stars reminiscent of a child's construction project. Like much of Yevonde's work, the reality of the scene gives way to artifice, an image that juxtaposes something dreamy, something classic.

J. had a room in our house painted to resemble the picture's sky, all scattered gold stars, stenciled to look like the white cut-out stars, some of them ghostly, with only the faintest trace of glitter.

*

THE SELF-PORTRAITS (DID YOU THINK I WAS DONE?)

1. A black-and-white print of a black cat wearing a tiny oval frame hung from a ribbon bow tie. Inside the frame is a tiny photograph of Madame Yevonde. The lettering on the picture reads "Junior and the Photographer."
2. Yevonde's body in profile, sitting, dressed as a harlequin, her face hidden in her arms.
3. A black-and-white picture of her giant camera. On the floor, next to the camera, tethered by a camera plunger, is a teeny Yevonde in hat and glasses.
4. A beautiful, smiling image of Yevonde, her face turned away from the camera, in a white wig, tricorn hat and fitted dress of an eighteenth-century aristocrat.
5. Yevonde poses exuberantly beside a massive camera, in a white satin blouse, long skirt, and the embroidered white gloves of a musketeer.

*

Introducing Madame Yevonde, Part 2

Yevonde Cumbers, later Middleton, was born in London, in 1893, to a well-to-do family. Her father manufactured colored inks (she received her first lessons in color during her visits to his office). She had a sister, Verena. There was theater, progressive schools (motto of one school: "Freely we serve because freely we love"), boarding school in Belgium, then Paris, then her discovery of the Suffragette movement. Though she was a committed advocate for women's suffrage, she had her (understandable) reservations, "I would cheerfully have burned churches, destroyed letterboxes and embarked on a career of wickedness and violence in order to claim political freedom, had it not been for the horror of prison hunger strikes and forcible feeding. I fancied very much the role of martyr but had not the courage to see it through."

The Second Wave of Feminism in this country had it easier than the Suffragettes of England, in the same way that the feminists of today (the Third Wave) have it easier than the Second Wave Feminists. Each turn of the movement secures gains, even if the work is unfinished. No matter what one's era, it is the more committed, the more radical women, who are really willing to risk it all, make life better for those who can't quite make that leap.

Yevonde couldn't manage the possibility of prison and force feeding (which often damaged the throat and broke teeth—and that's if you were lucky). I was more of a supporting player during my time, always aware that the more radical voices were doing the heavy lifting. I just didn't have it in me to be so relentless in my rhetoric, so inflexible in my stance. And I've thanked them every day for what they did for me.

I love the way the smart girl in her comes through, the girl who is realistic about the world and herself and has a sense of humor about it (those "cheerfully burned churches"). She has something of the wry observer about her, avoiding getting into the thick of it, which I entirely get.

Madame Yevonde is exactly my kind of feminist.

When Yevonde was trying to sort out her very young, still-in-her teens life, she came up with this idea, "I might take a lover, then go to the bad. But mother would be frightfully upset." This is Pure Good Girl, entertaining the possibility of dissipation, then rejecting it because it would upset her mother (we love stories of the girls who defy their parents, but what about those girls who happen to love their parents?).

Madame Yevonde later wrote, "By great good luck I had adopted an art-trade-profession-science that like myself, was not properly grown up."

(Women were professional photographers from the beginning. In this way, women never had to break into the profession, making it seem that every battle had been won—except it hadn't. Think of it this way: Imogen Cunningham still lost out an obvious photography assignment to her friend, Ansel Adams; Ruth Orkin still stayed home while her husband made movies; Tina Modotti still put Edward Weston's name on some of her pictures, as did Lee Miller with Man Ray, and who still wasn't permitted to be a war photojournalist, even when taking picture of the war.)

Her father staked her in her first photography studio on the strength of a single completed photograph that Yevonde took when apprenticing under successful socialite photographer Lallie Charles, which must make him the most supportive parent in the history of supportive parents. Lallie Charles made pictures with pink hues, in her pink studio where she hired female assistants. Yevonde learned to touch-up pictures, in between walking Charles's little dog, Chang.

When Yevonde was twenty-one, she opened her studio, taking several pictures of her sister, Verena, in various costumes and hairstyles, giving the impression of many clients, and placed them as advertising in the window. This is what happens when your father brings you to the office, stakes you on the strength of a single photograph, and both parents send you and your sister to Paris and Belgium to progressive schools. Her sense of independence, support of women's suffrage, and lightness about life didn't just happen.

*

A Teenage Yevonde Cumbers Tries to Decide Her Future

a. Being a doctor. Exams too difficult. Training too expensive though rather fancied myself as the "healing physician."
b. Being an architect: Exams too difficult.
c. Being a Farmer: Very interested. Hankered after wide open spaces. Family hostile.
d. Being an Author: Had an itch to write. Didn't know how to set about it.
e. Being an Actress: Ditto. Ditto. Wasn't particularly stage struck but had written and acted in plays since the age of seven.
f. Being a Hospital Nurse: Not sufficiently self-sacrificing. Hated the thought of bed-pans, night-duty and smells.
g. Devoting myself to the Suffragette cause: Tempting. Would not solve economic problem.

A girl after my own heart. My lists weren't exactly like hers but, written in the privacy of my bedroom, they weren't far off.

Kate Salway, her biographer, writes, "She was vivacious, knowing, energetic, sharp, critical, whilst full of wise cracks that made her so popular."

Independence was important to her from a very early age. In 1914, a nascent photographer, barely out of her teens, she was asked by a very successful male photographer if she would like to enter into an advantageous (for her) business partnership.

She declined.

*

More About My Dad

My dad never engaged in all that "my daughter's not dating until she's thirty" business, and thank god. My interests didn't bore him, and he shared his with me if I asked. His bottomless curiosity made us *simpatico*. He didn't get people, and he didn't get children, so he made some interesting parental choices (like the massive corsage he bought for me to wear on the last day of sixth grade). When I was nine years old, he bought all three of us kids $1.00 Diana cameras from Thrifty Drugstore to take on a family vacation, making no distinction between my brother and me. For my twelfth birthday he bought me the camera of my dreams: a Kodak Instamatic with rotating flash cube. I wanted nothing more in life than that camera. It was so perfect. (My mother bought me a white gold ring with a large, blue-gray aquamarine, my birthstone, set in the center of a white gold rose, that nearly dwarfed my finger.)

When I was in first grade in 1961, in those days when girls had to dress like girls, including not being allowed to wear pants to school, I decided I wanted to wear my brother's white button-down shirt. It had French cuffs, so my dad gave me a pair of his cufflinks (faux gold, set with a small jade stone, one of the cufflinks lightly damaged). And when I asked for a necktie as well, he gave me a smoky gray knit necktie and taught me how to tie it. I wore cufflinks and neckties, off and on, until I was in my early thirties. By that time I had added (starting when

I was twelve) boys' dress slacks, boys' sweaters, vintage men's suit jackets, vintage men's trousers, a soldier's gas mask bag as a purse (along with a binocular case, and camera lens bag), a beloved Boy Scout belt. I wore these things, off and on, with women's clothing, but my masculine clothing began with my dad, who was agreeable to my dressing this way, even though this began in 1961 when kid's clothing was pretty well gender differentiated. This is my way of saying that my dad always let me know that I could be anybody I wanted to be.

It's also my way of saying that I think I understand a little about some of the father-daughter relationship of Madame Yevonde.

My father allowed me so much breathing room because he never wanted to be anyone's boss. Literally. He wasn't good at managing people under him at work, preferring they sort themselves out. The only person he ever got fired was a married secretary that he had a brief affair with, and that was because in the 1960s if a man had an affair and his wife called the office to complain, the secretary was let go, so it was my mom who was the one who got her fired, but *really* it was the social mores of that era. It wasn't fair, but it's the way it was, something that gets lost in the current nostalgia for the *Mad Men* years.

However, my mother, who worked in advertising where the sexual and office dynamics were fun even if they didn't favor the women, was having an affair with her much older, married boss. While nobody got fired for affairs, a young man showed up one day, threatening to murder the art director for sleeping with his fiancé, who was something of an innocent.

My father and mother were as mismatched as the chance meeting on a dissecting table of a sewing machine and an umbrella.

In the middle of the divorce it was my father, a man who might very well have been a touch on the highest end of the spectrum (as they say), who recognized the struggle that I didn't even know I had with the demise of their marriage because my mother, the "emotional" parent, was so in tune with her own heart that she failed to see into any of the other ones around her. This was partly because she worked off the idea that her happiness would be the key to everyone's happiness (one can imagine how well that worked in practice). My dad, who couldn't read anyone, who had a hard time even embracing anyone (including us) did something for me that was so correct, so thoughtful that it sometimes still astonishes me. I mean, who sees a twelve-year-old girl?

My parents, so different, so flawed. I loved them.

A few months before my novel with the Madame Yevonde-inspired jacket was published (and the inspiration for the starry room in my house), we were in New York, having just passed through Houston where we had spent the previous week with my dad and his second family, when I got a call that he had died.

I wasn't surprised; I was sad and relieved, because that's how it is with terminal illness. You begin with hope for a cure, then end with a prayer for mercy. My father had Parkinson's, which took its sweet time dismantling him until he was speechless and immobile. It had been several months between visits (we had a two-year-old at the time and lived halfway across the country). When we arrived at his house, a caregiver carried him from his bedroom to the living room. He was so ravaged I had a hard time recognizing him, my own father; he looked like someone who wouldn't be out of place in a concentration camp, and that isn't making a comment about those camps, but just to explain how unthinkable and visually accurate his appearance.

I won't write about that week because I never, ever want to be there again.

*

Color Is Considered Feminine

All of which is to say—the willingness to be amused by life, willing to be entertained by the world; the commitment to the cause of women, the love of women in all their glamour, the artistic, the eccentric, the singular and resplendent pictures— that Madame Yevonde, right down to her whimsical moniker, is my kind of girl.

She was said to be charming.

She was willing to financially support her husband (who lost money in investments) with her own earned income.

She was involved with the Women's Rotary Club, giving a talk on photography saying it's an art and a science and a business and a profession. The same thing can be said of writing.

In the mid-thirties, professional photography began to fall off. It did for Yevonde, too.

By 1936 she wanted to do only color, even with its challenges. She would tell the lab not to "correct" her colors, not to bring them down.

Color is radical because color is often, has often, been considered "lesser" in photography (consider how we still view black-and-white photographs or films, the way their shades of dark and light assume the importance of Art, the sigh of nostalgia).

Color was often considered feminine.

*

There is a collection of love letters from Frida Kahlo to Diego Rivera written in different color inks. Recall Yevonde influenced by the colorful inks her father manufactured.

*

A List of Madame Yevonde's Props

Butterflies, glass fish, a stuffed bull's head festooned with flowers, rubber snakes studded with rhinestones; silk flowers, fake branches; shiny metal (deep green, like seaweed, affixed to the model's hair as she looks down, the ribbons of metal flow upward, as if she is a mermaid under the sea); gold stars, white stars, paper stars, fabric stars; yards of colored fabric backdrops in more stars, mauve, red; yards of pastel tulle, a stuffed bird in a bird cage. Blue iridescent butterflies. Butterflies. Fur. Pearls. An arrow, a Nazi helmet, a handgun. Laurel leaves. A stuffed owl. Fake fruit. Gold. A cornucopia. A painted wig, a seashell crown. Pearls. Pearls. Pearls. Perfectly applied makeup, very thirties when taken alone, timeless in the context of the entire picture. A gold frame. A cat. A camera.

*

A List of Items Currently on My Desk

A large glass paperweight of a color wheel (a gift from Joy). A vintage brass postage stamp box, a deck of color spectrum playing cards, photos of Obama and Georgia O'Keeffe, a paperweight of the earth nestled in a bowl of stars, a small metal zebra, vintage, made in France next to a tiny brass and oxidized dog made in Germany. A one-of-a-kind Italian-inspired ex-voto with a faded purple velvet back; a miniature shadow box of *Two Fridas,* a tin of ink. An old set of Vasa cubes, two pencil holders—one, a child's tin cup, the other a decoupaged tin can with Mary on it wearing a gold crown—a large paper weight of the phases of the moon. An ashtray from La Coupole, purchased at La Coupole. Post-its, paperclips, pens, a white eraser shaped like a bust of Einstein. Souvenirs: Spain (sterling silver cart drawn by two horses and driven by an angel; a tiny sterling St.

Jordi used to extinguish a cigarette), Paris (a two-inch metal Napoleon), Tokyo (a miniature replica of a tenth-century writing box in brass), Venice (a teeny gondola). A clear, diamond faceted crystal called a "Novagem" from eastern Europe and set into brass so it could hang on a 435-foot tower called the Tower of Jewels, at the Panama-Pacific International Exposition in San Francisco in 1915. The Tower was hung with 102,000 Novagems in eight colors—ruby, emerald, pale yellow, aqua, purple, sunflower yellow, pink, and diamond clear (my color). The "jewels" hung freely from their brass hangers, illuminated by fifty-four search lights for the better part of a year. It was rumored to be breathtaking.

*

A Brief Collection of Artists and Color

The photographer Yasumasa Morimura is a Japanese appropriation artist who frequently, though not exclusively, portrays women in history. My favorite Morimura photograph references Man Ray's picture of Rrose Selavy, Marcel Duchamp's alter ego. Morimura's version is in blacks and whites and golds, a green background, red lips, white face powder. It is a picture of a man (Morimura) dressed as a woman (Selavy) who is a man (Duchamp) dressed as a woman (Selavy).

Where the original Man Ray photo is in black-and-white, Morimura's version shimmers with color. There are two sets of arms, one white, one brown. He uses makeup as identity: feminine, Asian, European, theatrical, and hastily applied, calling attention to skin tone (can race ever be far from discussions of color?).

Morimura, like Yevonde, is making photographs that are elevated by color. In the same manner of David LaChappelle's excessive, extravagant pictures would fall apart in black-and-white. Or Pierre et Gilles and their glittering fantasies of mermaids and sailors and saints, where costumes, colors, and backgrounds dominate the image, reducing glamorous movie stars to little more than props. Lorette Lux, too, makes pictures as pastel and pure and spare as LaChappelle, and Pierre et Gilles's are over the top, yet just as exaggerated, something she achieves by slightly enlarging the heads of her child models.

I'm drawn, time and again, to the same sort of beautiful peculiarity in these pictures, each photographer—LaChapelle, Pierre et Gilles, Lux, Yevonde—never pretends to be making anything that even remotely resembles ordinary life. If black-and-white photography is, paradoxically, thought to be "realistic," even though it's *black-and-white* and most likely showing an image just as manipulated (cropping, dark room effects)—it's often because the goal is different. LaChapelle, Pierre et Gilles, Lux, Yevonde are working within their own reality—not your reality, not my reality—they aren't just interpreting what they see around them—they are working from within as surely as any painter. These constructs are natural to them; they aren't using soft focus, or some weird juxtaposition of objects, like the Surrealists. They aren't offering up dreams. They aren't on a search for the odd, or disturbing, image. Instead they build a whole other thrilling, unbridled world. In a sense, these photographers are working in their own category: not painting, not straight photography, not abstract photography, not Surrealism, but a universe apart.

How could the viewer not want to step inside?

*

A cyanometer, invented in 1789, is an instrument for measuring "blueness," specifically the blueness of the sky. There are fifty-three paper squares ranging from white to blues to black and pasted together in a large ring that is held up to judge the color of the sky.

The painter, Florine Stettheimer, once sent a young relative, who was summering in Nantucket, a postcard of seven shades of beige to dark brown in brushstrokes resembling fingerprints, asking him to identify his current skin tone so she could paint his portrait.

I have an old glass prism that I found in a junk shop. I bought it because I have pleasant memories of prisms when I was in grade school and how they produced color. Isaac Newton was the person who discovered that white light refracted through a prism projected color. The nineteenth-century artist James McNeill Whistler connected painting with music, often naming his pictures as arrangements, or nocturnes or harmonies using colors in the titles. Lately, all I think about is painting color wheels.

Many years ago, J. and I traveled to Washington, DC, where we visited the Freer Gallery. Charles Lang Freer was a self-made man of wealth who was an avid art collector. His collection—thousands of objects, including the largest personal collection of Asian art—is the largest of Whistlers. I like James McNeill Whistler, and I like John Singer Sargent, a pair of painters that I was raised, culturally speaking, not to like. The first was too closely associated with *Arrangement in Grey and Black No.1* (recall the Whistler connection between music and color), more commonly called *Whistler's Mother,* a painting I can only associate with Bugs Bunny cartoons and other send-ups.

John Singer Sargent was a society painter for the ruling class during the Edwardian Era. He was best known for the scandalous *Portrait of Madame X,* which fairly undid him. I never knew anyone who talked about his work, or knew much about it, or cared about it, even if everyone recognized *Madame X.* When I was young and wandering around a small New York museum, I

242 · WHITNEY OTTO

come across the Sargents and I wondered why it was wrong to love these pictures? I think the answer lay in the social changes of the 1960s and 1970s, and fear of being bourgeois. Yeah, anything but *that*. And then one day I found myself in that small museum in New York asking, *How could I have allowed myself to dislike something I had never really seen?*

Charles Freer was that rare bird who not only liked art, but the artists that came with the art. He believed the art he bought was only on "loan" to him, and he would allow the artists to "borrow" it back. While there were many remarkable pieces in his gallery, the thing that astonishes is *Harmony in Blue and Gold: The Peacock Room,* commonly known as just *The Peacock Room.*

The *Peacock Room* began its life in the London townhouse of a wealthy shipping magnate who wanted a room dedicated to his porcelain collection. The room, done in a Tudor-style (including the ceiling treatment and hanging lights), with pomegranates and red roses and rugs, ended up in the hands of Whistler when Whistler's painting *Rose and Silver: The Princess From the Land of the Porcelain* was featured above the fireplace, and the original designer of the room's remodel took ill. When Whistler went in to do the finish work, he decided, unilaterally, that the colors of the room (all those reds) were clashing with his painting, and could use a little touch-up, which is the exact moment that things began to get out of hand. Whistler described what happened, *Well, you know, I just painted on. I went on—without design or sketch—it grew as I painted. And toward the end I reached such a point of perfection—putting in every touch with such freedom—that when I came round to the corner where I started, why, I had to paint part of it over again, as the difference would have been too marked. And the harmony in blue and gold developing, you know, I forgot everything in my joy in it.*

The final result was a blue-green paneled room, glazed and embellished with gold-leaf. The wealthy magnate-owner took one look at this unapologetically, wildly colored blue-green and gold room and went nuts. In all fairness, Whistler's employer was absent during this period of redecoration (the lesson here is that taking a vacation when your house is being worked on is a sort of homeowner's roulette).

Getting paid was now out of the question, especially after Whistler informed his patron, *I have made you famous. My work will live when you are forgotten. Still, per chance, in the dim ages to come you will be remembered as the proprietor of the Peacock Room.* Whistler, no shrinking violet (see: the court case Whistler v. Ruskin), snuck back into the *Peacock Room* when his former employer wasn't around, and painted—in gold—a pair of peacocks fighting over a scattering of coins. Whistler titled his illicit graffito, *Art and Money or, The Story of the Room.* Then he sat back to enjoy the spectacle of burning the equivalent of a professional four-lane suspension bridge. This tale is only one of the reasons why I am a Whistler devotee. (He later made another peacock caricature called *Filthy Lucre* aimed at you-know-who.)

How did I come to be standing in the middle of this wondrous room in Washington, DC, that began its life in London, one autumn day? Freer bought the room in 1904—not just the contents of the room, but *the entire room, walls and all*—from the magnate's heirs, then reassembled it in his own Detroit mansion, before moving and reassembling it again, in 1919, in the gallery he built, bearing his name, in Washington, DC.

(Side note: I was once invited to read at a library in Philadelphia, where yet another rich man decided that it wasn't enough to donate the books from his personal library—he wanted the library to have the entire room. They moved his private library—walls, windows, and all—to a room within the public library, authentically reassembling *it* down to the photographs hanging just outside the windows, offering an accurate view of the rich man's view from the library when it was still in his home. There was something disorienting about being inside that room, as if I were pretending to be an author in a giant dollhouse.)

It also brought to mind the James Turrell exhibition I visited in Los Angles in 2013, an exhibition of colored lights that surrounds you, using your own biology to alter the colors of the lights that change with the way your eyes process and perceive light and darkness and color. A standout moment was walking up eight steps, shoeless, into an enormous room with a large opening, like the proscenium of a stage. In this white room it is nearly impossible to make out where the floor or ceiling meets the walls; even more so once the lights gently change over the next eighteen minutes, as you stand around this nearly empty space (only a few people allowed in at a time), immersed in evolutions of pink, or green, or red, or blue. The experience is soothing, tricky, and beautiful. Once you get into the "rhythm" of the lights (the pace is so slow, the changes so gradual, that you don't notice them happening as much as they suddenly dawn on you), the request to leave is jarring.

Gertrude Stein

Gertrude Stein belongs in any discussion about painting or art if for no other reason than for her attempt to make her writing do what visual art does, which is provide a kind of connection to visual modern art. She wasn't writing modern novels; she was trying to paint on the page. A kind of "leap across" of art forms. Stein made "word-portraits" where she repeated words, or short strings of words, when describing someone, though she said these repetitions weren't repetitions at all, but "emphasis." Stein said, "Is there repetition or is there insistence. I am inclined to believe there is no such thing as repetition."

Cubism shows all angles at once, the subject flattened and exposed, nothing hidden because there is no backside. Stein, a literary Cubist, wanted to pile up objects that are part of a subject's exterior life, in order to understand the interior life.

Stein is not interested in rendering, exactly; she is interested in perception, something that she thinks traditional biography or novels cannot reach, believing they are too limited by the relating of past events, with no attachment to the present; ironic because she finds the retelling of events that have already taken place ("repeating the past") as dull and useless when trying to understand someone, even though she relies on repeated words and phrases. She doesn't care about memory. Stein is also after rhythm and tones, sounds and specific words, the way they trip off the tongue. She will repeat a single word, or a phrase, then make a very slight adjustment—perhaps add a word, subtract a word, or break a sentence into more than one piece. In this way, her work connects to James McNeill Whistler, who heard musical notes and saw colors. She hears her words, too, and spreads them evenly across the page like paint on a canvas.

When I was a child I saw words in colors and patterns. Sometimes, certain alphabet letters appeared in this way as well. I thought everyone thought this way—how could I know otherwise? I mean, I wouldn't ask someone if words came to them in colors and patterns, I would just assume they did. Then, one day when I was twelve years old, I said something about a girl's name, Lindsay, and how it was sometimes orange-red and solid and sometimes pale pink with white lace, that it depended on which Lindsay came to mind.

The kid listening to me stared and said, What are you talking about? I said, You know, when words and names are colors? The expression on the other person's face silenced me. I understood, in that moment, that this wasn't common at all. I went home and asked my mother about a word and what it looked like to her. She didn't know what I was talking about either, nor did she pay much attention (this is a generational thing; my generation so not coddled that we grew up often coddling ourselves, which was arguably beneficial). I never mentioned the word-colors again and worked at trying to stop it. It was only in my forties, when talking to a novelist friend, that I learned the word "synesthesia." She said, you're a synesthete.

Florine Stettheimer

Florine Stettheimer, the marvelous, singular, naif painter, was the sister of Ettie Stettheimer, who was friends with Alfred Stieglitz and Georgia O'Keeffe. The Stettheimer sisters came from privilege: they "summered" in luxe locales, they "did Europe." Her mother raised her three daughters to live for art and pleasure. Florine was a modernist who never married or had children, held salons, and painted nude self-portraits where she never aged. She decorated her rooms in very specific styles that involved cobalt-blue walls, gold trim, airy white curtains. She also wrote poetry, free verse, and along with Gertrude Stein (libretto), Virgil Thomson (composer), and Eva Jessye (musical director), designed the sets and stage in her trademark fantastical style for *Four Saints in Three Acts.* The opera premiered in 1934, and featured an all-black cast, radical for its time.

Alfred Stieglitz and Georgia O'Keeffe came into Florine Stettheimer's life by way of her sister Ettie. Florine was the painter (and poet), Ettie was the author. Their third sister, Carrie, made the Stettheimer Dollhouse (1916–1935), a two-story structure complete with a collection of miniature paintings and sculptures made by established artists and hung on the tiny dollhouse walls.

Florine's paintings use color and figures and words and embellishments (like stars and tungsten lights), making her "cathedrals of" series depicting locations like Broadway or Wall Street, celebrations of a young, brash, emotionally sunny city. Related to ideas of cubism, Stettheimer's pictures "explore dislocation of time and space, allowing numerous activities and advantage points to be captured on a single canvas." These bustling cathedral paintings—large, dense with humanity—often give me the sense that I'm listening to them as well as seeing them. I always associate New York City with very specific sounds, Stettheimer just cranks up the volume.

I first saw Stettheimer's work at a show in New York in 1995, five years after discovering Madame Yevonde. I hadn't heard of Stettheimer before, but her pictures struck me much like Madame Yevonde's work—the whimsy, the sly humor. Her painted portraits, whether of places or people, are figurative and busy with detail: alive, decorative, fluid, bristling with information and electricity.

The portraits were less about her models' interior lives, and included words, and objects referencing their professions, or interests, or personal landscapes, made her portraits both factual and fantastic.

She painted a lot of flowers, that because of their profusion of color, or their size (sometimes substantially larger than the models, and wandering all over the picture plane), her flowers were anything but "natural." She wasn't showing life as much as enhancing it.

Stettheimer's Portraits and Women

Looking at Florine Stettheimer's portraits all I could think was, *Where have you been all my life?* In my mind they twin with Romaine Brooks' portraits, since I love each artist's work with the same sort of enthusiasm, and somehow I associate them with Madame Yevonde, which is how I ended up on this leg of my lengthy digression on various artists. Stettheimer and Brooks were contemporaries, refiguring the history of portraiture without abstracting it, with very different, but equally pleasing (for me) results. Stettheimer painted her family, and famous people, like the photographer Baron de Meyer (1923), or Marcel Duchamp, always capturing something essential in the pictures which are more idiosyncratic than realistic.

In the Duchamp portrait, the colors are more pastel, less assertive. There are two figures surrounded by a lot of space: Duchamp, of course, and his alter ego, Rrose Selavy, who sits on a very high stool, clad in a rose-colored dress. An endless series of *DMs,* Duchamp's initials, cut from wood, are affixed to the entire frame.

In 1928, Florine painted a portrait of Stieglitz, "depicting the sixty-four year old photographer as a vigorous man striding purposefully around his gallery in a black cape, surrounded by images and symbols of the artists he championed . . . an ermine-cuffed hand opens the door, signaling the entrance of Baron de Meyer . . . a foot paired with a cane symbolizes Demuth. Arther Dove sits leafing through a book at the left . . . Marin, Hartley, Strand. The palette is black-and white [Stieglitz as a photographer]. Stettheimer did not include an image of O'Keeffe but inscribed her name . . . near a profile drawing of her head carved in paint," and a reference to the first picture, a 1915 painting, a Stieglitz favorite by O'Keeffe, and to Lake George, and New York skyscrapers. This is Gertrude Stein-in-paint, a modernist, visual "word-poem." No one will ever see this picture of Stieglitz, despite the shaky realism of the figure, and say that it doesn't look like him. In fact, anyone seeing this painting will say it looks *exactly* like him.

Like Madame Yevonde, Florine Stettheimer made a handful of self-portraits, more interpretative than visually factual (see the earlier mention of her ageless nudes. Paint more forgiving than film). They twin, for me, with the use of color and whimsy (different from fantasy). Unlike Yevonde, Stettheimer painted men more often than women. Yevonde, being a photographer, necessarily worked from a model, then incorporated props, backdrops, then manipulated the film, transforming the picture into an art piece. Stettheimer often worked from memory, a dream of color and unstable line, the realism coming through in the form of biographical details.

*

Every time I've shown Madame Yevonde's photographs, either in a slideshow, or on the page, people are surprised to learn that most of what they're seeing was made between the two world wars. It isn't simply the embracing of theatrics, or the skilled use of saturated color that makes it feel contemporary; it's the women at the center of the pictures, and Yevonde's suffragette sensibilities that placed them there.

*

"If you think you are emancipated, you might consider the idea of tasting your own menstrual blood—if it makes you sick, you've got a long way to go, baby." I read these words in high school when I was reading Germaine Greer. I was seventeen and the 1970s had barely begun and I was already leaning into feminism in my Good Girl not-drawing-attention-to-myself fashion, and picking up Germaine Greer's *The Female Eunuch* to further my understanding. I had only had a period for a couple of years and was still wrestling with the knowledge that I would have to deal with this situation for decades.

Greer said that women don't realize how much men hate them and advocated revolution as she talked about women's sexuality. My personal experience of the world was pretty limited, and her language incendiary, forceful, and I remember thinking, I have to sample my own menstrual blood? This wasn't the adult scenario I had envisioned. My future ran more along the lines of *When I'm a grown-up I'm going to do whatever I want,* something that, unsurprisingly didn't include fusing the bathroom and the dining room. And what about the part where "men will hate me"? One of the sole advantages of being a Good Girl is that you seldom engender hatred, if only because you present a persona that isn't polarizing enough to hate. And frankly, I'm less of a revolutionary and more of a seether-slash-designated driver of life. Not that I enjoy being either of those things.

My high school was without a central clique running the place. Instead, it was a collection of groups (jocks, song girls, stoners, intellectuals) and races (everybody) and social classes and people like me who are like extras in the movies, providing scenery and context. I was always impressed by the vocal, smart political girls at my school who wore Levis and work shirts, or dresses cut up to there. They had sexual "relationships" and got accepted to excellent colleges. Their parents took them abroad. Some of them had money, but mostly they came from solid, well-educated backgrounds. Not all of them were nice, not that it mattered, but an intellectual snob doesn't even bother with you unlike the dim bulb bully.

I didn't hate high school—that's my dirty little secret— because the people watching (all those groups!) was interesting for anyone remotely observant. The social lessons were priceless, the class issues were illuminating, and it was entertaining. Like my hero Madame Yevonde, I was amused by the whole experience. I didn't fight or argue with anyone, I talked to various people from various groups (I was socially fluid and inconsequential), I liked my teachers (another interesting lot, most of them clearly on board with feminism), and my two best friends were smart, engaging, and one of them was as amused and jokey as I; the other a bit more serious, and a photographer.

The year I graduated high school abortion had been settled (or so I thought, given recent events in this country), so there was that.

Then my freshman year of college I joined a women's consciousness-raising group led by a sophomore named Cora who wore wire-rimmed glasses and no underwear and had a very sunny personality. We met once a week in an empty classroom where the conversations covered men who held the door open for a woman and referred to their cars as "she." This made the group very pissed off. There was the Masturbation Summit where everyone related their masturbation practices, then someone passed around what looked like a textbook of women masturbating in various domestic locales, like the shower or the sofa. The photographs were black-and-white, very 1950s since the book was literally from the fifties, with black rectangles over the women's eyes to disguise their identities. It was like a literary *Reefer Madness,* only with solo sex. When the book came to me I nodded knowingly, I might even have uttered a *yes,* like I was standing next to Madame Curie when she made her scientific breakthrough.

One night, Cora hopped up on the desk at the front of the room, lifted her floor length hippie dress, and inserted her personal plastic speculum. She did this in a very fluid motion since she wasn't hindered by underwear, then invited each of us to examine her cervix. She encouraged us to visit the Student Health Center and pick up our own personal plastic specula which I did the next day, without a clue of what I would do with it. It seemed that the speculum was part of the feminist toolkit, and if I was going to take this seriously I needed not only to experience the flavor of my period, but to observe the orifice from whence it came. Then Cora informed us that if we looked closely we could see *her* period that was about to begin. "See the blood just coming through?"

I should add that I rarely talked in these sessions because I couldn't trust my slapstick self and this was not a humorous crowd. They were still too angry over the car thing. After The Night of Cervix, all I could think was that the professor using this desk tomorrow would have no idea that Cora's naked ass and her PMS genitalia had spent an evening on it (prefiguring my involvement with hand sanitizer).

In another meeting, someone was talking about how vexed she got when her boyfriend always expected her "to roll the joints instead of doing it himself." Everyone treated this complaint like he was asking her to have a Rusty Nail waiting when he came in the door, and maybe a nice relish plate. More stories about slights, or small requests were discussed. And the fact that almost none of their mothers worked and how could they be expected to respect her? They were so excited when I told them about my working mother, adding that she worked *because she wanted to,* not because she had to, though I left out the part where all I wanted was her there when I got home from school. I couldn't tell them that without making myself look like the joint-rolling girl's sexist boyfriend.

I did mention once that all I really wanted was equal pay and a level playing field. They nodded, then went back to talking about the patriarchy and panty hose.

On Sundays we met with the men's consciousness-raising group who only talked about one thing: crying. They talked about wanting to cry, or the times they cried, or wishing they could cry. They were almost crying as they enthusiastically supported the women as they explained why they, the women, hated wearing nylons (with their poor-fitting crotches), which only existed to make them sexually attractive to men. There was an undercurrent of sexual attraction between the men's and the women's groups so that when the women called the men out on their sexism and the men quickly capitulated, making the meetings almost like some sort of gender political S&M foreplay.

I dropped out after a few weeks. But here's what I learned: the nitpicking social complaints ("My boss called me honey," "He told me I could be so pretty if I wore a little lipstick" or "I was sent home for wearing pants to work") were related to the anger and radicalism of many feminists of the time. It wasn't in me to rush into the fray or to complain because someone feminized an object—and I had my own irritations and angers about the way I was talked to or treated because of my gender, having had jobs, for example, that required me to wearing stockings until my mid-twenties—but I always, always knew that those women like Germaine Greer, or those girls who wouldn't let the little things go unremarked (where is the place where petty moves toward important?), were the ones who made it easier for me since they were doing what I couldn't see myself doing. I wasn't passive; I just wasn't picking up the gauntlet. I was more passive resistance with the occasional clever remark, like Yevonde, like the Good Girl that I am.

*

I mentioned abortion a few paragraphs back and let it drop. This is as it should be, because it's a legal medical procedure done at the discretion of the woman. Nothing changes a woman's world as irrevocably, as fundamentally as motherhood. Yes, fatherhood changes the lives of men, too, but not in the same way it does a woman. Biologically. Professionally. Legally. Even now, in the twenty-first century, motherhood can still be seen as a woman's desire and destiny. When I was in high school, I read a book by a journalist who explained, at length, why she didn't want to have children. The book was popular and she took some flak; legal abortion was still a few years away anyway.

My siblings and I had a babysitter one summer, a sixteen-year-old blonde who was the quintessential California girl. One afternoon, as we lay around our pool (she was always around the pool; working on her tan meant there was no possibility of any of us drowning), her sixteen-year-old friend from school came over to say good-bye. She and her boyfriend were on their way to Mexico to get married. "Why?" I asked. "Because she's pregnant," said our sitter, then went back to tanning. Legal abortion still years in the future.

The thing that is so deeply wrongheaded about the anti-abortionists is that they are making life and death decisions for which they aren't held accountable, and are so smug and self-righteous about it. As if they are really saving lives, but without lifting a finger. Not to mention that it's a class issue as well. I can't imagine a more terrible life then being born to someone who doesn't want me, who might not be careful with me, who might not expect anyone else to be careful with me either. How can any human being force any girl or woman to have a child and still sleep at night?

The thing about abortion is if you need one, what you feel is relief. You don't fret over it because your choice is pretty clear-cut. You appreciate clarity. You know there are people who might judge your "cavalier attitude," even if you could say, *you are confusing cavalier with being a realist.* And you never regret it; you know why you did it; you were grateful to have the option; what you mostly felt was pure, uncomplicated relief.

*

Women were Madame Yevonde's politics and her subject, whether photographing or lecturing. In 1921, when she was twenty-seven years old, she gave a lecture to the Congress of Professional Photographers on the topic of women and portraiture. She visited ten working female photographers, borrowing the slides that formed the foundation for her talk. She wore a Chinese shawl, spoke with a great sense of "theater," pretty much upsetting the room.

Here are some of her distressingly provocative statements:

- "Women have done much to popularise portrait photography . . . it would have languished and died but for the interest of women . . . mothers wanting portraits of their sons, daughters—for their fiances, society beauties every time they buy a new hat, the charming actress who must be photographed often and always."
- "Women seem to possess all the natural gifts essential to a portraitist . . . such as personality, patience and intuition. The sitter ought to be the predominating factor in a successful portrait. Men portraitists are apt to forget this; they are inclined to lose the sitter in a maze of technique luxuriating in the cleverness and beauty of their own medium."
- "A pleasant personality goes further to make a successful portrait than a perfect print."
- Women outside of the UK and America "have not had the opportunity for self-expression and development . . . which people sometimes forget in judging women's creative work in art." Then goes on to say that some women break through but the vast majority simply don't have the ". . . means of direct self-expression."
- And this: "The quickness with which a woman's brain works is an enormous help in dealing with sitters. . . . Our intuition here is of much more value than a man's much-prized logic."

It's nothing short of radical to state that you can do something better, *and* that the skill that it takes is inherent in your sex.

*

In *Eight Girls Taking Pictures*, I write about a British photographer, fun-loving, ambitious, well-liked, an amused suffragette who falls in love with a difficult, but not unkind man. He goes off to the Great War. She volunteers for service, doing a stint in the country, though she is barely able to stand being in her own skin for worry over his safety.

He returns, physically unharmed, but emotionally and psychologically "rearranged" by the war, in ways that he can (mostly) control. She ends up embracing color work with the idea that she can "remake a world" negating the effects of the war. He loves her for her fools' errand, and she loves him for understanding her attempt. Throughout their lives, they are an unlikely couple.

In 1919, Yevonde met Edgar Middleton, "journalist, author, promising playwright. She was twenty-six . . . after a whirlwind courtship, they married on Friday, February 13, 1920, six weeks after they met. She asked if she should give up her work. He said, 'it would be a mistake.' He also said that he didn't want children—a great disappointment to her." They loved each other, though she was social and he was not, she was friendly, charmed by the world, he was at odds with the world. They loved each other; throughout their lives they were an unlikely couple.

*

Women, she said, were naturals to work with color because color is intrinsic to a woman's daily life: her clothing, her makeup, her nails, her jewelry, home decor, gardens and flowers. Women live in a world of color.

Telling the photo lab "Don't correct anything—just print." She didn't want the colors muted or ladylike, as she made her bid for art, taking women (often) as her subject; the embrace of wild color as a way of making her pictures singular and "not doled out by the dozens."

So maybe this is the other place where what I do as a writer—or what I *try* to do, would be more accurate—intersects with Madame Yevonde's work. All my novels could be distilled into three main subjects: women, art, and feminism (I find it inconceivable to write about women, either fiction or nonfiction, and not also write about feminism). My handling of material is light, maybe too light to be taken seriously (my version of color). If I came to my own novels purely as a reader, I might not see what's underneath it all either.

In Yevonde's era, color photography was considered gauche, garish, savage, unserious, unsophisticated, an impatient child grasping at the nearest shiny thing. And there she was with her high wattage lights, her large prints, the flood lights, the colored cellophanes. The stuffed birds, and animals, and blue iridescent butterflies and glass fish; the pearls. The stars. The blondes and yellow, the redheads and reds. The fantasy, the dream.

*

Color is sensual; line is logic; color, like emotions (emotions are often rendered in colors), line is singular, mono. Line is masculine, rational; color is feminine and chaotic. Or so some critics have claimed.

Rousseau said that without line, color had no effect.

Charles Blanc, critic, color theorist, sometime Director of the Arts in 1848 in France identified color with the "feminine" in art; he asserted the need to subordinate color to the "masculine" discipline of design and drawing, writing, ". . . *[color] had to be subordinated—like a woman. . . . Color signifies the mythical savage state out of which civilization . . . color was coded in the feminine . . . it was coded in the primitive. For both, color is a corruption, a lapse, a fall*" [italics mine].

He goes on to say, "color is both secondary and dangerous; in fact, it is dangerous because it is secondary."

It's also "low down in the hierarchy of the painter's skills."

I think, probably too much, about wanting to paint color wheels, and color palettes like the sort one makes in a beginning painting class; graphs of color, lines of color, dots of color. The organization of color. It thrills me that color can be considered transgressive and uncontrolled. And feminine.

I think about Matisse (*The Red Studio*), and Rothko, Ellsworth Kelly's Spectrum paintings. Cezanne said, "Color is the place where the brain and the universe meet." I think about Joni Mitchell and her tunings, aural color. Isaac Newton, with a love of harmonies, "divided the spectrum into seven colors into order to make it correspond to the seven distinct notes in the musical scale." There's a room in Dresden, rebuilt after the war, called the Green Vault because the pillar bases and capitals were painted green.

Kate Soloway said that "Yevonde felt that most photographers possessed no sense of color, or what little they had had become non-existent through years of seeing tonally; they had become so engrossed in the beauty of light and shade that they thought the color photograph unnatural."

In Yevonde's color work you can see the reach of her ambitions, the playfulness more thoroughly displayed. Though her black-and-white work is beautifully composed it's when everything goes to color, you see *her*. In a sense, the introduction of color, in her era, explodes society's (photography's) norms; we have the "fall" that so tweaked Charles Blanc, then we have the elevation.

Yevonde's *Goddesses* embodied glamour, and play and camp, humor, beauty, innovation, modernity, classicism, and social class; they are the very women she once so admired with their evening gowns, sleek automobiles, and thick eye lashes.

Through color, Madame Yevonde becomes Madame Yevonde.

*

Chromophobia (Book); Commentary (Mine)

"White was the precondition for color; color was intensified by its proximity to white."

I went through a period of my twenties where I had five white cotton skirts. One white cotton slip from 1900 that I wore as a skirt (when my boss gave me my holiday bonus one year he handed me the check and said, "Buy yourself some outer garments"). Several white shirts, mens' white t-shirts, two white vests. I wanted ivory jewelry because I liked the worn look of it, though morally I couldn't manage it. I don't know what the white was all about. I also had five small black sweaters, two black vests, and two pairs of red shoes. One pair of beautiful red leather gloves. I guess I was having a highly graphic moment.

*

"Figuratively, color has always meant the less-than-true and the not-quite-real. The Latin colorem is related to celare, to hide or conceal; in Middle English, 'to colour' is to embellish, adorn, to disguise, to render specious or plausible, to misrepresent."

I'm a fiction writer.

*

"Color makes a mask, is duplicitous."

Madame Yevonde's pictures are surreal because of the props and costumes, but mostly because of the unrestrained color. Her pictures tapped into the subconscious as effortlessly as Man Ray's black-and-white photographs. Because his pictures relied on odd juxtapositions and shadows their dreamlike quality is unmistakable. Yevonde hides her dreams in plain sight. I've always hidden in plain sight myself.

*

"Warhol's signature failing to keep color in line . . . is one of his great successes."
Sometimes there's simply no place for you within the lines, then you realize that you don't mind being on the outside.

*

"Color threatens order and promises liberty."
A Surrealist would say that he "loves" women (their "eroticism,"), he "admires" and "worships" them because they are so "in touch with their creative, unfiltered natures" like, you know, children. Art historian Whitney Chadwick remarks: "We know more about Kiki of Montparnasse and Nadja than we do of Lee Miller and Valentine Hugo." The muse, that figure who rouses the artist and lends her body to his vision, is not unlike the women of the social revolutions of the 1960s. They were part of the revolution in their supportive roles (and, I'm guessing, rolling a bushel of joints), but it was only when they decided to have their own revolution that people knew their names, too. If a rose is a rose is a rose, then a secretary is a secretary is a secretary is a wife is a wife.

*

"To be called 'colorful' is to be flattered and insulted at the same time. To be colorful is to be distinctive and, equally, to be dismissed."
Surrealism in photography during that era was defined by Man Ray. And the women who ventured into surrealist pho-

tography, like Lee Miller, also worked in black-and-white. Color was childish and loud and unserious. Miller imitated her mentor, that is to say, the men. Madame Yevonde found her own interpretation of Surrealism by using the very thing that men dismissed as "feminine," pushing all that color as far as she could. She was no man's muse. There is something unfettered about Yevonde's work. Maybe this what Lee Miller meant when she said, at the end of her life, that she wished she's been more free with her "ideas." Her pictures were never as fully realized as either someone like Madame Yevonde, or someone like Man Ray. This is the result of being caught in the middle where you aren't you but you aren't them, either.

*

"Color doesn't conform well to language; we often point to a color, or compare one thing to another when describing color."

I write about women. Some women I admire (some in this book) aren't always obvious sex or gender rebels or revolutionaries; their progress to the lives they desire is much quieter, less showy. They leave home, they love whom they love, they make their art, they accept some realities of life, while rejecting what they can. They say *No* while giving the impression they are saying *Yes*. I wrote a novel that used *quilt* in the title and somehow that invited some people to dismiss my novel as glancing, domestic. I created a structure, and I invented a story about women talking though art that maybe didn't look the way people wanted a feminist story to look. No matter.

*

"An object may change color, but the color never changes."

*

Le Corbusier, Part I

For Le Corbusier, ornament, clutter, glitter and color were not so much signs of 'degeneracy' as they were . . . kitsch. . . . Chromophobia (fear of color) manifests itself in the many and varied attempts to purge color from culture, to devalue color, to diminish its significance, to deny its complexity. More specifically: purging color is usually accomplished one of two ways. In the first, color is made out to be the property of some "foreign" body—usually the feminine, the oriental, the primitive, the infantile, the vulgar, the queer, or the pathological. In the second, color is relegated to the realm of the superficial, the supplementary, the inessential or the cosmetic. In one, color is regarded as alien and therefore dangerous; in the other, it is perceived merely as a secondary quality of experience, and thus unworthy of serious consideration. Color is dangerous, or it's trivial, or it is both.

—David Batchelor, *Chromophobia*

Le Corbusier, Part II

So, Le Corbusier. *This guy*, as the kids say. According to Batchelor, Le Corbusier (real name: Charles-Edouard Jeanneret) "was a man who would later say that color was 'suited to simple races, peasants and savages.'"

And, of course, women.

Eileen Gray, an Irish architect and furniture designer born in 1878 whose work is still unbelievably relevant; as a matter of fact, any one with the smallest awareness of modern furnishings would immediately recognize a certain end table and a certain chair that are still around today.

She also worked with lacquer on furniture.

Gray was famous during her life until she wasn't. Yves Saint Laurent collected her, and in 2009, an armchair that she made in the early twentieth century sold at auction for over twenty-eight million dollars, setting a record. Her work was influential, classic, collected, revered as art (included as a part of a permanent collection at the National Museum of Ireland), and this reverence and modernity goes for her architecture as well. Her aesthetic was clean, uncluttered, pure. You can imagine the men loving it.

In 1929, when Gray was 51, she completed her masterpiece, a modernist villa called E.1027 (the name is code for the letters of the alphabet that correspond to the initials of Eileen (E) Gray (7) and her lover, a younger man named Jean (10) Badovici (2), located in the South of France, on the a cliff overlooking the sea. E.1027 took three years to build, with Gray herself often hauling debris, clearing bushes, camping on the site to memorize the light. She designed all the furniture. There were banks of windows, and a winding stairway up to the flat roof. It is not unlike Le Corbusier's famous Villa Savoye, *which was begun the year E.1027 was completed.* The timing matters.

I'm often conflicted when considering the personalities and actions of artists and writers and how it influences how I feel about their art and books. Sometimes I worry that I like the work because I'm so taken with the artist or writer; I'm charmed, beguiled if you will, by their lives, or their style (Lee Miller is an excellent example; I'm still more attracted to pictures *of* her than pictures *by* her). If I really don't like what I know of the artist or writer, it can affect how I feel about their work. I try really really really hard to keep the two things separate.

Here is how I came to dislike Le Corbusier.

Gray and Badovici broke up shortly after E.1027 was finished. She gave him the house, and went off to a nearby Menton to build another modernist house, where she again considered the effect of light in her home, and arranged the rooms so that the more private spaces were tucked away in the back, offering a view of the hills, while the more social areas looked out at the sea and the city (it's been said that the house was clearly divided between public and private through water view and mountain-scape). Some materials were used both inside and outside.

The story goes that Le Corbusier had been a frequent house-guest of Badovici's after the couple split. During a stay in 1938 and 1939, Le Corbusier decided to paint Gray's white walls, the walls that weren't just a color choice, but part of the entire design of the house, with eight colorful murals. The man for whom "ornament, clutter, glitter and color were not so much signs of 'degeneracy' as they were . . . kitsch," and who famously built his own sleek white house, and not to forget his assessment of color being for "simple races, peasants and savages," painted the white walls of E.1027.

Villa Savoye, Le Corbusier's landmark house, is a remarkable structure: clean, uncluttered, modern, pure. Its relationship to Gray's E.1027 is evident, though it isn't a replica. What *is* replicated is Gray's use of white, inside and out.

Le Corbusier was often nude when he painted the murals at E.1027 which featured some sexual imagery. Rowan Moore, an art critic wrote, "As an act of phallocracy, Corbusier's actions are hard to top . . . seemingly affronted that a woman could create such a fine work of modernism, he asserted his dominion, like a urinating dog . . ." All the easier to achieve if you're defacing someone's work while in the nude. Gray stayed away from the house because she couldn't look at his "vandalism."

A coda to this mess, *Le Corbusier's murals are protected as a national art treasure.*

The house itself wasn't protected. The Germans used the place for target practice during World War II. Squatters defaced it with graffiti in the 1990s. Villa Savoye, nearly as old as E.1027, remained untouched.

It was also thought for some time that Le Corbusier was the architect of E.1027 because of some confusion about Gray not attaching her name to the house quickly enough.

This is a case where color was used maliciously, as an insult, as theft.

And this is why I have a hard time loving Le Corbusier's Villa Savoye, a house I once wished that I could live in.

*

Edgar Middleton made money, then lost money; Yevonde was the breadwinner in a household with the husband with the difficult personality. His published autobiography was called *I Might Have Been a Success*. She was the lighthearted, easy-laugh girl and he was the stick. But he was the stick that she loved, adhering to the truth of being a non-traditional woman: you can really only be with a certain type of man. You are both reinventing the relationship wheel every day. Living with anyone is a compromise. When O'Keeffe was asked why she always returned to New York from New Mexico she answered, *Because my husband was there*. Demanding everything to be your way isn't feminist, it's unrealistic and petulant. Letting down your guard to allow yourself to love and be loved isn't capitulation. Sometimes a feminist doesn't look like a feminist and it means nothing that you can't recognize her.

In the twenty-first century, there's no real model for everyone's roles when they're upended; there certainly wasn't in 1919. Leaving off social norms for a minute, how do you live with someone who wrote a book about themselves called *I Might Have Been a Success*?

Edgar died at age forty-four, in 1939, having survived one war, he left before the arrival of the next war. He couldn't know, for example, that Colour Studios, the lab that processed Yevonde's prints (the ones she had to specifically ask them not to color correct) closed due to the war, or that her final color picture showed a Roman head wearing a gas mask, next to red geraniums; he couldn't know that her business waned, and her fear mounted, since she lived alone with her cats on a heavily bombed street in London, that she found her way to an underground shelter during one particularly bad hit, and another damaging hit that left her trapped in her studio, in the darkness, later deciding to live on the outskirts of the city; nor could he have known that during one attack she left the shelter, went out to the garden to see the sky lit up in colors of red and purple; flames and gas. He couldn't have known that when she stopped making color pictures, "The exhilaration went out of her work," and that her Royal Photographic Society membership identified her as Mrs. Middleton. For a suffragette, a professional woman, a breadwinner, an artist who named herself an exotic, sly name like Madame Yevonde (that name the foundation of her professional, artistic identity), using Mrs. Middleton is not a casual decision.

*

A Slightly Different Self-Portrait

Then there is the picture that is pure narrative, unmistakable autobiography. No costumes, no playing with scale or her cat, though the markers of her life are present: a butterfly, a glass plate, a goddess. The light feminist touch. It is 1940. Madame Yevonde wears a suit (for all the extreme color and fantasy of her work, her personal style recalls a cinematic idea of a librarian). She holds a glass plate in her rubber-gloved hand, a blue butterfly hovers. She is inside an ornate, gold frame, like that of an Old Master that, in turn, sits on a table. The frame is significant in that Yevonde believed that color photography was "closer to painting," and her large 15" × 12" prints announced, in a manner similar to the post-war Abstract Expressionists who painted on large, museum-sized canvases, that she was making art.

There is a picture of one of her goddesses (Hecate), and a collection of bottles filled with chemicals used for developing scattered about the table. It's all color, no black-and-white. She looks tired, worn; her husband, Edgar Middleton, passed away the year before.

My father preferred colored stones while my mother only wanted diamonds.

PSYCHOANALYSIS WILL HELP YOU

Grete Stern

A series of photocollages called the Suenos *("dreams" in Spanish), of women roughly the same age, somewhere between their mid-twenties and mid-thirties, nicely dressed, beautifully made up and coiffed, middle class or upper middle class. Along with the occasional secretary. There were originally 140 of these images—46 remain as originals; the rest were tossed once they appeared in the women's magazine,* Idilio, *its readership the Argentine housewife.* Idilio *was published in Argentina after the war, years after German photographer Grete Stern and her husband, Horatio Coppola, porteño photographer, moved to Buenos Aires in 1934. The* Suenos *were the accompanying illustrations for a column called "Psychoanalysis Will Help You" that ran from 1948 to 1951. "Richard Rest"—in reality Professor Gino Germani, a prominent sociologist, and psychologist and publisher Enrique Butelman, both blacklisted by the Peronist government—was the "doctor" making the psychological interpretations of the dreams sent to him by their female readers—the dreams that Stern spun into collaged images.*

*

269

In the mid-1990s while visiting Barcelona, my friend, Katherine Slusher, handed me a rather perfect and unusual hardcover book that served as the catalog for an exhibition of photographer Grete Stern at a museum in Valencia. The book was smaller than the usual monograph that accompanies a museum show, sky blue with a tiny sepia-toned Stern photograph the size of a postage stamp glued to the cover. Inside the reproductions of the *Suenos* were also sepia-toned. Katherine said, *you will love this,* in reference to my affection for Madame Yevonde; Katherine and I already spoke a common art language, understanding, for example, *why* I liked the impish, witty technicolor-feminism of Madame Yevonde, (in particular her *Goddess* series.) She was right, of course, the *Suenos* were right up my alley.

To understand a little of the effect of photocollage, here's a passage by John Berger about John Heartfield, the famous German photomontagist who pioneered the art form as a way of protesting Hitler and fascism. His pictures are so daring and provocative and frankly oppositional that you can't believe he survived the war.

"With his [Heartfield's] scissors he cuts out events and objects from the scenes to which they originally belonged. He arranges them in a new, unexpected, discontinuous scene to make a political point . . . the particular advantage of photomontage lies in the fact that everything has been cut out keeps its familiar photographic appearance. We still look first at things and only afterward at symbols."

Stern put her photocollages together in a couple of ways: one used a standard cut-and-paste technique, the other used an enlarger that selectively blocked out certain images in order to arrange them on a single sheet of paper. In a way, a photocollage can function like that attractive stranger you were too quick to trust. You become dazzled by the play of images, only to be shaken by meaning.

The *Suenos* are a collection of dark fantasies, the subconscious secret lives of women exposed; the fears, anxieties, frustrations, resignation, desires and displacement. A jumble of dreamscape images of marriage, motherhood, and work. Heartfield's Hitler and his fellow fascists are the waking nightmare, while Stern's *Suenos* are the thoughts that cannot be voiced. One is global; one is personal. For a woman to bring these troubling feelings into the open, especially when there wasn't much alternative to being a wife and mother, was to begin to dismantle her own life.

*

Grete Stern was born in 1904 in Elberfeld, Germany. She was a student of Walter Peterhans, a photographer who taught at the Bauhaus and who made pictures of close-up still-lives. Very precise, very lovely. "Peterhans' teaching involved using the theories of Kant, Plato and Pythagoras to show how beauty is constructed in the mind, and how it can be created in works of art."
Beauty is constructed in the mind.
It was through Peterhans that Stern met the woman who was to become her friend and business partner, photographer Ellen Auerbach. Together they opened an innovative photography studio called ringl + pit (their childhood nicknames) using equipment they purchased from Peterhans. It was a Berlin-based studio that specialized in pictures for advertising (a relatively new field), even winning awards, which wasn't bad for a pair of women still in their twenties.
Berlin between the wars (the Weimar Republic) was a period of progressive and regressive politics, social upheaval, artistic innovation (all fields), literary excellence, design innovation in architecture, in household goods and textiles; poverty, military defeat, reparations, rebuilding, youth, and an old guard, sexual freedom and degeneracy and freedom and experimentation,

and money for some. It was a hugely populated city, modern and vast and attached to Nature and industrialization by turns. The fluidity of class and sex offered opportunities for The New Woman, that girl who raced cars, or worked in an office, or opened her own advertising photography studio.

The work of ringl + pit was modern, playful, surreal. Gloves, hats, veils, metal screens, mirrors, human hair, mannikins, a real human hand coming through the backdrop in place of a mannikin's hand. Use of printed words. A picture of a table-top, scattered with a leafy branch, seashells, a pair of geometric protractors, sand, lens, marbles, and woman's compact mirror with the reflection of a woman. The collection of objects, combined with the image of a woman's reflection, resembled a collage (one that includes a woman). A *collage* effect.

Three of my favorite photographs are by Ellen Auerbach: one of a woman tying a corset, her hands behind her back. We see her trussed-up figure, the corset ending in a ruffle, and below that the curve of the woman's milk-white derriere and the tops of her milk-white thighs contrasting with her black stockings. It's all sex in the space between the bottom of corset and top of the stockings.

The second image is of a woman applying lipstick in a mirror. She leans in close, her fingerless lace gloved hand presses against the glass. Very *Berlin Stories*. She doesn't care who's watching.

Finally, there's Grete herself, wearing glasses.

Auerbach made a scrapbook for Stern for her birthday in 1931 called *ringlpitis*. In a series of self-portraits, the women dressed in costumes, wore theatrical makeup; they are male, female, androgynous, role playing, sending up societal expectations; the two young women at play. Grete in a fake beard and long black gloves, dressed like a French sailor, sitting back in a chair as Auerbach, sporting angel wings, balances on top of her.

ringl + pit opened in 1930. Stern continued studying with Peterhans at the Bauhaus until 1933. During that time she met Horatio Coppola, also, a photographer, originally from Buenos Aires. After 1933, she emigrated to England, the political climate in Germany being what it was, and Grete Stern being Jewish. It was there that she set up a new studio, where Ellen Auerbach (also Jewish) joined her. Stern had family connections in England that Auerbach did not, and England's immigration laws being what they were, even under these political circumstances, forced Ellen to leave.

In 1935, Stern and Coppola married and moved to Buenos Aires, where they eventually had a boy and a girl and a divorce. Then the *Suenos*. In that order.

*

There simply is no better illustration, expression, or document of the anxieties of mid-twentieth-century women, trapped in traditions that didn't allow them to have lives other than the ones prescribed for them. A woman covers her eyes when she encounters an adult-size baby doll with its arms reaching out to her as she walks down a narrowed, walled path ; a woman's mouth has disappeared as she tries to speak on the phone; a woman in a living room with padlocks on the windows is terrified as a lion lunges toward her; a woman tries to climb a washboard so as not to drown in a laundry tub; a woman stands at a crossroads with unintelligible symbols for directions, suitcase in hand; a woman plays a violin with a broom; a secretary's legs have grown roots into the floor; a woman is trapped in a room so small she cannot stand or stretch. A clock whose hands are replaced by a woman, spinning around the numbers. A woman as a lamp, being turned on and off by a man, with the title, "Electric Appliances for the Home."

Or a woman who looks into a hand mirror and is shocked to see a man's reflection staring back.

Some time ago I read that educated, middle class, and upper-middle class American housewives began taking the tranquilizer Miltown in the 1950s, with consumption rising steeply in the early 1960s. Anyone who has ever been a stay-home parent understands the mind-dulling sameness of the day (unless you are that rare bird that loves to clean and care for babies and toddlers, who are awfully cute but don't really give a lot back in their early years conversationally speaking, and who can be kind of fun if you don't have anything else to do, you know, like cook, clean, market, laundry, shower, not to mention the pressure of making sure they don't have some horrible accident when your back is turned. I mean, just for starters). Most post-war families in America had three or more children, so all of what I just said, multiplies.

*

My mother began her work life when she was fifteen years old at B. Altman and Company, a department store located at 5th Avenue and 34th Street. This was part of a high school work-study program, working in the tearoom every other week. It wasn't long before she transferred to the credit office, a position she preferred in part because it allowed her to see the accounts of the famous people who shopped at the store. This is a job perk the voyeur in me can relate to.

When she was seventeen years old she worked for an advertising agency on Madison Avenue. Then at another on 57th Street, around the corner from Carnegie Hall. She said there were three professions women went into (my mother was born in 1926): teacher, nurse, or secretary. She hired on as a secretary, but "quickly noticed other jobs within the office," passing through two of them before becoming a media director.

She was still a teen at her first advertising firm where she would leave her office, take an elevator down to the lobby, then walk to a nearby hotel to use their ladies' room. Every day. The reason she didn't use the one on her floor was because she had to pass by the office of the art director who was always saying things to her like, "Come here and sit on my face."

There were four girls, all Italian American like her, who went through school together. Three of them were married (my mother had a couple engagements of her own along the way) and when the fourth, her best friend, Sena Pepe, told my mom that *she* was getting married, my mother, whose contradictory relationship with traditional female roles/progressive desire to have a business career, was similar to a silver ball in a pinball machine, lost it.

Enter Jean Olivet, who happened by for dinner (my mother, like good Italian girl she was, still lived with her folks), and said, "Let's move to California!"

This will tell you a key thing you need to know about my twenty-four-year-old mother: she jumped at the chance to leave, deliberately missing her best friend's wedding because "she couldn't handle going." My mother got a place in Los Angeles, except Jean Olivet never showed up. So my mother moved again, this time to an apartment in Beverly Hills where she met my dad, newly arrived from three years in Saudi Arabia. He would time his departure from his apartment every morning to coincide with my mother catching the bus and offer her a ride. She would time walking out of her apartment every evening at dinner time whereupon he would take her out.

They ended up eloping to Las Vegas in the early 1950s, then settled down in Pasadena, California. Then had a son and a daughter (me) and a son and a daughter and a divorce. In that order.

*

It should be clear by now that I like photographic series, particularly ones that are about women: Ruth Orkin photographing Central Park and the New York skyline from her window; Cunningham and her botanicals; Sally Mann and her children; Dater and her women. Stieglitz's visual love poem of a young Georgia O'Keeffe. Grete Stern and her *Suenos*. The single photograph is a single frozen moment, a pause, a cessation where we can only guess at the before and after. It can suggest a story, without being a complete story. But the series? The series is a flip book. The piling up of images, whether sequential or not, the story unfolding. The images contextualized by their accompanying images.

I'm a novelist at heart. I see the long game.

*

A word about Ruth Bernhard. The woman who made *Billie with Glass, 1971*. Who crisscrosses with the other photographers, writers, and artists in this telling, including my photographer friend, CS.

Ruth Bernhard's nudes—all women—are nothing but beautiful, and timeless, Bernhard's desire directed her toward classism. Her women exist in the space between idealism and realism; they're like breathing statues, homages to the importance of being female.

The bodies are sometimes fragmented (Stieglitz and O'Keeffe), or pushed into the place of perfection (Mapplethorpe, classicism), or shown as pure form (Edward Weston).

Edward Weston was Bernhard's mentor, her friend, the most important man in her life next to her father, Lucien Bernhard (echoing Lee Miller). She met Weston in Los Angeles in the 1930s. "When I first saw Weston's work, I burst into tears. It was a complete revelation. . . . His photography allowed me to accept my own work at higher value. It was as if I were hearing the music of Bach for the first time." A sentiment I understand so completely it almost moves me to tears.

(When I learned that my friend CS had known Ruth in San Francisco, she said, "You can ask me anything about her," Ruth having done for my friend in terms of photography what Weston did for Ruth, that sort of creative awakening. I still haven't asked my friend anything.)

Bernhard and Weston were close friends, close enough that Charis Weston (Edward's second, significantly younger, wife) sometimes thought Ruth a rival. The friends would flirt, and even though Ruth was more interested in women, an encounter with Weston was never a complete impossibility. He took a series of portraits of Ruth during her first visit that were "absolutely me," she said, though the images were slightly damaged due to a leaking developing tank. The whole situation: the pictures, the developing mistakes, Weston's ease with the portraits and the problems allowed her to see what was "human and endearing." She said that she saw Weston, now living in Carmel, California, as often as she could. "I adored him. He was enthusiastic . . . charming, witty, and a great raconteur. He was my type."

The print Weston asked for of Bernhard's was of a doll's head called *Creation, 1936*. She had been photographing the head while working at a doll hospital in Hollywood where she took portraits of the children of movie stars. (Ruth Orkin, in California, took pictures of movie stars as a child.)

Weston, emotionally and professionally, gave shape to Bernhard's work.

Lucien Bernhard, Ruth's father, influenced his daughter's photography in an entirely other manner.

Ruth was born near Berlin in 1905. Her father, who she says, was "at center stage, where he remained all my young life." Lucien Bernhard, a natural storyteller, who invented and reinvented his own biography, though he was a famous graphic artist (creating 36 typefaces) who also painted and sculpted. His paintings of women were of the "pinup girl" genre. Her parents had Ruth young, divorced young, then her mother left. Ruth said Lucien Bernhard wasn't "like a father" in that he showed up in her life (she lived at boarding schools and with relatives) in the form of the fairy tales he sent, too often busy with his art and women and another family. He was something of a romantic, artistic figure, very glamorous. (Her mother was absent and eccentric, insisting that she and Ruth be introduced as sisters.)

Ruth had her first love affair with a married man when she was seventeen. He was thirty-seven.

Eventually, she joined her father when he went to New York (a city that he was in love with), photographing images in patterns, like Lifesavers or straws, the light and shadows abstracting the objects, not unlike Margarethe Mather and Tina Modotti (also like Modotti she liked puppets; Modotti made dolls. All three women involved with Weston).

He introduced her to his contacts at magazines.

She met photographer Berenice Abbott, who had been Man Ray's assistant before Lee Miller.

She met Stieglitz who introduced her to O'Keeffe, saying they would have a lot in common. O'Keeffe invited Bernhard to join her in Santa Fe. Ruth said, "it seemed she had some interest in me. I declined."

And here's the heart of the matter, with this father and daughter, this pair of artists who both loved and made pictures of women. Ruth said:

They were all about the female body and my father's attitude toward women. As a girl growing up I had been in love with my father. As a young adult, when I observed him and realized how badly he treated women, I found him out. I always knew, when he looked at a girl, how he judged her, and I know that I would never qualify. I was not his pretty little daughter. Nor was I his son.

And this:

I remember the nudes of the 1939–1940 U. S. Annual. There was a girl on a stool flirting with a photographer. She was supposed to be pleasing everyone. It made me mad! . . . I wanted to express the dignity and simplicity of what it is like to BE a woman without thinking in terms of sexual interest.

I don't feel that one needs to do anything to make the body appear more sensual. Men have photographed a nude as if she belonged to them.

There it is again, that complicated father-daughter relationship that seems to mark so many of these photographers' lives, and Ruth's is furthered complicated by:

1. Choosing to make women her main subject (like her father did with his painting and sculpture) and
2. Loving women.

*

It is nearly impossible to know if Bernhard's women are from the 1940s or 1970s (when many of them were made), or last week. In this way, they are artistically similar to Yevonde's *Goddesses,* all beauty and displaced time. Politically the message is more overt: not enough has changed.

In the Box, Horizontal, 1962 a young woman, naked, lies inside a long box that has been placed on its side. The woman is herself inside the open box, her knees bent, her body a reclining *contrapposto,* with one arm fully outside the box, reaching behind her. It's a remarkable image in every way, one of those brilliant things that just worked out. Ruth said of that picture—its inspiration came from a box she saw in the street that someone had tossed. She ran down and dragged it up to her studio—"This picture has had a life of its own. Everyone gives it a different meaning," she said.

*

The Dinner Party, 1974–1979 by Judy Chicago

Here is a list of the 39 women (real and mythical) with places at the triangular table, with 13 place settings on each side of the triangle (the number 13 and the triangle significant). This is considered an important feminist work of art. Chicago and her some 400 helpers used ceramics and embroidery. The piece is not without controversy, both in the way it was made, and the choice of the women (largely white). It also bounces between being judged as art or artifact. I tend to think of it more as an artifact, a timepiece, a reminder of *then*.

Wing I: From Prehistory to the Roman Empire
1. Primordial Goddess 2. Fertile Goddess 3. Ishtar 4. Kali 5. Snake Goddess 6. Sophia 7. Amazon 8. Hatshepsut 9. Judith 10. Sappho 11. Aspasia 12. Boadicea 13. Hypatia

Wing II: From the Beginnings of Christianity to the Reformation
14. Marcella 15. Saint Bridget 16. Theodora 17. Hrosvitha 18. Trotula 19. Eleanor of Aquitaine 20. Hildegarde of Bingen 21. Petronilla de Meath 22. Christine de Pisan 23. Isabella d'Este 24. Elizabeth I 25. Artemisia Gentileschi 26. Anna van Schurman

Wing III: From the American to the Women's Revolution
27. Anne Hutchinson 28. Sacajawea 29. Caroline Herschel 30. Mary Wollstonecraft 31. Sojourner Truth 32. Susan B. Anthony 33. Elizabeth Blackwell 34. Emily Dickinson 35. Ethel Smyth 36. Margaret Sanger 37. Natalie Barney 38. Virginia Woolf 39. Georgia O'Keeffe

And this:

THE ADVANTAGES OF BEING A WOMAN ARTIST, 1988
BY THE GUERRILLA GIRLS

Working without the pressure of success.
Not having to be in shows with men.
Having an escape from the art world in your 4 freelance
    jobs.
Knowing your career might pick up after you're eighty.
Be reassured that whatever kind of art you make it will
    be labeled feminine.
Not being stuck in a tenured teaching position.
Seeing your ideas live on in the work of others.
Having the opportunity to choose between career and
    motherhood.
Not having to choke on those big cigars or paint in Ital-
    ian suits.
Having more time to work after your mate dumps you
    for someone younger.
Being included in revised versions of art history.
Not having to undergo the embarrassment of being
    called a genius.
Getting your picture in the art magazines wearing a
    gorilla suit.

*

Around the time I was joining my first (and last) consciousness
raising group, many female college graduates were joining with
their male counterparts in back-to-the-land dreams. Utopia in a
yurt. Drugs everywhere but in childbirth. People had been gathering in various communes with various philosophies (including having no philosophy at all) for several years. I was not a

commune sort of gal; I'm more of a private idealist. Also, the whole hippie thing wasn't really for me because I was too neurotic not to think that if you "go with the flow" you would probably end up with cancer, serious diseases being a consequence of inattention. Unless you get that disease that comes from outer space and manifests itself in threads that emerge from your pores, because no one can guard against turning into a family room sofa. When the Manson Family (a commune) unleashed itself, I was glued to the news, along with reading everything written in the *Los Angeles Times* (our newspaper), and while I knew they weren't true hippies, even if they looked the part, it just didn't help my fourteen-year-old world view at the time.

The trouble with the back-to-the-land homesteading movement is that it seemed to me to be some sort of punishment. You know, we've invented all these easy, timesaving devices because life had to be more than waking with the sun to churn your own butter, sew your own clothes, harvest your own wool, bake your own bread, ferrying your own water, deal with your period with cloth and an outhouse, and push out a baby in your free time. To me, this wasn't just a move back to living simply—it was a life of radical domesticity.

My sister-in-law lived in a remote Colorado cabin for two years from ages seventeen to nineteen with a man nearly ten years her senior. This was in 1978. *1978.* They didn't have electricity, so she sewed with a treadle sewing machine. They didn't have any plumbing, so she used an outhouse, and bathed in a tin tub in a field. They only ate what they grew, augmented by grains picked up at the store in town, a place I could only picture with an elderly man who lets you buy on credit, and offers you a choice of penny candy while the horses from the Wells Fargo wagon are watered down for the run to the next town. Everything was made from scratch and when she got to the part where once a month she treated herself to a bottle of Coca Cola, I began to feel that I was talking to a historical re-enactment hobbyist.

"And you did this *voluntarily?*" I asked, knowing my tendency to conflate "remote cabin" with the image of a middle-aged white male who makes unsuspecting hikers in isolated areas get on their knees so he can shoot them at the base of their skulls in ritualistic killing fashion. Do not get me started on lakes, i.e., the places where you dump the body.

"We just had to be sure to get out before getting snowed in because then we would be in trouble." *Did you have a horse named Wildfire?* I wanted to ask. During the few non-cabin months, the boyfriend did something with pools and she got paid work, then it was back to the mountains where their only neighbor was an old misanthrope who called her a whore because she wasn't married to Jeremiah Johnson, so I guess going to him for help in an emergency was out. Life is unforgiving in the nineteenth century.

*

Ruth Bernhard's nudes and love of dolls in her photographs (their heads anyway); the Stettheimer Dollhouse; Mrs. Glessner Lee's murder tableaus, the *Nutshell Studies of Unexplained Death;* Tina Modotti's dolls; Joseph Cornell's obsessive depiction of ballerinas and actresses in boxes and collages; Hans Bellmer and his dolls (the meanings sometimes murky)—it isn't any sort of leap at all to see the relationship between a model (particularly if she is a muse) and doll.

Mrs. Glessner Lee's little murders and accidents all take place in the home, the domestic sphere. And the Stettheimer Dollhouse, begun casually, soon took on an unexpected sophistication, removing forever any notion that it's a child's plaything (it is a grown woman's plaything).

If you're going to examine the lives of women (the dreams of women) you must begin with the home. And maybe dolls and dollhouses.

I started making box art assemblages in 1990. They began because I kept my jewelry in a collection of boxes, large and small, and when I needed to think something through I would gather up these boxes, and remove all the jewelry, arrange it on the floor, then put it all back in no particular order. Take it out, look at it, put it back.

My theory about the jewelry business is that it connected to the abstraction that is writing. All that world-building is largely in the mind, the manuscript a blueprint. I needed something tactile, tangible, and dimensional.

Anyway, the jewelry business led to making these decorative, fanciful boxes of various themes. They each had something unexpected inside, along with space for the owner of the box to add something of his or her own, as if the box I made was unfinished.

Then one day, the elaborate exteriors, went interior, and I began making shadow boxes, around 1994, I think, when my friend Susan Segal's novel *Aria* was published. I made a small shadow box inspired by the novel that showed a sailboat on a rough sea of broken mirror.

Not long after the *Aria* box I discovered Joseph Cornell in a big way, that is, Cornell didn't inspire me to make shadow boxes, which was probably a good thing since many people so love his work that it's almost impossible not to try to emulate it and I would've been no different. In my case it was the jewelry, then the decorative boxes, then my friend's novel/shadow box, then my own box assemblages.

When I was a kid I scavenged my father's workshop for pieces of wood, bits of metal, and glass to make my own toy house (which was more of a studio apartment—a kind of prophecy of many of the places where I would live as an adult) and "furniture" (matchboxes, cotton, cloth, junk). I made an outdoor area (more found stuff transformed). Even as a child, I would take this stuff out, arrange it, or rearrange it, then put it away.

(My first published novel was written as if it were pieces of a quilt. My first short stories, decades ago, were written as literary collages.)

I've always loved architecture, thinking I would be an architect one day (one of my many career desires). I think of my "found objects" house that never had dolls living in it, as working three-dimensional imagination while thinking about the various lives that would inhabit this house, and having a list of things I wanted to do with my life and, knowing I couldn't do all of them, chose instead to be a writer where I could live them all.

*

My second novel was about a disappearing woman. It touched on cultural perceptions of women and their various roles; social visibility and invisibility (I often thought about Ralph Ellison's *Invisible Man*), and women aging, and how you are judged physically when you step into the room and hoping that someone will talk to you so they will see that you are more than your age, more than your face.

I was also thinking of the Hostess Mentality where you allow everyone's needs and desires to come before your own; the Hostess as first cousin to the Good Girl. She wants to make sure other lives are in order before attending to her own. Sometimes, you forget you have a life at all. It can be exhausting, wanting to please everyone. In my novel the main character is often (literally) disappearing, and every time she tries to tell her own story, to try and understand what is happening to her, she ends up talking about the lives of her friends and family. A book reviewer criticized the novel, saying, "the main character doesn't even talk about her own life" and I wanted to say, *yes, exactly.*

*

Grete Stern worked with images, taking them (the jewelry, for example, in my case) out of their original context (the jewelry box), then combining them with other images, putting them all together to create a new image (leftover wood can become a house; a matchbox a bed). Her photocollage dreams of the interior world of the post-war middle-class housewife does what straight photography couldn't do and have the same impact, the same accuracy. This is because on any given day, no, at any given moment, everything is true and not true about women in the home. No set-up tableaux could've managed it, which is why any sort of set-dressed idea of domesticity too often resembles a send-up, something more satirical where the female model seems in on the joke.

Collage, with its myriad pieces, not only changes the original meaning of its parts, but it offers a certain intellectual, or visual, precision; it can lay the heart bare.

*

The writer Jodi Angel wrote, ". . . nobody tells you when you have a child that you are putting shoes on your own heart."

My father was emotionally distant (something I very much came to appreciate later). He couldn't read people, those mysteries that surrounded him. And children were more mysterious still. He was a sidelines guy, an observer, but people? People were pure dada, a place where the nonsensical and disparate meet.

My mother was emotional to the point of being an open book, one that was often entertaining, fun to read, yet maddening. She was the little Italian girl with class aspirations, an intrinsic glamour and a longing for excitement who, in another life, might have graduated from college and went even farther in her career (though what she did was impressive enough). She loved the business world. She might have gone into law. Most importantly, she loved people. She loved their stories and socializing. She loved it best when they were interested in her. Later on, she married her married boss (eighteen years her senior) with whom she had a two-year affair, then was widowed by age forty-seven, never to remarry unless you count the quasi-marriage she has with my brother. (My mother also dated *significantly* younger men after my stepfather passed, years before Cher; my parents were never fully how they appeared.) She loaned her gowns to her gay male friends and went to their weed parties. She asked me why the guests passed around the same "wet little cigarette and why didn't they just have their own?" She was more concerned with the lack of hygiene than the fact that weed was still an illegal drug, something that concerned her not at all. Since she didn't smoke I asked what happened when they passed the "wet little cigarette" to her? "Oh, I tell them I quit."

These two people created the parental emotional imbalance of my upbringing: the minimal, almost elliptical connection with one parent, and a nearly suffocating avalanche of passionate yearning from the other.

Then, one day, I became a parent myself only to discover that I loved my kid so much I sometimes found myself pushing against it, pretending a breeziness I never felt. I again found myself marooned between a longing to let the mad love for my kid rule my (our) lives and the restraint that would let him know that, no matter what, I'd be okay without him, that I wasn't his responsibility. I knew that I was never going to be a helicopter parent or a tiger mom which all seems like a swing in the wrong parental direction.

My mother made me her audience and her confidant, despite our age difference and worldly experience. This sort of closeness with a parent, especially one as charismatic as my mother, can be intoxicating to a child. You do all the listening because you don't have any stories to offer—not like her stories—and she tosses in some valuable life lessons (my Greatest Generation parents had all kinds of friends, for example), but then the line gets crossed and she forgets how young you are when she's talking to you about adult subjects, stuff you have no business knowing. Later she will say, *you were just so precocious, so smart and funny.* Really what you were was an available audience. This "friendship" creates a closeness that doesn't wear well. And I loved her, so I was inclined to be on her side, which made things dicey when she demanded my loyalty against my father before, during, and after they parted. What you learn from all this is to relax your judgement and see the world prismatically. You also say to yourself, *If I ever have a child I will be his mother and not his friend, I mean, I will be a friendly mother but not confide in him, even if he confides in me, I will be his mother and not his peer, or make him my peer, or confidant, and I hope like hell he won't think I'm just being distant, but I don't want to risk everything by emotionally crowding him and making him think he is the moon and stars even if he is the moon and the stars.*

Everything was further complicated by not wanting to be defined by my child; I didn't want to burden anyone with my dreams. I needed to keep in touch with my own dreams, though it felt that it sometimes came at the expense of being a mother (childrearing and artistic creation drawing on a similar interior well as they do). I still had dreams. I still have dreams.

I also had a relationship with J. that I didn't want replaced.

I had friends.

And I still wrote.

Then I saw the work of Sally Mann, Ruth Orkin with instant recognition.

Then I saw the *Suenos* and I knew other dreams wouldn't be out of place with those dreams.

*

I knew my mother didn't want to be home with us kids. We weren't interesting enough, motherhood wasn't interesting enough. She would say it was because my brother was such a handful, so off to work she went, leaving my sister and me without her. She would let me stay home from school if I claimed to be sick, even though it meant staying home alone.

My working mother outsourced her domestic duties: house-keeping, childcare. We had a cornucopia of caregivers—some who lived with us full-time or part-time or not at all—that were young, old, middle-aged, white, Black, European (two from the Netherlands), Latina (one from Guatamala, another Mexican American), sweet, bitchy, bored, fun, religious, male and female.

Our next-door neighbor, with whom we were friends, believed for more than two years that two sisters lived in our house: the pretty, glamorous one who drove off each morning in her white Cadillac, and the plain, mousey one who took care of the house, who she only saw on the weekends. Not only is this a fairy tale in the flesh, but it gave my father a cachet that no one would believe even if it were true.

What you learn from all this is to relax your judgement and see the world prismatically.

*

Joseph Cornell

Joseph Cornell was a twentieth-century artist best known for his shadow box assemblages of various themes (France, the bal-

290 · WHITNEY OTTO

let, film stars, birds, pharmacies, observatories, celestial themes, hotels), often using Victoriana, bric-a-brac, or thrift store finds. Many of his shadowboxes were portraits (including one of Lee Miller). He made paper collage (including one of Lee Miller), and experimental "collage" films from old film stock.

In *Rose Hobart* (1931), his most well-known film collage, he took a Hollywood movie (*East of Borneo*), then cut out all the scenes that did not feature the leading lady. He bathed the entire nineteen-minute film in blue. Just blue, the film falls out of categories of black-and-white or color movies. It is its own thing. The effect is poetic and absorbing. At a showing of *Rose Hobart*, Salvador Dali leapt from his seat, accusing Cornell of "stealing from my dreams."

Whistler combined music and painting, and Stein combined words and painting. This essay that you're reading, in fact this entire essay collection that you're reading? It's a Cornell box.

*

Joseph Cornell was the master of the three-dimensional collage. His work is yearning, poetic, dreamy, nostalgic, archival, whimsical, reverential. The penny arcades and planets and birds only masquerade as playful; there is a kind of precise elegance, but not play. It's hard to pin down why Cornell's boxes provoke any sort of feeling given how they're so very weird. The Surrealists were right to recognize him as one of their own, despite the insistence on the part of Cornell that he was definitely *not* a Surrealist. From where I sit, I would argue that he was confusing intention with results since it may not have been his *intention* to mine the subconscious, but the *result* suggests a dreamer in full. It is the sole non-ambiguous aspect of his art, I think.

His shadow boxes—the medium he is best known for, though he also made movies and paper collages, and assembled "dossiers" on public figures (usually the actresses and ballerinas he so obsessed over). These files were not mean to be art as much as to lay the groundwork for shadow boxes yet they still read like portraits of a sort, disturbing and engaging and more revealing about Cornell than about his subject. Sort of like putting together characters without writing the novel.

He often made boxes for the artistic, performing women he favored, romantic tokens of his shy affection, though there weren't many takers. It was unnerving to be the focus of this odd, birdlike man, who was reserved almost to the point of emotional paralysis, proffering these strange, glassed-in, timeless worlds, sometimes (but not always) using their images. The boxes, too, sometimes suggested confinement.

The shadowboxes cover a variety of obsessions, among them women, often actresses and ballet dancers. Women were his fixation. He made boxes, films, dossiers about the women and girls that caught his eye, some famous, some not. He wrote about them in his diary. His interest has been described as, "sentimental, creepy and painfully innocent."

The common image of Cornell is that of a recluse, locked away in his basement of stuff, in the house he shared on Utopia Parkway with his domineering widowed mother, and his much-loved brother, Robert, who was confined to a wheelchair. When he was away from home, he wandered Manhattan like a magpie, acquiring found objects from vintage shops and drugstores, or buying old movie film stock. He liked to stop for something sweet, or maybe just observe the young women that he was too repressed to approach.

Except he wasn't reclusive; he was extraordinarily shy. Many visitors—art collectors, and artists—made the trek to his shared home, where he offered them terrible supermarket pastries while giving most of his attention to the women that sometimes accompanied the men. Cornell had trouble letting go of his shadow boxes (often making "variants" for himself). These variants, I think, had something to do with his need to hold on to them: If he had the boxes then he could stand next to them while his guests admired them. It was a visual way of explaining himself without saying a word, a little like the shy gift-giving: Art as a conversational shortcut. The assemblages, those collaged objects illustrated the man with their penny arcades, Victoriana, interests in history (the Renaissance), hotels (freedom, France, travel), the stargazing, the birds, and, finally, the celebrities and personalities (Lee Miller, Lauren Bacall, Audrey Hepburn), laying out who he was by showing us what he loved.

(This collection of people and things is the key to this book. This book, a key to me.)

Any expansiveness in Cornell's life was contained in those shadow boxes—in a way, any *life* he had could be found there. They were his travel, his romantic attachments to those unattainable women, his worlds of stars and maps. His was a lopsided life where his imaginative self loomed larger than his everyday self as the reticent, gray man who looked older than his age, who lived on cheap mass-produced coffee cakes, with his bossy mother and much-loved brother while his "box" life was vivid and daring.

*

Joseph Cornell belongs with Ruth Bernhard, with Grete Stern, with their women-centric art. He is even closer to the artist-wives-mothers who made their art in the small spaces of their homes, and the even smaller spaces between their domestic duties since Cornell's family was dependent upon him, not just financially, but physically, placing Cornell, for me, squarely in the company of woman artists locked into domesticity, an assessment he might not have minded.

Stern's *Suenos* depicted the anxieties of women, that uncontrolled subconscious. Art is a way to leave without leaving. (Orkin, Cunningham.) Cornell was a Francophile who never left the country, though that didn't prevent him from using French in his work, or "inventing France," his dream of romance, of travel and freedom, seen most clearly in the *Hotel* boxes.

*

Joseph Cornell joined the Christian Science church when he was twenty-one. He had chronic digestive issues, not helped by an almost exclusively sugary diet. His brother, Robert, was confined to a wheelchair by his cerebral palsy. Cornell wouldn't be the first person to look elsewhere when conventional medicine failed. Call it a gateway situation.

Cornell's mother wasn't happy about her son's choice to follow a metaphysical religion founded in the nineteenth century by a sometimes problematic woman (Mary Baker Eddy), and it seems appropriate that Cornell embraced one of the only religions founded by a woman (I can only think of one other one offhand—Theosophy—and I believe that Madame Blavatsky founded it with a couple of men).

Most people think of Christian Scientists as people "who don't believe in doctors" (the Santa Claus phrasing is theirs). They, the non-Christian Scientists, have it right and wrong; adherents of the religion often choose not to turn to doctors— the reasons for this decision are the foundations of the faith—but if they do seek medical treatment it doesn't change their standing in the church. No one is shunned or demoted or excommunicated or punished or anything. Nothing happens to you.

The religion pulls its ideas from a man named Phineas Quimby (a mesmerist, among other things), Hinduism, Emersonian Transcendentalism, and Judaism.

So, here is the heart of the story of my Greatest Generation parents: they had a little boy who passed away when he was three years old. They were not religious. They took their child to doctors in Los Angeles and New York. Then he died.

They were as flattened by grief as one can imagine. I was five months old and clocking serious time down at the neighbors, the formerly midwestern people by the name of Smedley to whom my mother wanted to give me because she couldn't bear her own life. All of which led them to Christian Science.

My parents didn't care all that much about the medical part of the religion, they just cared that they were healed of their grief. My dad also liked it because it's a faith devoid of ritual and is more of the mind than the all too human mess of emotions. No one kneels, or makes hand signals, or eats crackers. No magic, no mystery, none of what makes religion halfway entertaining, or reassuring.

Anyway, this is how I came to be raised in Christian Science (Joseph Cornell's adopted faith), a religion where non-Christian Science parents would frequently remind me that, if push came to shove, my parents would "let me die before taking me to a doctor." I was too polite to answer, *Funny you should say that because my parents did take my brother to a series of doctors and, well, let's just say it didn't end well. But thanks for the judgement, and the heads up. You know I'm just a kid, right?* It isn't alarming or anything to have *adults* inform you that your parents are so casual about your mortality.

Or people would always tell me The Story of the Babysitter whose young charge died of appendicitis because the parents were Christian Scientists, sometimes the babysitter died because *her* parents were Christian Science. There was always a fair number of fatal appendix instances. Sometimes peers and their parents insisted that I was Church of Religious Science, or Seventh Day Adventist, or Jehovah's Witness, or, my personal favorite, a Scientologist, as if I didn't know my own religion. Or kids would scoff "so, if you jumped off a cliff, you're saying that God would save you," to which I would look confused and say, "Why am I jumping off a cliff?"

Christian Science is not a converting, door-to-door, let's talk deal. It's kind of on the down low, and that's how I kept it.

My parents weren't hardcore and didn't care what church or synagogue I attended on the weekends as long as I went somewhere, though they did keep me unvaccinated, and I was made to sit in the hall if the school nurse walked into the classroom to hand out polio vaccines on sugar cubes, or give a health lecture. The school hallway was the location of punishment where I had to explain to passing fellow students that I wasn't in trouble, even though I quickly realized that it was easier to be considered a troublemaker than part of a religion thought to kill its own children.

Anyway, after a youth spent reading the encyclopedia that took up an entire shelf of my bedroom and included my sole medical education, I began to develop a kind of "hypochondria lite." Hypochondria is really the crossroads of a little information and a lot of imagination, those two things, in my case, enhanced by faith-healing. By the time I left home at eighteen, I left Christian Science as well.

*

Here's what I can tell you about Christian Science (in a nutshell): it is about the spirit and not the body. There is, in fact, a fairly radical separation from the corporeal world. Sin, disease, death are an illusion; Love, God, goodness, health are reality. Jesus isn't a savior or a redeemer of our sins (they don't believe in sin) or the magical son of God, or seen in any traditional Christian role. God is dual-gendered, "father-mother-God." You have a problem with someone? You must love them. They're awful to you? You must love them. God is love and love is the Truth. The body, that old shell? Meaningless.

I'm not convinced that Cornell was drawn to Christian Science solely on the basis of his and his brother's physical issues, or that he thought of Mary Baker Eddy as a "Houdini" making ailments "disappear like elephants."

I think it's very possible that he liked the religion because it allowed him to take the focus off his (troublesome) body, reducing its importance.

For Cornell, who may have finally lost his virginity at the outer edges of middle age, and who—more importantly—was tethered to a domestic situation that, until his mother and brother died, he temporarily escaped with city walks and making art in the basement. The *Hotel* series (and all of his Francophilia) was about the transitory life of travel, of getting away, of losing yourself within time, of being unencumbered, of not being home, of not answering to anyone, having no particular place to be, and maybe taking a walk along the Seine. The *Hotel* boxes are empty rooms that suggest a temporary resident, someone who just stepped out, maybe to wander the city, collecting found objects like souvenirs.

By freeing himself from the physical preoccupations of the body he could "travel" (in his mind), eat whatever he chose without regard to health, and ignore the mind-body problem of erotic desire.

In his hotel box *A Serenade for Juan Gris* (mid-twentieth century), there is a sense of an expansiveness contained within a small space. The shadow box is nearly empty, yet it provokes a strong response, as if you can sense Cornell's relief of being lifted out of his housebound, prescribed domestic life, his inner self alive with dreams of being somewhere else (maybe being someone else)—the very thing that connects him to Ruth Orkin or Imogen Cunningham.

Or Grete Stern.

It's so easy for me to see the *Suenos* and to see Cornell's boxes, especially the *Aviaries* (birds caught up in branches, or tethered to a perch, or living in an enclosure), and the *Hotels,* those boxes that feel almost spiritual, airy, and weightless, absent the clutter of some of his other work which can feel cluttered, beautifully so, but cluttered.

*

The shadow boxes aren't unlike a book—the variants as chapters—the story comes together in pieces. A writer places things in a book like a box and asks the reader to interpret them.

*

Many of Cornell's boxes remind me of snapshots, stopped time. Why the collection and arrangement of his objects creates that feeling for me I cannot say, only that they don't tell a whole story as much as they seem to interrupt a story that I cannot quite grasp.

*

The Mind-Body Problem Illustrated

In 1962, when Cornell was sixty-one years old, he became involved in his first romance, with an eighteen-year-old unmarried mother who worked as a waitress in a Manhattan diner. Joyce Hunter was, by all accounts, somewhat plain, somewhat plump, financially strapped, and minimally educated. He frequented the diner where she worked; she talked to him; she came out to the house. He gave her boxes, which she sold. This went on for a few months, he notes in his journal that he kissed her, then she disappeared. His *Penny Arcade* series were made with her in mind. He behaved as someone who had denied his physical longing for nearly his entire life would behave: recklessly, foolishly, hopefully.

By the next year, she showed up at his house with a friend, asked for one more box, but he said no.

Interlude of a couple of other women, exhibitionist artists, one of which he was sexually involved (to a point), until 1964 when Joyce Hunter returned with a friend and stole nine boxes worth roughly $1000 each (though that is over $8000 in today's dollars, his work sells for considerably more) from where he kept them in his garage. A former dealer contacted Cornell and turned her in; whereupon Cornell did everything to get her off the hook. He semi-looked after her, sending her money, having her over to the house. She was murdered later that year.

*

Lee Miller photographed Cornell. Cornell made two pieces with Miller in mind. Lee Miller who said, at the end of her adventurous, extraordinary life, "I keep saying to everyone, "I didn't waste a minute of my life—I had a wonderful time, but I know myself, now that if I had it to do over again I'd be even more free with my ideas, with my body and with my affections."

Joseph Cornell said, at the end of his quiet, geographically and emotionally limited life, that he "wished he had been less reserved."

*

A few women-centric objects in my house: my original 1972 ERA bracelet, sold by the League of Women Voters, purchased when I was in high school. A menorah made of individual women standing on crescent moons in sterling silver and copper and made by a jewelry store in Oregon run by women. A glass mermaid from Provincetown. A painted portrait of a nude woman on a blue sofa, and another of a nude woman with blue hair, and an etching of a woman with naked women in her hair, all by Jesus de Vilallonga, a Catalan painter. A contemporary tintype of a woman wearing a black lace mask. A collection of sterling silver Madonnas from various trips to Barcelona and Madrid.

*

Joseph Cornell's *idee fixe* with women dominated his art and his life. His single-mindedness inevitably became a stumbling block to ever truly knowing women. He invented them instead.

Ruth Bernhard made such flawless photographs of women that they seemed plucked from heaven and sculpted by light. The women are so perfect there is almost no space for eroticism, a fetish without the sex.

Cornell's women are really Cornell (housebound and yearning).

The complexity of Cornell's *relationship* to women is more about his distancing elevation of them.

Bernhard's women are wishes.

Neither artist, Cornell or Bernhard, creates art that tells us *about* women.

Virginia Woolf writes about the unpleasantness of being "locked out" and how it is "worse perhaps to be locked in." She was talking about women, and how being excluded, that is, outside of expectations, can be an advantage. The female mind doesn't seek to emulate the male mind; instead it becomes something new. We see it all the time in movies and books, the person who suddenly finds herself on the outside, suddenly finds herself. Or Joseph Cornell whose art took all his little obsessions, locked them away in a glass-fronted box that, paradoxically, also put them on display.

Being "locked in" can mean being imprisoned in societal roles. Men, for example, might feel the constraints of societal expectations. But the difference between the genders has often been one of choice. Men have long had alternatives.

Bernhard's elegant nudes are a response to the inability to photograph a naked woman as a man would (as her father would), forcing her to develop a separate visual language that both references the classicism of the past in the form of a contemporary woman.

Cornell is simply an uncommon (for his time) male artist who was both locked in and out, a situation that is decidedly feminine.

Stern's women are excluded and trapped. Night after night, dream after dream, they can't escape their female roles and they can't settle into them, either. The column "Psychoanalysis Will Help You" in *Idilio* was a brilliant way of inviting women to share the aspects of their lives that they dare not complain about openly. It allowed them to relate dreams (in the Freudian sense), those rogue thoughts that no one can be expected to control. Who knows what it all means? These peculiar tableaux where a husband has the head of a lizard, or a wife clings to a rock located just above the violent surf, or she gazes into a black mirror, or has her head transformed into a paintbrush that the man uses to paint their home. The *Suenos* were a way of giving voice to women without them saying a word, because what kind of person would you be if you had all the creature comforts, with all your husband provides, and what about those children that are supposed to give you the satisfaction of the fulfilled maternal promise and you said, I'm not sure this is who I am?

In *A Room of One's Own* Virginia Woolf writes about a moment where during an Oxbridge luncheon, a woman spies a tailless cat outside. She is momentarily distracted by the little cat, her thoughts derailed. One of the ideas behind this incident is to illustrate the life of the woman writer, the one who cannot retreat to the solitude of her own room. As a wife/mother/writer I'm all too familiar with the tailless cat. A ceramist artist friend of mine and I used to call it "fish on the lawn." It was a reference to her husband returning from a fishing trip, laying out his catch on the lawn, then interrupting her work, asking her to come and see it.

The thing about the Manx and the fish is that they catch your attention. Sometimes, you welcome the break, even if the timing is someone (or something) else's timing. After all, you love the cat and the fish, you married them, you gave birth to them, they mean everything to you, and you're always fighting against your own predisposition to distraction anyway when you're working. Art, books, music: it's all so fraught and complex and exhilarating and risky that if someone mentions a Manx or a salmon, it's almost a relief, that is, until it undoes you.

EPILOGUE

Revisiting *The Advantages of Being a Woman Artist*, Thoughts on Writing, and One Question

The Advantages of Being a Woman Artist, *1988* by the Guerrilla Girls

Working without the pressure of success.

If you write a novel with the word "quilt" in the title, then you deserve to be dismissed by the men *who are dragged* to your readings (as you've been told more than once) by their wives or girlfriends. You will be asked, by a man, where you were invited to talk about your novel to an audience of 1,200 people, if you plan to write a book about cooking next? He will be very proud to have said this to you, in front of 1,200 people, so everyone will know just how much he devalues what you've written.

Not having to be in shows with men.

You will only be asked to participate on "women-themed" panels, never plain writer panels, because you are a "woman writer" who seemingly doesn't write about the human condition but only about women. Sometimes, just trying to parse this out made your empty little lady head hurt.

Having an escape from the art world in your 4 freelance jobs.
I made the mistake of getting more serious about teaching in academia when I was in my mid-forties. (I had seen male writers do the same and get hired.) I mistakenly thought that my publishing record, MFA from a good university, and experience would matter more than age. Then I was reminded that I lived in the real world.

Knowing your career might pick up after you're eighty.
Um. Ha?

Be reassured that whatever kind of art you make it will be labeled feminine.
Four words: "Quilt" in the title.

Not being stuck in a tenured teaching position.
Yes, being an adjunct is the Holly Golightly of academia. You love the freedom.

Seeing your ideas live on in the work of others.
More than once. Not in the right way, and not because I think I'm all that great.

Having the opportunity to choose between career and motherhood.
This is what happens when love becomes multiplied beyond the hours of the day. You think you are doing both things simultaneously: writing and mothering. But really you are doing them in an alternating pattern so hectic that it only appears that both are happening at the same time.

Not having to choke on those big cigars or paint in Italian suits.
My dream is to paint in an Italian suit.

Having more time to work after your mate dumps you for someone younger.

In my case, it was just enough that the work place that preferred someone younger. Because, you know, all older women are so difficult and intractable. Really, we're quite monolithic in our personalities.

Being included in revised versions of art history.

I wish.

Not having to undergo the embarrassment of being called a genius.

I think I would have to change my name to Jonathan, or Michael, or David. For a start.

Getting your picture in the art magazines wearing a gorilla suit.

We're all in gorilla suits.

*

Thoughts on Being a Writer

Joseph Cornell said, *"Life can have significance even if it appears to be a series of failures."*

Writing is one of those professions marked by ongoing failure and success. Success and failure tend to be fluid in their definitions when applied to writing or the arts. Sometimes your best goes unnoticed; sometimes you can't judge your own work. Sometimes you read something you wrote and you don't even see the words on the page, you only see your life at the time you were writing those words, it's all you remember. Sometimes it's just another part of your life where the love is larger than you can manage, and the tumble harder than you thought.

*

Gertrude Stein, *The Making of Americans,* "*I write for myself and strangers.*"

This pretty much sums up the impossibility of the profession. If you ask me.

*

"*Ladies, there is no neutral position for us to assume.*"
—Gertrude Stein

A reminder that if you speak up, you are out of line and unlikely to get what you want (still, which is amazing to consider). And if you remain silent, you are unlikely to get what you want (still, which is amazing to consider).

*

From *Everybody's Autobiography* by Gertrude Stein:

It always did bother me that the American public has more interest in me than in my work. After all there is no sense in it because if it were not for my work they would not be interested in me so why should they not be more interested in my work than in me. That is one of the things one has to worry about in America.

As if there isn't enough pressure on the writer, now you have to be a celebrity, too. Do you become, like Hemingway, the public's version of you? Do you need a persona to be a success in the arts? Isn't the art itself persona enough?

*

The Pillow Book of Sei Shonagon

Sei Shonagon, born in the tenth century in Japan, was a lady of the Japanese court. She married, had children, and married and maybe married again. Her pillow book is a collection of poetry, and short, lyrical entries detailing things she loves and things she doesn't love. It's like a personal miscellany that wouldn't be out of place if written today.

Lady Murasaki, another court lady and the author of the *Tales of Genji,* had a rivalry with Shonagon, though Murasaki won in the only way that writers can win: by writing important work that lasts. I imagine the two women as the Imperial Japan equivalent of Lillian Hellman and Mary McCarthy with their ongoing feud that culminated with McCarthy saying, "Every word she [Hellman] writes is a lie, including 'and' and 'the.' (Side note: I borrowed this line when I wrote to George W. Bush protesting entering Iraq in the two weeks before the invasion.)

It's said that Shonagon lived out her days as a Buddhist nun in poverty, which is how you *know* she was a writer.

In her final entry Shonagon writes of her pillow book: ". . . *odd facts, stories from the past, and all sorts of other things, often including the most trivial material. I concentrated on things and people I found charming and splendid; my notes are also full of poems and observations on trees and plants, birds and insects, I was sure when people saw my book they would say, 'It's even worse than I expected. Now one can tell what she is really like.'"*

*

Why do I write?
Was there ever a choice?

ACKNOWLEDGMENTS

Writing is a solitary endeavor, but making a book takes the proverbial village. As always, I couldn't ask for a better agent (or friend) than Joy Harris, who is something of the mayor of my village. Thank you, too, to Mad Creek Books: the wonderful Kristen Elias Rowley and the marvelous Rebecca Bostock. Thank you, Tara Cyphers, Samara Rafert, and Jessica Melfi.

I remain deeply grateful to the writers of the biographies, newspaper articles, interviews, monographs; the numerous art exhibitions at museums and galleries that I read, studied, visited over the years. There are almost too many books and places to name (and a more formal bibliography can be found at the end of my novel *Eight Girls Taking Pictures,* the companion piece to this book for anyone interested in the stories of many of these artists and writers), but I'd still like to mention a few more books here that weren't mentioned there (this is as very short list):

Chromophobia by David Batchelor; *The Life and Art of Florine Stettheimer* by Barbara J. Bloemink; *Take Care of*

Yourself by Sophie Calle; *Don't Kiss Me: the Art of Claude Cahun and Marcel Moore* edited by Louise Downie; Mapplethorpe by Patricia Morrisroe; *A World Through My Window* by Ruth Orkin and Arno Karlen; *Georgia O'Keeffe* by Georgia O'Keeffe; Roxana Robinson's *Georgia O'Keeffe: A Life*. *Ways of Seeing* by John Berger.

Thank you, David Shields, always. Thank you, Katherine Slusher, Camille Solyagua, Michael Brod, Katherine Vaz (who told me about synesthesia), and Steven Josefsberg for your wonderful gallery and for introducing me to Herman Leonard. Thank you, Joan Takayama-Ogawa, for the fish on the lawn.

Thank you, Jan Novotny and Simone Seydoux. Sloane Lowell and Bill Otto. When I published my first book in 1990, I ended every reading or talk with a long quote from James Baldwin. A kind of touchstone. It ends like this:

The finest principles may have to be modified, or maybe even pulverized by the demands of life, and that one must find, therefore, one's own moral center and move through the world hoping that this center will guide one aright. I consider that I have many responsibilities, but none greater than this: to last, as Hemingway says, and get my work done.

I want to be an honest man and a good writer.

Thank you, John and Morganfield, for the cheap entertainment that is life with you guys. You are the most fun anyone could ever have without leaving home.

Whitney Otto is the author of five novels, including the *New York Times* bestseller *How to Make an American Quilt,* which was later made into a movie of the same name, and *Eight Girls Taking Pictures.* Her work has appeared in the *New York Times,* the *Los Angeles Times,* the *San Francisco Chronicle,* and in several anthologies. She lives in Portland, Oregon, with her family.

21st CENTURY ESSAYS
David Lazar and Patrick Madden, Series Editors

This series from Mad Creek Books is a vehicle to discover, publish, and promote some of the most daring, ingenious, and artistic nonfiction. This is the first and only major series that announces its focus on the essay—a genre whose plasticity, timelessness, popularity, and centrality to nonfiction writing make it especially important in the field of nonfiction literature. In addition to publishing the most interesting and innovative books of essays by American writers, the series publishes extraordinary international essayists and reprint works by neglected or forgotten essayists, voices that deserve to be heard, revived, and reprised. The series is a major addition to the possibilities of contemporary literary nonfiction, focusing on that central, frequently chimerical, and invariably supple form: The Essay.

Art for the Ladylike: An Autobiography through Other Lives
WHITNEY OTTO

The Terrible Unlikelihood of Our Being Here
SUSANNE PAOLA ANTONETTA

*Warhol's Mother's Pantry: Art, America, and the Mom in Pop**
M. I. DEVINE

Don't Look Now: Things We Wish We Hadn't Seen
EDITED BY KRISTEN IVERSEN AND DAVID LAZAR

How to Make a Slave and Other Essays
JERALD WALKER

Just an Ordinary Woman Breathing
JULIE MARIE WADE

My Private Lennon: Explorations from a Fan Who Never Screamed
SIBBIE O'SULLIVAN

*On Our Way Home from the Revolution: Reflections on Ukraine**
SONYA BILOCERKOWYCZ

Echo's Fugue
DESIRAE MATHERLY

This One Will Hurt You
PAUL CRENSHAW

---

*Annual Gournay Prize Winner

The Trouble with Men: Reflections on Sex, Love, Marriage, Porn, and Power
DAVID SHIELDS

Fear Icons: Essays*
KISHA LEWELLYN SCHLEGEL

Sustainability: A Love Story
NICOLE WALKER

Hummingbirds Between the Pages
CHRIS ARTHUR

Love's Long Line
SOPHFRONIA SCOTT

The Real Life of the Parthenon
PATRICIA VIGDERMAN

You, Me, and the Violence
CATHERINE TAYLOR

Curiouser and Curiouser: Essays
NICHOLAS DELBANCO

Don't Come Back
LINA MARÍA FERREIRA CABEZA-VANEGAS

A Mother's Tale
PHILLIP LOPATE